THE YACHT RACING RULES:
A COMPLETE GUIDE

THE YACHT RACING   RULES:
A COMPLETE GUIDE

MARY PERA

NAUTICAL

Commentary copyright © Mary Pera 1985
Rules extracts copyright © International Yacht Racing Union 1985
All rights reserved. No part of this publication may be reproduced
or transmitted, in any form or by any means, without permission of
the publishers.
ISBN 0 85177 343 5
First published in Great Britain 1985 by
Nautical Books
an imprint of Conway Maritime Press Ltd
24 Bride Lane, Fleet Street
London EC4Y 8DR

Line drawings by Mike Collins
Jacket designed by Ray Harvey
Jacket photograph by Patrick Roach
Book design by Tony Garrett

Typeset by Witwell Ltd, Liverpool
Printed by R J Acford, Chichester

Contents

How to use this book   7

The yacht racing rules and commentary   9
(Rules 14–17, 28–30, 47, 49 and 67 do not exist)

Introduction and Part I (no numbers to rules)
**Status of the Rules, Fundamental Rules
and Definitions**   14

Part II 1–13 **Management of Races**   32

Part III 18–27 **General Requirements**   59

Part IV 31–46 **Right of Way Rules**   68

Part V 50–66 **Other Sailing Rules**   148

Part VI 68–78 **Protests, Penalties and Appeals**   167

Appendices   204

A universal index to the yacht racing rules   219

Abbreviations

CYA	Canadian Yachting Association
FIV	Federazione Italian Vela
IRPCAS	International Regulations for Preventing Collisions at Sea
IYRU	International Yacht Racing Union
KNWV	Koninklijk Nederlands Watersport Verbond
NYA	Norwegian Yachting Association
RYA	Royal Yachting Association
USSRYRF	USSR Yacht Racing Federation
USYRU (or US)	United States Yacht Racing Union

Yachts: I, inside; O, outside; P, port-tack; S, starboard-tack; L, leeward; W, windward; M, middle (or intervening).

NA	national authority	PC	protest committee
N of R	notice of race	RC	race committee
FR	fundamental rule	SI	sailing instructions
OA	organising authority	IJ	international jury

How to use this book

The rules under which sailing yachts, multihulls, centre boarders and sail boards are raced are revised every fourth year, after the Olympic games. The complete rules for 1985–88 will be found in this book together with four of the appendices issued by the International Yacht Racing Union (IYRU) in its rule book.

This book helps you by providing a commentary on each rule to explain its use when sailing, before or after a race or series, or for the protest room. Much of this commentary is case law as issued by the IYRU, the United States Yacht Racing Union (USYRU) and the Royal Yachting Association (RYA), as well as some other national authorities. The main sources for the cases are from the USYRU appeals decisions (US1, US2 etc) and the RYA annual booklet YR5 (RYA 84/2 etc.). Selected cases from these publications and their equivalents in other countries are published annually by the IYRU as interpretations. There is also my opinion, sometimes shown by the phrases 'I believe' or 'I suppose'.

It is nowhere written that a protest committee must follow a published decision, but it would be very unwise of it not to do so. IYRU Regulation 6.3.3 merely states: 'IYRU interpretations of the yacht racing rules are recognized as authoritative interpretations and explanations of the rules'. A national authority appeals committee will be unlikely to upset one of its own rulings and doubly unlikely to upset one confirmed by the IYRU. Some of these interpretations arise from very unusual incidents never likely to be exactly repeated, others interpret a rule for some class of boat or for some special set of circumstances; others yet again interpret a word or phrase for everyone everywhere and these, sooner or later, become the basis of a rule change incorporating the point in question.

The rules themselves start off with fundamental rules and definitions, then Parts I to VI, followed by Appendices 1–13, of which 1–4 are reproduced here.

In Part I, after the fundamental rules, the definitions fix and limit the meaning of each word or phrase. When a word is used in its defined sense in the rules it is printed in *italics*. The definitions cannot be altered, and any attempt to do so in sailing instructions is automatically void. Part II, management of races, is addressed to race committees. It authorizes and sets the stage for the organization, conduct and judging of races. Part III is addressed to owners; it contains the rules they must comply with before bringing their boats to the starting line. Part IV, the right-of-way rules, controls the situation between boats when they meet. It is 'where the action is' and about half this book is devoted to it. Part V consists of the rest of those rules that affect a yacht while she is racing. Part VI has no rule that can be infringed, being entirely concerned with the procedure for protests and appeals. However if a yacht fails to observe some of the requirements of this part, she may lose her right of action and, indeed occasionally lay herself open to disqualification (under rules 33.2 or 52).

Do not forget that there is no substitute for reading the rules themselves. Many of them are self explanatory. All the comment in the world will not be of any avail, if sailors or juries fail to read each sentence and each word in the relevant rule.

In this book a boat called *Daisy* plays a part; so many sentences start 'when a yacht ...', that I have preferred to put 'when *Daisy* ...'. Boats are feminine, people masculine throughout – feminists and yachtswomen forgive me! Yacht is the accepted formal term for anything from a sailboard to a maxi, but most of us use 'boat' in normal everyday parlance, and I have used both; after all, distances in the rules are expressed still as boat-lengths, not (thank heaven) as yacht-lengths. The terms 'give way' (British), 'burdened' and 'obligated' (American) are all used to describe the yacht that has not got the right of way.

The book ends with a unique 'Universal Index to the Racing Rules' . The figures in it refer to rule numbers (not page). Often a subject appears three times in the rules, in a definition, in Part II as it affects the race committee and then in Part IV as it affects the competitor. It is therefore possible to trace 'premature starter' or 'proper course' as the ideas they incorporate are developed through the rules.

Since 1959 the world has had one set of racing rules and subsequently international interpretations. At a championship with starters from more than a score of countries and a jury from, say, five, we can all rely on a consistency and common understanding without which it would be impossible to enjoy such racing.

I am very much aware that a large part of this book is not written by me. The many extracts from the appeal cases have been written over the last 25 years, in a number of countries, by devoted, unpaid and often anonymous judges. They have given their time on appeals committees unstintingly to try to ensure fair results in competitions from the humblest club racing to the Olympic Games. Many of them are friends and colleagues and I should like to thank them. I am also grateful to the various national authorities and the IYRU for permission to publish the cases and to Bryan Willis for reading the proofs and pointing out a number of improvements.

Mary Pera 1985

1985–88

International Yacht Racing Rules

CONTENTS

Part I—STATUS OF THE RULES, FUNDAMENTAL RULES AND DEFINITIONS

page

Status of the Rules 14

Fundamental Rules

A Rendering Assistance 14
B Responsibility of a Yacht 14
C Fair Sailing 15

Definitions

Racing 17
Starting 18
Finishing 19
Luffing 21
Tacking 22
Bearing Away 23
Gybing 23
On a Tack 23
Close-hauled 23
Clear Astern and Clear Ahead;
  Overlap 24
Leeward and Windward 25
Proper Course 26
Mark 29
Obstruction 30
Postponement 31
Abandonment 31
Cancellation 31

Part II—MANAGEMENT OF RACES
Authority and Duties of Race Committee

Rule   page

1 Authority for Organising,
  Conducting and Judging
  Races 32
2 Notice of Race or
  Regatta 36
3 The Sailing Instructions 37
  3.1 Status 37
  3.2 Contents 38
  3.3 Distribution 42
  3.4 Changes 42
  3.5 Oral instructions 42
4 Signals 43
  4.1 Visual signals 43
  4.2 Signals for starting a
    race 46

4.3 Other signals 48
4.4 Calling attention to
  signals 48
4.5 Visual starting signals
  to govern 49
5 Designating the Course,
  Altering the Course or Race 49
6 Starting and Finishing Lines 51
7 Start of a Race 52
  7.1 Starting area 52
  7.2 Timing the start 52
8 Recalls 52
  8.1 Individual recall 52
  8.2 General recall 54
9 Marks 55
  9.1 Mark missing 55
  9.2 Mark unseen 55
10 Finishing within a Time Limit 56
11 Ties 56
12 Races to be Re-sailed 57
13 Award of Prizes 57

Part III—GENERAL REQUIREMENTS
Owner's Responsibilities for Qualifying his Yacht

18 Entries 59
19 Measurement or Rating
  Certificates 60
20 Ownership of Yachts 61
21 Member on Board 62
22 Shifting Ballast 63
  22.1 General restrictions 63
  22.2 Shipping, unshipping or
    shifting ballast; water 63
23 Anchor 63
24 Life-Saving Equipment 63
25 Class Insignia, National
  Letters and Sail Numbers 63
26 Advertising 66
  26.1 Basic rule 66
  26.2 Exemption for yachts 66
  26.3 Exemption for events 67
  26.4 Dispensation 67
  26.5 Warning and penalties............ 67
27 Forestays and Jib Tacks 67

Part IV—RIGHT OF WAY RULES
Rights and Obligations when Yachts Meet

Section A
Obligations and Penalties

31 Disqualification 69

32   Avoiding Collisions 69
33   Rule Infringement 70
     33.1 Accepting penalty 70
     33.2 Contact between yachts
          racing 71
34   Hailing 74

Section B
   **Principal Right of Way Rules
   and their Limitations**
35   Limitations on Altering Course 75
36   Opposite Tacks—Basic Rule 85
37   Same Tack—Basic Rules 88
     37.1 When overlapped 88
     37.2 When not overlapped 88
     37.3 Transitional 88
38   Same Tack—Luffing and
     Sailing above a Proper
     Course after Starting 88
     38.1 Luffing rights 88
     38.2 Proper course limitations 88
     38.3 Overlap limitations 89
     38.4 Hailing to stop or
          prevent a luff 89
     38.5 Curtailing a luff 89
     38.6 Luffing two or more
          yachts 89
39   Same Tack—Sailing below a
     Proper Course after Starting 99
40   Same Tack—Luffing before
     Starting 100
41   Changing Tacks—Tacking
     and Gybing 101
     41.1 Basic rule 101
     41.2 Transitional 101
     41.3 Onus 101
     41.4 When simultaneous 102

Section C
   **Rules that Apply at Marks and
   Obstructions and other Exceptions
   to the Rules of Section B**
42   Rounding or Passing Marks
     and Obstructions 106
     42.1 When overlapped 106
     42.2 When not overlapped 106
     42.3 Exceptions and limitations 107
     42.4 At a starting mark
          surrounded by navigable
          water 107
43   Close-Hauled,
     Hailing for Room
     to Tack at Obstructions 134

43.1 Hailing 134
43.2 Responding 134
43.3 Limitations on right to
     room to tack when the
     obstruction is also a mark 134
44   Returning to Start 142
45   Re-rounding after
     Touching a Mark 144
46   Person Overboard; Yacht
     Anchored, Aground or Capsized ..146

Part V—OTHER SAILING RULES

**Obligations of Helmsman and Crew in
   Handling a Yacht**
50   Ranking as a Starter 148
51   Sailing the Course 148
52   Touching a Mark 154
53   Casting Off, Anchoring,
     Making Fast and Hauling Out 158
     53.1 At the preparatory signal 158
     53.2 When racing 158
     53.3 Means of anchoring 158
54   Means of Propulsion 158
     54.1 Basic rule 158
     54.2 Actions that are prohibited 159
     54.3 Actions that are permitted 159
55   Aground or Foul of an
     Obstruction 160
56   Sounding 160
57   Manual and Stored Power 161
58   Boarding 161
59   Leaving, Crew Overboard 161
60   Outside Assistance 162
61   Clothing and Equipment 163
62   Increasing Stability 165
63   Skin Friction 165
64   Setting and Sheeting Sails 165
     64.1 Changing sails 165
     64.2 Sheeting sails to spars 165
     64.3 Spinnaker; Spinnaker boom ... 165
     64.4 Headsail 166
65   Flags 166
66   Fog Signals and Lights 166

**Part VI—PROTESTS, PENALTIES
   AND APPEALS**

Definitions
Rules 167
Protest 167
Party to a Protest 167
Protest Committee 167
Interested Party 167

Section A
Initiation of Action
68 Protests by Yachts 169
68.1 Right to protest 169
68.2 During a race
—Protest flag 170
68.3 After a race 172
68.4 Informing the
protested yacht 173
68.5 Particulars
to be included 174
68.6 Time limit 174
68.7 Fee 175
68.8 Remedying defects
in the protest 175
68.9 Withdrawing a
protest 176
69 Requests for Redress 176
70 Action by Race or
Protest Committee 181
70.1 Without a hearing 181
70.2 With a hearing 181
70.3 Yacht materially
prejudiced 183
70.4 Measurer's
responsibility 184

Section B
Protest Procedure
71 Procedural Requirements 185
71.1 Requirement for a
hearing 185
71.2 Interested parties 186
71.3 Protests between yachts
in separate races 186
72 Acceptance or Refusal
of a Protest 187
72.1 Accepting a protest 187
72.2 Refusing a protest 187
72.3 Notification of parties 188

73 Hearings 188
73.1 Right to be present 189
73.2 Taking of evidence 189
73.3 Evidence of
committee member 191
73.4 Failure to attend 191
73.5 Re-opening a hearing 192
74 Decisions and Penalties 192
74.1 Finding of facts 192
74.2 Consideration of redress 193
74.3 Measurement protests 194
74.4 Penalties 195
74.5 Alternative penalties 197
74.6 Points and places 198
74.7 The decision 198

Section C
Special Rules
75 Gross Infringement of Rules
or Misconduct 199
75.1 Penalties by the race committee
or protest committee 199
75.2 Penalties by the
national authority 200
76 Liability 201
76.1 Damages 201
76.2 Measurement expenses 201

Section D
Appeal Procedure
77 Appeals 201
77.1 Right of appeal 201
77.2 Time limit and deposit 201
77.3 Interpretation of rules 201
77.4 Withdrawal of appeal 202
77.5 Interested parties 202
77.6 Power to uphold
or reverse a decision
77.7 Decisions 202
78 Particulars to be
Supplied in Appeals 202

APPENDICES
1 Definition of an Amateur and Eligibility Regulations 204
2 Sailboard Racing Rules 207
3 Alternative Penalties for Infringement of a Rule of Part IV 210
4 Team Racing Rules 214
5 Olympic Scoring System
6 Protest Committee Procedure
7 Protest Form
8 Terms of Reference of an International Jury and Conditions
for its Decisions to be Final
9 Excerpts from the International Regulations for Preventing
Collisions at Sea—1972
10 Weighing of Wet Clothing (Racing Rule 61)
11 Photographic Evidence
12 Sailing Instructions Guide
13 Guide for Principal Events

Part I—Status of the Rules, Fundamental Rules and Definitions

Status of the Rules

The International Yacht Racing Rules have been established by the International Yacht Racing Union for the organisation, conduct and judging of the sport of yacht racing, and are amended and published every four years by the IYRU in accordance with its Constitution.

A national authority may alter or add to these rules by prescription, with the exception of the rules of Parts I and IV and rules 1, 3, 26 and 61, unless permitted in a rule itself.

The sailing instructions may alter rules only in accordance with rule 3.1, (The Sailing Instructions).

Fundamental Rules

A. Rendering Assistance

Every yacht shall render all possible assistance to any vessel or person in peril, when in a position to do so.

It is a basic rule of the sea that you should try to rescue a drowning man (or woman). By providing a carrot and a stick, the IYRR do their best to ensure that a fanatic racing skipper does not overlook this. The carrot is to be found in rule 69 (b), where redress is made available to those rendering assistance. This fundamental rule is the stick. Disqualifications for failing to help are few and far between, but they are not unknown.

In IYRU 38, one boat went to the assistance of another without being asked. She was considered to be entitled to redress because 'a yacht in a position to assist another that may be in peril is bound to do so. That she offers assistance not requested is irrelevant'. This case is further discussed under rule 69. IYRU 66 discusses the relationship between this fundamental rule and other rules. However, since here the rescue boat was a spectator craft, not bound by the IYRR, the case is discussed under rules 59 (Leaving, Crew Overboard) and 60 (Outside Assistance).

B. Responsibility of a Yacht

It shall be the sole responsibility of each yacht to decide whether or not to *start* or to continue to *race*.

This straightforward rule was the subject of US 209. Prior to the start of the fourth race of a Sunfish series, one boat informed the race committee that she did not believe the weather was suitable for racing and that the race should not be started. She then withdrew. Nevertheless the race committee ran the race and the Sunfish requested but was refused redress. The US Appeals Committee remarked: 'The decision to start, postpone or abandon a race is a matter solely within the jurisdiction of the race committee. If a yacht decides not to race, she cannot claim her finishing position was prejudiced.'

In addition to preventing such claims for redress, the rule protects race committees in the event of accidents. Only the owner – or the helmsman – of a boat can know whether she is seaworthy or not. It would be beyond the bounds of possibility for a committee to check the soundness of hulls and gear or to know the competence of crews. Whether the race committee can be relieved of all responsibility probably depends on the law of each national authority's country.

If six rescue boats were scheduled to be on the water and only one was present when there was an accident, some of the responsibility might well be held to rest with the race committee, particularly in a race for children. The competitors would have started under false pretences, expecting help to be available that was not in fact there. Again in, say, a Trans Atlantic race, an inexperienced competitor might be entitled to expect that suitable safety regulations were prescribed and that the boats were checked for conformity with them.

In general, I believe, that if it were found that a race committee had been negligent in failing to provide the safety organisation that could reasonably have been expected, or which had been promised, this rule would not prevent liability to damages.

C. Fair Sailing

A yacht shall participate in a race or series of races in an event only by fair sailing, superior speed and skill, and, except in team races, by individual effort. However, a yacht may be penalised under this rule only in the case of a clear-cut violation of the above principles and only when no other rule (except rule 75, Gross Infringement of Rules or Misconduct) applies.

One of the reasons it is a mistake to try and compare the IYRR with criminal law, and why such words as 'guilty' and 'innocent' should be avoided, is that the IYRR do not question the intention of the rule infringer. In fact you will notice that it is the yacht that infringes a rule. and wood and glass fibre can hardly be 'guilty' or 'innocent'. There is all the difference in the world between a man borrowing his wife's car and his taking (with the intention of keeping it) a stranger's car from a car park. One is a crime, the other is not. It is not the taking of the car but the intent of the taker. This is not so in the rules. The most obvious example is fairly common. A helmsman intends to tack and put his helm down. Something happens –

perhaps a foul jib sheet – and he never gets beyond head to wind. He is protested for tacking. But in fact the boat did not tack – she remained on a tack – and the committee will decide on this fact, not on the helmsman's intention. When the helmsman's intention is to cheat he lays himself open to action by the race committee, or the protest committee under rule 75.1 – or the national authority under rule 75.2 – for misconduct, bad sportsmanship or gross infringement of the rules.

My own view is that the Fair Sailing Rule should be used when a yacht (notice that it is aimed at yachts and not people) breaks an unwritten rule, but her helmsman does not make himself liable to penalties under rule 75. The penalty for infringing the Fair Sailing Rule is disqualification (or penalisation); under rule 75 a helmsman can be excluded from a whole series or worse.

In case law another rule has always been infringed, except in two cases, RYA 69/9 where a boat was deliberately heeled to touch another, and IYRU 107 which concerns hailing.

'An experienced helmsman of a port-tack boat hailed "Starboard!" to a beginner who, although on starboard tack, not being sure of himself and probably being scared of having his boat holed, tacked to port to avoid a collison. No protest was lodged. One school of thought argued that it was fair game, because if a helmsman did not know the rules, that was his own hard luck. The other school rejected this argument, on the grounds that it was quite contrary to the spirit of the rules to deceive a competitor in that way. It was known that such a trick was often played, particularly where novices were involved, and therefore guidance was sought on whether a protest committee should or should not take action under the Fundamental Fair Sailing rule.'

The RYA ruled: 'A yacht that deliberately hails "Starboard" when she is on port tack has not acted correctly and is liable to disqualification under Fundamental Rule C – Fair Sailing.' Even this case would have needed little before it became a matter for rule 75. Perhaps all the rules that should be written down, have been written down!

Definitions

*When a term defined in Part I is used in its defined sense it is printed in **italic** type. All preambles and definitions rank as rules. Further definitions of terms used in Part VI will be found at the beginning of Part VI.*

Racing—A yacht is *racing* from her preparatory signal until she has either *finished* and cleared the finishing line and finishing *marks* or retired, or until the race has been *postponed*, *abandoned*, *cancelled*, or a general recall has been signalled, except that in match or team races, the sailing instructions may prescribe that a yacht is *racing* from any specified time before the preparatory signal.

There are 17 definitions in Part I and they may not be altered. The 'Status of the Rules' and rule 3.1 prevent any national authority or race committee laying down that, for example, a yacht becalmed is not to be considered 'on a tack.' Such a prescription would vary the definition of 'on a tack' and would therefore be automatically void. Whenever a word is used in its defined sense it is written in italics in the IYRR and the meaning in each place is therefore tightly controlled. Some definitions, such as 'starting' and 'proper course' express complex acts and trail clouds of case law behind them. Others, 'gybing' for instance, say little more than we expect from the word's ordinary everyday meaning.

Definitions must be read carefully, for each word counts. When you meet, say, 'proper course' in other rules (38, 39, 42, 45) check that you know the defined and detailed meaning of the two words. Do not rely on what may be a less than perfect recall of what the definition says.

Note that the preamble includes the instruction that preambles rank as rules. Of these, the preamble to Part IV is the most important. The definitions 'rank as rules', but this is of no great importance as there is nothing to obey.

Phrases such as 'while *racing*', 'before a yacht is *racing*', 'before or after *racing*', appear in a number of rules (eg 4.1 'Y', 33.1 and 33.2). The definition identifies the precise moment when *racing* begins and when it ends. It begins at the same instant for all yachts, at the preparatory signal. Yachts sailing around in the vicinity of the starting line are, for obvious reasons, already subject to the rules of Part IV (see preamble to Part IV) rather than International Regulations for Prevention of Collisions at Sea (IRPCAS) but only at the preparatory signal do they become liable to disqualification for infringement of the rules (there are rare exceptions to this in rule 31.2).

In match or team racing, however, *racing* may begin before the preparatory signal at a time specified in the sailing instructions. This exception is usually superfluous; it is quite possible to extend pre-start *racing* time by altering rule 4.2 and making the preparatory signal ten minutes before the starting signal instead of the usual five.

Racing may end at the same moment for everyone, when a race is *postponed*, *abandoned*, *cancelled* or a general recall is signalled, but usually it ends at an individual moment for each yacht – when she has either *finished* and cleared the finishing line and the finishing *marks* or retired. We shall see in the definition of *finishing* that a yacht may *finish* but still be on the line. So now she must clear the line (in either direction, rule 51.5) and if while so doing she touches a *mark* she so to speak 'unfinishes' and must re-round it in accordance with rule 52 and finish again, clearing line and marks before she can safely consider herself as no longer *racing*.

In US V99 (Fig. 1) A luffed head to wind to finish, her genoa came aback and she was forced onto port tack. B hit her and protested under rule 41.1. It was clear that A had infringed either rule 41 or rule 36, the question being only whether or not she was still *racing* and therefore subject to disqualification under rule 33.1. The US Appeals Committee stated: 'It is

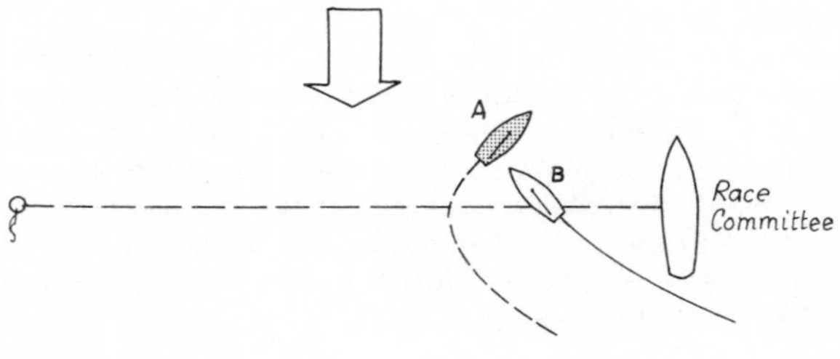

Fig. 1

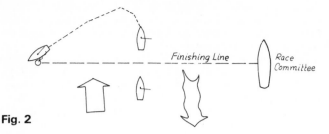

Fig. 2

held that when no part of a yacht's hull, equipment or crew remains on the finishing line, she has cleared it'. There being no question of rule 31.2 being invoked – failure to clear the finishing *marks* – A escaped penalisation. Since B had also finished A could not be disqualified after *racing* for serious hindering another that was *racing* (rule 31.2).

US 136 (Fig. 2) discusses the phrase 'and cleared the finishing *marks*'. A was disqualified under rule 52 for failing to re-round and re-finish, after touching a finishing *mark* (see rules 52 and 52.2 (b) (ii)).

The appeals committee reversed the decision stating: 'The intent of including "finishing *marks*" as one of the criteria in determining when a yacht is no longer *racing* is to prevent a yacht that finishes so close to a mark that she is unable to avoid touching it, from escaping penalty through the circumstance of having cleared the line at the time of touching. The official diagram showed the yacht in this case to be some six lengths from the mark which she subsequently touched, so that at the time she cleared the line she was well clear of the mark. Her contact with the mark was no part of her finishing manoeuvre. It was, therefore, a separate incident, occurring when the yacht was no longer racing.'

Starting—A yacht *starts* when, after fulfilling her penalty obligations, if any, under rule 51.1(c), (Sailing the Course), and after her starting signal, any part of her hull, crew or equipment first crosses the starting line in the direction of the course to the first *mark*.

Starting, in its defined sense, means starting correctly. It is possible to start prematurely without *starting* and to rank as a starter without *starting* (rule 50). Do not worry about these paradoxes, they do not cause trouble in practice. A yacht *starts* 'when . . . any part of her hull, crew or equipment . . . crosses the starting line . . . '. The dots represent qualifications to this basic statement.

1 '. . . when . . . after the starting signal . . .' If *Daisy* crosses before the gun she is a premature starter (and that includes her anchor if she is kedged with it on the 'wrong' side of the line – RYA 1950/11). When she is a premature starter she must return and start correctly.

2 '. . . when, after fulfilling her obligations, if any, under 51.1 (c)' This is the Round-the-Ends rule, which may or may not be in force. If it is and the yacht has infringed it, she must return correctly outside the committee vessel or ODM before she can start correctly.

3 '... first crosses' ... Once started she cannot 'unstart.' Few races start in a flat calm, but if *Daisy* were to start and clear the starting line and then drift back across the line she would be subject to rules that apply after starting, such as rule 38, while those boats that had not yet started would be subject to rule 40. However timely postponements should avoid such possibilities.
4 ' ... in the direction of the course to the first mark' This phrase not only prevents yachts from starting in the wrong direction, but stops race committees from trying to use the starting marks as rounding marks!

Now look at what the definition does not say. It does not lay down a last moment when a yacht can start. RYA 82/13 tells the story of *Jessie*. *Jessie* sailed the wrong side of the outer distance mark, thus failing to cross the starting line and failing to *start*. At the end of the first round she crossed the line and *started*. Later in the race she retired. The race committee posted her as DNS, but on appeal it was held that she had *started* at the beginning of her second round and should have appeared in the results as DNF. A yacht, said the appeals committee, may ignore her previous course and *start* as long as the starting line remains open. (Note however that rule 53 requires her to be off moorings at the preparatory signal.)

The rules do not expressly require a yacht to wait for the starting signal on the pre-start side of the line (except when expressly forbidden by SIs with such rules as the Round-the-Ends Rule or the Five Minute rule).

The rules differ before and after the start and each will be dealt with under its own rule number, a brief list is given below. Sometimes the rule changes at the starting signal or even before, sometimes when the yacht starts and sometimes when she has started *and* cleared the starting line. *Always* check the rule in question, it is easy to forget which changes when.

Daisy acquires:

1 the right to luff as she pleases when she has luffing rights (38.1) as opposed to 'slowly' (rule 40);
2 an obligation not to sail above a proper course when she is a leeward yacht with no luffing rights;
3 the rights and obligations of a new overlap (38.3);
4 the qualified obligation not to bear away on a free leg of the course (rule 39);
5 the rights and obligations of rule 42, in so far as it refers to the marks (not obstructions). Before a yacht starts, a *mark* has no required side (rule 51.3), thus a boat over the line at the start can, just because she has not *started*, return to the pre-start side of the line on either side of the line *marks* (always supposing that the Round the Ends rule is not in force);
6 rights and obligations at a starting *mark* surrounded by navigable water (rule 42.4);
7 right-of-way over premature starters returning and still on the course side of the line (rules 44 and 51) and over boats exonerating themselves under rules 46/52 or Appendix 3.1.

Finishing—A yacht *finishes* when any part of her hull, or of her crew or equipment in normal position, crosses the finishing line in the direction of the course from the last *mark*, after fulfilling her penalty obligations, if any, under rule 52.2, (Touching a Mark).

Daisy finishes when the finishing line is cut (it is always spoken of as 'crossed' – but crossing is not necessary – rule 51.5) by any part of her hull,

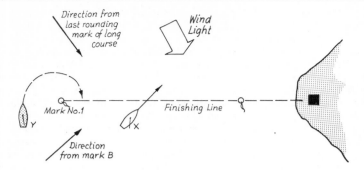

Fig. 3

crew or equipment in normal position. The last qualification prevents an arm or a spinnaker pole being pushed forward.

Unlike starting, a boat that finishes can 'unfinish' and have to finish again. If *Daisy* touches a finishing mark she is not considered to have finished until she has exonerated herself (see rule 52.2 (b) (ii)), and, until she has cleared the finishing line, exonerate herself she must. So, if her stem crosses the line (and she gets a gun) she has finished, but if she then drifts onto the finishing mark before she has cleared the line she has 'unfinished'! She must then exonerate herself in accordance with rule 52.2, and finish again, this time correctly. Remember that she does not stop *racing* until she has finished and cleared the line and marks.

Daisy can only finish correctly 'in the direction of the course from the last mark', a prescription that regularly gives rise to difficulties. Sometimes it is inconvenient for race officers and they would prefer a 'hook finish'. Sometimes when a course is shortened the direction to the finishing line automatically changes, but the SI for the finishing line has not been altered. In no case can the definition be altered. See also Fig. 98 in rule 51.1 (a).

In IYRU 102 (Fig. 3) after one race that finished from N to S, the RO set a shorter course for a second. Because of other classes that were also racing, he deliberately ordered the finishing line to be crossed in the same direction as before although the direction from the last mark was now S to N. X crossed as required by the definition, Y as required by the SIs.

The race committee posted Y, which had crossed from N to S, as first. X requested redress on the grounds that she was the first boat to finish correctly. The protest committee agreed that X had finished correctly, in accordance with the definition, but then proceeded to give redress to Y. X appealed on the grounds that the protest committee had defeated the purpose of the definition. The appeal was upheld. 'It is not open to a race committee to override the definition of *finishing*. The results are to be based on the finishing positions of the yachts that finished in accordance with the definition. If the PC is satisfied that the course ordered was such that the other yachts were prejudiced, so as to alter the results of the race, it is open to the committee to award points to such yachts, but it would not be equitable for such yachts to rank higher than those yachts that finished correctly.'

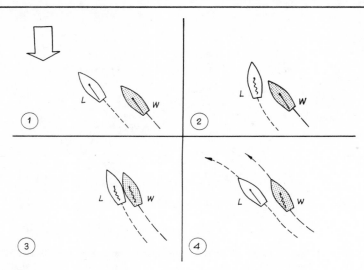

Fig. 4

Luffing—Altering course towards the wind.

Luffing begins when *Daisy* begins to alter course towards the wind. It ends when she resumes a steady course, bears away or tacks. When she reaches head to wind she must either fall away on the other tack, thus beginning to tack, or bear away on the same tack as before. But before she does either she may remain head to wind for an appreciable time, and during this time she will not be tacking. In IYRU 58 (Fig. 4) L and W were closed-hauled on starboard tack, with L just clear ahead and slightly to leeward. L luffed to begin tacking, admittedly having forgotten W's presence. As soon as W saw L's bow approaching, W hailed and L bore away as quickly as possible. W also luffed hard, but contact occurred. L did not go beyond head to wind during her luff. W protested L under rule 41.1. L having admitted attempting to tack in contravention of that rule was disqualified. Reversing the protest committee's decision, the KNWV stated: 'L was wrongly disqualified because her intention to tack was of no relevance. It was established as fact that during her preliminary luff she did not go beyond head to wind. Therefore, while she intended to tack, she in fact had exercised only her right to luff as permitted by rule 38.1. W is disqualified for failing as a windward yacht to keep clear as required by rule 37.1'.

Luffing, its right and obligations, is discussed under rules 34.1, 35, 37, 38, 40, 42 and 43.

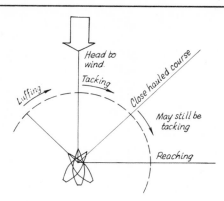

Fig. 5

Tacking—A yacht is *tacking* from the moment she is beyond head to wind until she has *borne away*, when beating to windward, to a *close-hauled* course; when not beating to windward, to the course on which her mainsail has filled.

Tacking, which is invariably preceded by luffing, begins at 'the moment she is beyond head to wind'. We have seen under the definition of luffing that even when *Daisy* intends to tack, she is still not tacking until she reaches this point (IYRU 58, RYA 85/6). Head to wind will be judged from the direction of the hull relative to the wind, the sails obviously cannot be full and will be all over the place. (Fig. 5).

While she is in the act of tacking *Daisy* has no rights at all (except in respect of yachts that have made mistakes and are returning to exonerate themselves under rules 44, 45 or are doing their 720° turns). It is therefore of the greatest importance to be quite clear at what moment she completes her tack and becomes on a tack.

Two situations are defined. First, when beating to windward she is tacking until she has *borne away* to a close-hauled course. IYRU 32 states that when beating, a yacht has completed her tack when she is heading on a close-hauled course, regardless of her movement through the water, or the sheeting of her sails. So there is *Daisy*, with no way on and her sails all no-how, but her hull is on the close-hauled course, her tack is completed, and she is on a tack, US 186 confirms this.

Secondly, when not beating to windward, she is tacking until she has borne away to the course on which her mainsail has filled. (The definition seems to think that she would let her main out first and then bear away to fill it). There is no problem with this after the start. Tacking at a mark *Daisy* bears away onto her new course, a beam reach, and has then completed her tack. It is in pre-start manoeuvring, particularly in match racing, when both boats are endlessly circling, never settling to a course, that the moment is difficult, or impossible, to identify. The definition was not written with this in view. The identification of this moment is however of vital importance because, as will be seen in rule 41.2, when *Daisy* tacks onto starboard, the port tack yacht need then and only then begin to keep clear – and she must be able to do so.

Bearing Away—Altering course away from the wind until a yacht begins to *gybe*.

No comment is needed; except for an appearance in the definitions of *tacking* and *proper course*, the words are not used elsewhere in the rules.

Gybing—A yacht begins to *gybe* at the moment when, with the wind aft, the foot of her mainsail crosses her centre line, and completes the *gybe* when the mainsail has filled on the other *tack*.

This definition has thrown up no case law and needs no comment. The act of gybing is swiftly completed and the main usually fills on the new tack almost simultaneously with the boom crossing the centre-line of the boat. Rule 41 governs the obligations of a yacht that *gybes*.

On a Tack—A yacht is *on a tack* except when she is *tacking* or *gybing*. A yacht is on the *tack* (*starboard* or *port*) corresponding to her *windward* side.

A boat that is neither *tacking* nor *gybing* is *on a tack*. So far so good. The definition then states: 'A yacht is on the *tack* (*starboard* or *port*) corresponding to her *windward* side.' This sentence links with the definition of *leeward* and *windward* and, theoretically at least, there are problems when a boom is held up against the wind, but in practice no cases have come to appeal, and common sense has so far prevailed.

RYA 85/6 and IYRU 58 holds that a yacht that has luffed until head to wind remains on a tack until she *tacks*. See under rule 41.

US 138 illustrates the line drawn between the definitions of *tacking* and *on a tack*. Fig. 6 shows A head to wind by the mark and B hitting her stern and thus nudging her round into a tack. On appeal it was stated: 'The RC found as facts that, when A came within two lengths of the mark, she was clear ahead of B, that on reaching the mark she luffed head to wind and that while head to wind she was struck by B. Since A was head to wind she had not yet started to tack and was still on the port tack. Rule 42.2 (a) therefore applied ... and B is disqualified for failing to keep clear'.

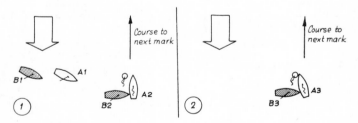

Fig. 6

Close-hauled—A yacht is *close-hauled* when sailing by the wind as close as she can lie with advantage in working to windward.

A yacht working her way to windward as best she can is *close-hauled*. It depends on her hull direction not on the setting of her sails. *Daisy* may be sailing with her sails pinned in but she may still be on a reach. It may, or rather does, vary enormously between boats, close-hauled for a family cruiser would be practically a broad reach for twelve-metre. In protest commitee diagrams the angle to the wind is commonly shown as 45° but a Dragon will sail at about 40° and most modern racing hulls closer. Cruisers and multihulls in particular sail to a larger angle. Wind and water conditions alter this angle.

Clear Astern and *Clear Ahead; Overlap*—A yacht is *clear astern* of another when her hull and equipment in normal position are abaft an imaginary line projected abeam from the aftermost point of the other's hull and equipment in normal position. The other yacht is *clear ahead*.

The yachts *overlap* when neither is *clear astern*; or when, although one is *clear astern*, an intervening yacht *overlaps* both of them.

The terms *clear astern, clear ahead* and *overlap* apply to yachts on opposite *tacks* only when they are subject to rule 42, (Rounding or Passing Marks and Obstructions).

Two boats must be *clear astern* and *ahead* of each other or overlapped, they cannot be both at the same time, for one precludes the other (Fig. 7). (Naturally there is a partial exception to this rule in rule 38.3, where, for the purposes of that rule only, an overlap ceases to be effective at more than two boat lengths.) IYRU 21 (Fig. 8) shows clearly that the courses of the two boats may differ by almost 180° but they are still overlapped with all that this implies.

Circumstances will decide which of the two has right-of-way when overlapped. Opposite-tack boats are affected by the definition when not beating and when rule 42 applies. Same-tack boats will be governed by rules 37, 38, 39, 40 or 42 as appropriate. When a third boat intervenes the rules permit it to form a link between the other two, causing them to remain overlapped. But the intervening yacht must be between them, not outside. Fig. 9 shows the positions.

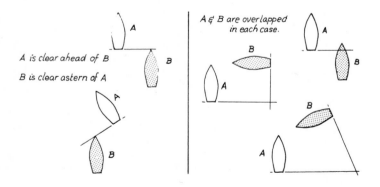

Fig. 7 *Clear ahead, clear astern and overlap with two boats.*

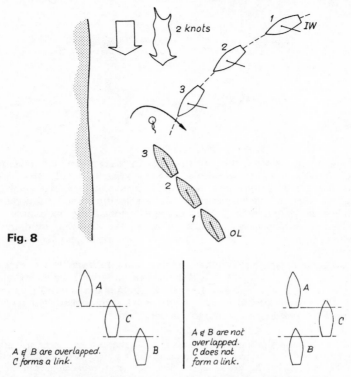

Fig. 8

Fig. 9 *Clear ahead, clear astern and overlap with three boats.*

Leeward and *Windward*—The *leeward* side of a yacht is that on which she is, or, when head to wind, was, carrying her mainsail. The opposite side is the *windward* side.

When neither of two yachts on the same *tack* is *clear astern*, the one on the *leeward* side of the other is the *leeward yacht*. The other is the *windward yacht*.

A definition that is more successful in practice than in theory perhaps. *Daisy* is carrying her mainsail to starboard, starboard is therefore, by

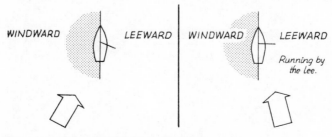

Fig. 10 *Definitions of windward and leeward.*

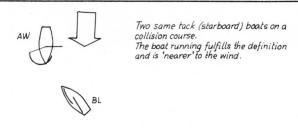

Two same tack (starboard) boats on a collision course.
The boat running fulfills the definition and is 'nearer' to the wind.

Fig. 11

definition, her *leeward* side, and the other, in this case port, is her *windward* side. It follows that a boat running by the lee has the wind on her leeward side (Fig. 10). The definition is not entirely satisfactory however when *Daisy* sails backwards or holds her main aback and for this reason it is modified for sailboards in Appendix 2. Their propensity for sailing backwards – and indeed all which ways – makes it necessary. Deriving from the first definition, the second defines which of two overlapped yachts is L and which W.

Confusion sometimes arises when two same-tack yachts approach each other as shown in Fig 11. It is a dangerous situation because the closing speed may be very high – perhaps 20 knots. A is the windward yacht and must keep clear (an awkward moment with her spinnaker!), B is on A's lee side and therefore, according to the definition, L.

Proper Course—A *proper course* is any course that a yacht might sail after the starting signal, in the absence of the other yacht or yachts affected, to *finish* as quickly as possible. The course sailed before *luffing* or *bearing away* is presumably, but not necessarily, that yacht's *proper course*. There is no *proper course* before the starting signal.

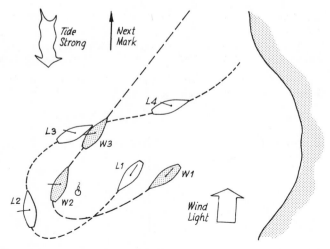

Fig. 12

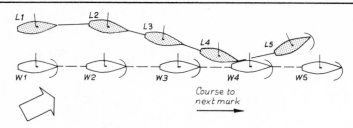

Fig. 13

Even between yachts in the same class there may be more than one *proper course*. Those who race in tidal waters will be well aware of this. IYRU 25 (Fig. 12) held that both L and W were on a proper course and illustrates the fact that there can be more than one proper course. Which of two different courses is the better cannot be determined in advance and is not necessarily proven by one yacht reaching the next mark ahead. Two of the criteria for the proper course are whether the yacht sailing it has logical reason for its being a proper course and whether she applies it with some consistency. (Under rule 37/38 we shall see that when both yachts are on a proper course, but these converge, W must keep clear).

IYRU 97 shows that this consistency is important, (Fig. 13). W sailed straight for the next mark. L had a spinnaker problem and headed up while she put it right. In doing so she hit W. L claimed that she was sailing a proper course because she would have reached the mark sooner (ie 'finish as quickly as possible') by sailing the higher course until her spinnaker was pulling. The US Appeals Committee disagreed:' IYRU 25 cautions against too free an interpretation of proper course by saying that two of the criteria are whether a yacht sailing it has a logical reason for its being a proper course and whether she applies it with some consistency.' The definition of 'proper course' itself indicates similar limitations: 'The course sailed before luffing or bearing away is presumably but not necessarily, a proper course.' Those words work in two directions. First, they imply that conditions can change to such a degree that a different course is justified. Conversely, they imply that, as IYRU 25 concludes, some consistency in applying a different course, is required. It cannot, normally, be a temporary change of course or be changed frequently. A leeward yacht without luffing rights is not entitled to use a temporary condition to justify a luff, particularly when that condition was caused by her own poor seamanship or sail handling.

US 74 discusses a free leg of the course (where W was bound by rule 39 as well as L by rule 38.2) and states: 'The proper course that W was not permitted to sail below and L was not permitted to sail above, while having the same objective, was not necessarily the same proper course . . . The fact that W was carrying working sails while L was reaching with a spinnaker, could have had a bearing on what each construed to be her proper course.'

US 79 shows (Fig. 14) that the tidal effect can make the course 'proper', although a yacht does not point towards a mark. Normally a proper course will be above close-hauled but at a mark this may not be so.

US 6, a case where L was held to be on a proper course even though she was sailing well above the direct course to the mark because a rough sea

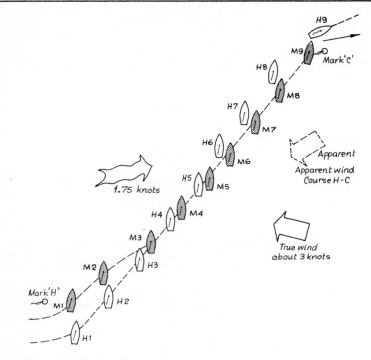

Fig. 14

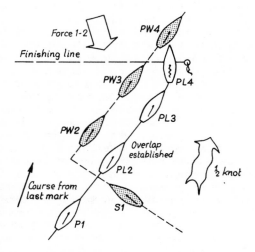

Fig. 15

was causing her to make considerable leeway, states 'When there is doubt that a yacht is sailing above her proper course she should be given the benefit of the doubt'.

RYA 1975/6 illustrates this point (Fig. 15) where L luffed head to wind, sails empty, in order to try to shoot the mark . . . and in doing so hit W. W maintained that L took room to which she was not entitled and the RC asked whether L was sailing a proper course and that the phrase 'to finish as quickly as possible includes pinching, shooting head to wind or generally wiggling round the mark during the existence of an inside overlap'?

The RYA, to put it briefly, replied that it was permissible; even in the absence of PW, PL would have pinched or shot head to wind in order to finish as soon as possible. RYA 1982/14 confirms this. (Rule 42 does not require the inside leeward yacht to sail a proper course in so many words, but it refuses her more room than necessary for a rounding or passing which perhaps, in these circumstances comes to much the same thing). In team racing *Daisy* may wish to manoeuvre against her opponent rather than finish as soon as possible. However the definition remains the same, her object is still to finish and her proper course must be based on this.

Mark—A *mark* is any object specified in the sailing instructions that a yacht must round or pass on a required side.

Every ordinary part of a *mark* ranks as part of it, including a flag, flagpole, boom or hoisted boat, but excluding ground tackle and any object either accidentally or temporarily attached to the *mark*.

'. . . any object. . .' The Fastnet Rock, a light vessel, a committee boat, and, most commonly, a buoy laid by the race committee – each can be a *mark*. Even an imaginary point can be a *mark*, such as Point 'A', sometimes prescribed as the northern limit in Trans Atlantic races to keep boats clear of the ice.

'. . . specified in the sailing instructions . . .' It is fundamental that competitors be informed which objects are to be marks of the course, and that this information be given clearly and unambiguously. In RYA 74/1, the race committee set a two-round course: 'ABC – ADC, all marks to port'. When some boats went direct from C to A without passing through the starting/finishing line they were disqualified. Their appeal was upheld; the race committee should have written 'ABC – outer limit mark – ADC, all marks to port' if it intended the line to be included between C and A. Competitors could not be expected to 'know' what was meant.

'. . . on a required side . . .' A mark has a required side for each yacht at some time during the race, not for the whole time. A starting mark has no required side until *Daisy* starts, or is approaching the line to start (see rule 51.3) yet she may not touch it from any time after the preparatory signal (rule 52). Likewise a finishing mark ceases to have a required side for *Daisy* when she finishes, but even thereafter she may not touch it until she has cleared the finishing line. A rounding or passing mark only has a required side for a yacht while she is on a leg that the mark begins, bounds or ends. (see rule 51.3).

Occasionally a buoy that has a required side is not a mark. When organisers are using a starting area (rule 7.1), the buoys marking it are not to rank as marks.

IYRU 94 discusses the distinction between marks and obstructions when the mark is, or is on, an island (see 'Obstruction' Fig. 16).

There is only one sort of mark. The definition covers starting, finishing, limit, rounding, passing, indeed any kind of mark that can be conceived. However, a buoy (or other object) may be specified as a mark in the sailing instructions yet fail to qualify. An intended starting limit mark on the pre-start side of the starting line, or an intended finishing limit mark on the post-finish side of the finishing line, unless very close to those lines, do not rank as marks and are not part of the course. (rule 51.3 and Figs 102 and 17).

Obstruction—An *obstruction* is any object, including a vessel under way, large enough to require a yacht, when more than one overall length away from it, to make a substantial alteration of course to pass on one side or the other, or any object that can be passed on one side only, including a buoy when the yacht in question cannot safely pass between it and the shoal or object that it marks. The sailing instructions may prescribe that certain defined areas shall rank as *obstructions*.

An *obstruction* spells danger; it is something that a boat needs to avoid. The definition distinguishes objects that can be passed on either side and those that cannot. Those that cannot are obvious; large lumps of land, in all its shapes and forms, shoals, sandbanks, rocks, beaches, jetties etc. etc. form insuperable obstructions to the forward movement of any yacht.

The definition spells out what is an *obstruction*; how to deal with such an animal will be found in rules 34.2, 42, 43 and 55. By and large these rules provide that a yacht meeting an obstruction may ask for room from others to enable her to get out of the danger without compromising her position in the race, provided she does so early enough. Frequently the obstruction is a right-of-way yacht. A starboard-tack yacht for example which P must avoid. What she can do about it is discussed under rules 42 and 43. (IYRU 20, 4, and 91 illustrate situations where S, W and the clear-ahead yacht respectively form obstructions. In IYRU 67 a right-of-way yacht forms a continuing obstruction).

On modern inland waterways governmental rules sometimes lay down prohibited areas. Now these are not obstructions in the old-fashioned sense, they do not represent a danger to the yachts, but nevertheless competitors must not sail into them. The last para of the definition permits sailing instructions to define an area as an obstruction. This will presumably allow a same-tack leeward yacht approaching the invisible line to call for room to tack under rule 43 just as if she were nearing a rocky shore. RCs must take care to distinguish whether the buoys, withies or what have you that bound these areas are to be considered as marks. If so they can be rerounded, (if not they may be touched with impunity). Each situation should be carefully considered.

What is not an obstruction? IYRU 45 shows a case where P was held not to be an obstruction to S (see rule 42.3.) IYRU 94 discusses the situation when an island forms a rounding mark (Fig. 16). The RYA stated 'when the sailing instructions prescribe that an island is to be rounded or passed on a required side it ranks, by definition, as both a mark and an obstruction. In its condition as a mark, only its above-water parts must be considered; as with the ground tackle of an ordinary mark the submerged portion below the water's edge, need not. Therefore, a yacht that goes aground in shoal water near that island is not touching a mark within the meaning of rule 52. She merely fouls an obstruction.

Fig. 16

On the other hand, a yacht that touches any above-water part, including a projecting rock or jetty, of an island that ranks as a mark infringes rule 52 and is subject to the re-rounding provision of that rule.'

The fact that a certain rock may at low tide be part of the mark and at high tide only an underwater obstruction need not worry us. The boat ashore, if she dries out is on the mark, but IYRU 94 protects her (see rule 55).

It is not always easy to decide what is an obstruction. Take a tall solid post six inches thick. A yacht close-hauled, at one boat's length in fine conditions will probably need only the merest touch on the helm to avoid it – it not an obstruction; but suppose she is running with spinnaker set and mainboom right out, at one length she may not be able to avoid it with even the most violent of efforts, so it is an obstruction after all. I believe both are right and that an object can sometimes be an obstruction and sometimes not. However, when there is doubt, it should be resolved in favour of the yacht that maintains that the object is an obstruction. It is the safer way.

Postponement—A *postponed* race is one that is not started at its scheduled time and that can be sailed at any time the race committee may decide.

Abandonment—An *abandoned* race is one that the race committee declares void at any time after the starting signal, and that can be re-sailed at its discretion.

Cancellation—A *cancelled* race is one that the race committee decides will not be sailed thereafter.

A *postponement* which may be made at any time until the starting signal, may be for five minutes or for a month. It is made available to the RC in rule 5.3 and its signals are in rule 4.1 'AP'. A race can only be *abandoned* after the start. It cannot be abandoned at the RO's discretion; he is bound by rule 5.4 only to abandon in certain circumstances. A race can be abandoned after it is finished but only after consideration has been given to redress (rule 5.5). The signals for *abandonment* are to be found in rule 4.1 and 'N' over 'X'.

A race that has been *postponed* or abandoned can, when it is not possible to resail it, be *cancelled*. A race can be cancelled at any time for any reason before the start (rule 5.3(c)) and after the start with the same controls as for abandonment. The signal for *cancellation* is in rule 4.1 'N' over '1st substitute'.

Part II—**Management of Races**

Authority and Duties of Race Committee

The rules of Part II deal with the duties and responsibilities of the race committee in conducting a race, the meaning of signals made by it and of other actions taken by it.

Part II is primarily for organising authorities and race committees. However helmsmen should study it so as to know what they may expect in a well-administered series or where an indifferently run one has gone astray. It would be nice to be able to say that there is no rule in Part II that a competitor can infringe, but rule 4.1 'Y' can certainly be, and other signals in the same rule need careful study even though the rule to be infringed if the signal were disregarded would be rule 51 – Sailing the Course.

1   Authority for Organising, Conducting and Judging Races

1.1   Regattas and races shall be organised by either:
(a) the I.Y.R.U.; or
(b) a national authority recognised by the I.Y.R.U.; or
(c) a club or regatta committee affiliated to a national authority; or
(d) a class association either with the approval of a national authority or in conjunction with an affiliated club or regatta committee; or
(e) an unaffiliated body in conjunction with an affiliated club or regatta committee,
which will henceforth be referred to as the organising authority.

All races shall be organised, conducted and judged under the rules of the I.Y.R.U. The organising authority shall appoint a race committee and publish the notice of race or regatta containing the terms and conditions of the event in accordance with rule 2, (Notice of Race or Regatta).

1.2   Subject to such direction as the organising authority may exercise, all races shall be conducted and judged by the race committee in conformity with the published terms and conditions. The term "race committee" whenever it is used shall include any person or committee that is responsible for carrying out any of the designated duties or functions of the race committee.

It will be seen in rule 1.1 that when races are properly set up, the organising authority is linked to the IYRU through the national authority, because it is an affiliated body (club, regatta committee or class association) or, when it is not affiliated, it will work in conjunction with an affiliated body; unless the national authority or the IYRU itself is to be the organising authority. Note that the races are to be run under 'the rules of the IYRU', meaning not only the racing rules (IYRR) but any other regulations concerning yacht racing that the Union may prescribe in its class rules, judges appointments etc.

The organising authority has two main jobs, to appoint the race committee and to issue a notice of race. When a small sailing club asks two keen club members to run an evening race for children the procedure will be quite different from when a large and powerful yacht club appoints a race committee of five or six to run a major international event. The notice of race may be a scribbled piece of paper on the club notice board or an elaborately printed document circulated widely months before the series begins. The principle is the same. Note that in rule 1.2 the 'race committee' means not only those specifically appointed by the organising authority but includes anyone delegated to do the race committee's jobs, the man laying the marks, hoisting the flags, writing down the results.

1.3   Unless otherwise prescribed by the national authority, the organising authority or the race committee may, before the start of a race or series, reject or rescind the entry of any yacht or exclude a competitor, without stating the reason. However, at all world and continental championships, no entry within established quotas shall be rejected or rescinded without first obtaining the approval of the I.Y.R.U. or the duly authorised international class association.

This rule gives the organisers the right to refuse entry to all except world and continental championships without giving a reason. 'Rescind' is intended, I believe, to cover the case where an entry has been accepted by mistake, a cheque cashed in when it should not have been or some such. The rule gives clubs the right to exclude unpopular members of the sailing fraternity without having to say – he drinks – she owes money – he cheats – or whatever. US 110 and US 239 confirm what is now in the rule, that this exclusion cannot be applied after racing begins.

1.4   (a) The race committee and all other bodies and persons concerned with the organisation and conduct of the races or regatta shall be governed by these rules, by the prescriptions of its national authority when they apply, by the sailing instructions, by the class rules (except when they conflict with these rules) and, when applicable, by the Sailboard Racing Rules as contained in Appendix 2 or the Team Racing Rules as contained in Appendix 4, and shall decide all questions in accordance therewith.

(b) The organising authority may modify class rules only for a race or regatta that is not subject to the control of that class association.

A race committee may, within limits, prescribe what it likes in sailing instructions, but once published it is bound by them and any other rules affecting the competition. For instance a race committee may not adjust a class rule when it is inconvenient (unless it conflicts with the IYRR) or ignore a sailing instruction because it suddenly suits it to do so. In RYA 83/3, *Nancy B* requested redress because the race committee had calculated the handicap of another yacht in a way other than that prescribed in the sailing instructions. She was granted redress and the results of the series were recalculated on the basis of a new correct handicap. The decision cited rule 1.4, adding: 'Council does not doubt that the handicap committee acted in good faith, but this cannot be accepted as a good reason for upholding actions that were not in accordance . . . the sailing instructions.'

RYA 83/2 confirms this: 'A race committee is bound by the wording of its own sailing instructions, although its intentions were otherwise' – this from a case where the course displayed on the course board did not send yachts where the race committee had wanted and meant them to go.

Note that, unlike the IYRR many of which can be altered by sailing instructions, class rules may only be modified for races that are not subject to the control of the class association. Any alteration of class rules takes the boat out of class. RYA 81/12 stated: 'Sailing instructions that purport to override measurement rules of an International Class either do not apply to a yacht in that class or, when they do apply, invalidate her certificate'. For reference, US 152, US 154 and US 228 uphold protest committee decisions that accord with class rules.

1.5   The receiving, initiating, hearing and deciding of protests and requests for redress shall be carried out either:

(a) by the race committee itself; or

(b) by a sub-committee thereof appointed by the race committee from its own members or from outside the committee or from a combination of them; or

(c) by a protest committee or a jury, separate from and independent of the race committee, appointed by the organising authority or the race committee; or

(d) by an international jury appointed by the organising authority in accordance with rule 1.6 and Appendix 8, (Terms of Reference of an International Jury and Conditions for its Decisions to be Final), that shall have supervision over the conduct of the races and power to direct the race committee, but only to the extent specifically provided in the terms and conditions of the regatta.

The term "jury", as used in yacht racing, means a panel of judges.

The long-established system of policing the sport through the protest and the protest hearing has stood the test of time reasonably well, if only because of the impossibility of finding any other effective way of controlling what goes on in the middle of a scrum at a mark. Rule 1.5 lists four types of protest committee:

(a) the race committee itself, its members coming ashore after a long day on the committee boat to hear the protest late into the evening;

(b) a sub-committee of the race committee, perhaps three wise men of the club, taking over while the race officers take a well-earned rest;

(c) an independent protest committee (sometimes called a jury) appointed by the organising authority dealing with protests throughout a championship or regatta;

(d) an international jury (also called a jury).

Because there is no appeal from the decisions of an international jury its constitution is strictly controlled: rule 1.6 states when an IJ may be appointed, Appendix 8 how. An IJ may have 'supervision over the conduct of the races and power to direct the race committee', but only as specifically stated in the notice of race. I think it is better for there to be no such powers specified. A series runs more smoothly when there is a good understanding between the jury and the race committee. By this I do not mean that the two should be in league against the competitors – rather the opposite. Unless it is absolutely necessary the jury should not interfere in anyway with the running of the races, thus remaining disinterested and unbiased in the event of requests for redress against the race committee. I say unless absolutely necessary, because I was once at an event where, owing to very unfortunate circumstances, the race committee virtually ceased to exist and to save the event the jury had to do the race committee's work, which was better than abandoning the whole event. Whatever the situation on paper, regular meetings between jury and race committee should be held to resolve the various problems that inevitably occur. Jaw-jaw is better than war-war.

1.6   International juries may be appointed in accordance with rule 1.5(d):

(a) for the Olympic regatta and similar regattas open to yachts from different countries and in such other international regattas as are under the jurisdiction of the I.Y.R.U. or a national authority; or

(b) for international regattas under the jurisdiction of an international class association; or

(c) for international regattas not included in (a) or (b) when the organising authority so advises in the notice of race or regatta or in the sailing instructions.

1.7   The right of appeal may be denied only when either:

(a) an international jury is properly constituted, except that a national authority may prescribe that its approval is required for international juries appointed in accordance with rules 1.6(b) and (c); or

(b) it is essential to determine promptly the result of a race or series of races that will qualify a yacht to compete in a later stage of the event or a subsequent event. A national authority may prescribe that its approval be required for such a procedure; or

(c) a national authority so prescribes for a particular event open only to entries under its own jurisdiction.

When the right of appeal is to be denied, the organising authority shall announce its intention in the notice of race or regatta and in the sailing instructions.

National prescriptions to the rules may (as they do in the UK) require national authority permission for the appointment of an international jury and for the denial of appeal. Appeal may be denied either because there is a properly appointed international jury or because the series cannot get on to the next stage until the first is determined. Failure to follow the requirements of these rules may result in the acceptance of an appeal. In RYA 83/4, the intention of the race organisers was to appoint an international jury, but the condition laid down in Appendix 8 for a minimum of five members was not fulfilled. It followed that competitors had a right of appeal and the appeal in question was accepted by Council. (And then dismissed!)

2   **Notice of Race or Regatta**

The notice of a race or regatta shall contain the following information:

(a) The title, place and dates of the event and name of the organising authority.

(b) That the race or regatta will be governed by the International Yacht Racing Rules, the prescriptions of the national authority when they apply (for international events, a copy in English of prescriptions that apply shall be available to each yacht), the rules of each class concerned, and such other rules as are applicable. When class rules are modified in accordance with rule 1.4(b), the modifications shall be stated.

(c) The class(es) to race, conditions of eligibility or entry and, when appropriate, restrictions on numbers of entries.

(d) The times of registration and starts of the practice race or first race, and succeeding races when known.

The notice shall, when appropriate, include the following:

(e) The scoring system.

(f) The time and place at which the sailing instructions will be available.

(g) Variations from the racing rules, subject to rule 3.1. (The Sailing Instructions).

(h) The procedure for advance registration or entry, including closing dates when applicable, fees and the mailing address.

(i) Measurement procedures or requirements for measuring or rating certificates.

(j) The course(s) to be sailed.

(k) Alternative penalties for rule infringements.

(l) Prizes.

(m)Denial of the right to appeal, subject to rule 1.7.

A notice of race is mandatory, rule 1.1 obliges the organising authority to publish one. No details are given, so presumably a notice on a club notice board would be sufficient. The obligatory clauses are minimal, only those facts essential to get the right boats to the right place at the right time and any information the competitor needs to prepare himself before he gets the sailing instructions. It is of course in the interest of the OA to ensure that there are no surprises on arrival at the regatta. For example, last minute, or non-published special regulations requiring the carrying of some unusual piece of equipment lead to the emptying of local chandlers and the impossibility of compliance for some. The first part (a-d) is mandatory, the second (e-m) mandatory when appropriate, for instance (j) 'the course(s) to be sailed'. Foreign visitors might want their own charts for offshore and would need to know the area required.

Note (b) 'When class rules are modified ... the modifications shall be stated'. This last point is of particular notice. It would be unacceptable for a race to be advertised for the International Finn class and when someone had lugged his dinghy across England he were to find that the class rules were so altered that it was no longer a class event and that he was so disadvantaged that it was not worth his racing.

When drawing up the notice of race try to think through what the competitor needs to know at that stage and tell him. Do not be stingy with information provided that it is reasonably firm and unlikely to be altered. Sailing instructions can (though there is no case law) override the N of R, but it is obviously undesirable to change unless unavoidable.

3   The Sailing Instructions

3.1   STATUS

These rules shall be supplemented by written sailing instructions which shall rank as rules and may alter a rule by specific reference to it, but, except in accordance with rule 3.2 (b) (xxviii), they shall not alter Parts I and IV of these rules, or rules 1, 2, 3, 26, 51.1 (a) or 61, or the rules of Sections C and D of Part VI, or the provision of rule 68.2(a), (Protests by Yachts), that International Code flag "B" is always acceptable as a protest flag. However, when so prescribed by the national authority, this restriction shall not preclude the right of developing and testing proposed rule changes in local regattas.

The IYRR may be divided into three groups:

a) rules that contain the words 'unless otherwise prescribed in the SIs' (eg rules 4.1, 10, 18 and many others). All such rules may be altered in SIs without any reference to the IYRR.

b) rules that contain no such 'unless otherwise ...' clause, and are not among those listed in (c) below. This second group may be altered but only if the competitor is warned. For example, the RORC has a fairly complicated penalty system which differs in some respects from the IYRR and the paragraph is headed by the words 'affecting IYRR 70.1, 70.2 and 74.4'. Rules 53.1, 58, 59 and 60 are also altered and the altered rule is specifically referred to. In some SIs (Cowes Week for example) a list of altered rules is given at the beginning. US 235 upholds this principle rigidly. The race committee changed the course two minutes before the start. The method for a course change had been written in SIs but did not refer to rule 5.1 which governs changing the course. On appeal it was stated: 'If a RC desires to substitute a procedure for changing the course different from that provided for in rule 5.1, it must comply with rule 3.1 and make a "specific reference" to rule 5.1 in its SIs; accordingly, the procedure followed by the RC was improper', IYRU 74 confirms this. When SIs alter an IYRR correctly, then the alteration will govern, however undesirable. In FIV 69/13 the SIs altered rule 71.1 – the right to a hearing – permitting a jury to disqualify on the spot without a hearing. The appeals committee said: 'This prescription was pretty drastic and may be justly criticised. However it does not alter any of the listed rules and therefore has the force of a rule. It follows that it must be respected by whoever has freely agreed to race when such a rule has been published. If a competitor does not wish to sail under such conditions he need only refuse invitations of this sort. If he accepts, however, he must abide by them'. Would he, I wonder, be entitled to recover his entry fee if confronted by an unexpected and unacceptable SI?

c) rules that may not be altered. Any attempt to alter the rules listed in rule 3.1 will be void. Let us look at them:

Part I Fundamental rules and definitions – not many attempts are made to alter these except for *finishing*. Hook-round finishes are a recurring problem, and the futility of trying to arrange them, or of accepting them if they happen are illustrated by Figs. 3 and 98 discussed under *finishing* rule 4.1 'S' and rule 51.1 (a).

Part IV – right of way between yachts. It would obviously be dangerous to allow local alterations, for competitors might unwittingly sail on different rules. The only exceptions are first, at night, when other rules may be prescribed (see under Preamble to Part IV and Appendix 9) and secondly for experimental development purposes when permitted by a national authority.

Rules 1, 2 and 3 (all in Part II). These rules, as we have seen form the framework for racing, judging and organisation and are not to be tampered with.

Rule 26, 51.1 (a) and 61. Rule 26 contains major IYRU policy decisions. Rule 51.1 (a) merely confirms that a yacht cannot *start* or *finish* except within the terms of the definition. Rule 61 deals with the safety aspects (weight) of clothing and equipment and is unalterable except in so far as 61.4 permits its exclusion for 'cruiser-racer type yachts'.

Sections C and D of Part VI. The ban on altering these protects a competitor's right of appeal and his rights under rule 75. Both are extremely important points which it would be wrong to permit a RC to change, however it is unlikely that it would *want* to do so.

Rule 68.2 (a). SIs may not prescribe that flag 'B' is not acceptable as a protest flag. Thus an SI which required white flags for protests would in reality mean white flags *or* code flag 'B'.

Finally note the most important part of this rule – SIs must be written. Rule 3.5, it is true, makes arrangements for oral instructions but these arrangements themselves must be in the written SIs. In US 55, there were no written SIs which was accepted without comment by the competitors and this was considered to bar later objections, (although the appeal was upheld on other grounds: later ambiguous oral instructions). It would however be unwise to rely on this appeal, a modern appeal might well go the other way and if all (or at any rate 99%) of competitors are to understand and get things right, clear written SIs are an absolute essential (see rule 3.2).

3.2   CONTENTS

(a) The sailing instructions shall contain the following information:

    (i)   That the race or regatta will be governed by the International Yacht Racing Rules, the prescriptions of the national authority when they apply (for international events, a copy in English of prescriptions that apply shall be included in the sailing instructions), the rules of each class concerned, the sailing instructions and such other rules as are applicable.

    (ii)   The schedule of races, the classes to race, and the order and times of warning signals.

    (iii)   The course or courses to be sailed or a list of *marks* or courses from which the course or courses will be selected, describing the *marks* and stating:

        1 the order, and either

        2 the side on which each *mark* is to be rounded, or

3 the side on which each *mark* is to be passed.

A diagram or chart is recommended.

(iv) Description of the starting line, the starting system and any special signals to be used.

(v) The procedure for individual and general recalls and any special signals.

(vi) Description of the finishing line and any special instructions for *finishing* a course shortened after the start.

(vii) The time limit, if any, for *finishing*.

(viii) The scoring system, when not previously announced in writing, including the method, if any, for breaking ties.

(b) The sailing instructions shall, when appropriate, include the following:

(i) Variations from the racing rules, subject to rule 3.1, or the class rules for a special race or regatta.

(ii) The registration procedure.

(iii) Location(s) of official regatta notice board(s).

(iv) Procedure for changes in the sailing instructions.

(v) Restrictions controlling modifications to yachts when supplied by the organising authority.

(vi) Signals to be made ashore and location of signal station(s).

(vii) Class flags.

(viii) The racing area. A chart is recommended.

(ix) The starting area.

(x) Course signals.

(xi) Approximate course length; approximate length of windward legs.

(xii) Information on tides and currents.

(xiii) Procedure for shortening the course before or after the start.

(xiv) Mark boats; lead boats.

(xv) Procedure for changes of course after the start and related signals.

(xvi) The time limit, if any, for yachts other than the first yacht to finish.

(xvii) Whether races *postponed* or *abandoned* for the day will be sailed later and, if so, when and where.

(xviii) The number of races required to complete the regatta.

(xix) Safety, such as requirements and signals for personal buoyancy, check-in at the starting area, and check-out and check-in ashore.

(xx) Any measurement or inspection procedure.

(xxi) Alternative penalties for rule infringements.

(xxii)   Whether declarations are required.

(xxiii) Protest procedure and times and place of hearings.

(xxiv) Restrictions on use of support boats, plastic pools, radios, etc. and limitations on hauling out.

(xxv)   Substitute competitors.

(xxvi) Prizes.

(xxvii) Time allowances.

(xxviii)Racing rules applicable between sunset and sunrise and night signals to be used by the race committee.

(xxix) Disposition to be made of a yacht appearing at the start alone in her class.

(xxx)   Denial of the right to appeal, subject to rule 1.7.

(xxxi) Other commitments of the race committee and obligations of yachts.

It is depressingly easy to write bad sailing instructions and no experienced race officer would dare boast that he had never misled competitors, never been ambiguous, or indeed had simply never made a mistake. For this reason, before SIs are printed, never be too proud to ask an outsider to read them through and comment. An outsider cannot rewrite them because he (or she) does not know the circumstances, but he can ask questions, or make remarks. For example: 'It is not clear when Class A's new start would be after a general recall'; 'What happens if only one yacht comes to the start?'; 'Why alter rule 68.3?' etc. Such comments and questions call the race committee's attention to the point, and it can then consider them and decide what to do – if anything.

Sailing instructions consist of a mixture of essential information for, and instructions to competitors. They are the basis of a good race, or rather, since further ingredients are necessary to achieve success, poor sailing instructions can spoil one. Here are some points:

1 SIs should be written in simple clear English, based on a clear idea. Legal language however pompous will not clarify a muddled concept, it will only serve to hide it until some desperate competitor brings the ambiguity out into the open at a redress hearing.

2 they should be revised each year; only too often an outsider gets caught by the fact that SIs have not kept pace with events. For example, the name of a buoy, familiar for years in the neighbourhood, is changed on the charts but not in the SIs: fine for the locals (*everyone* knows) but hopeless for the visitor!

3 SIs should alter the IYRU rules as little as possible, (and of course only within the limits permitted by rule 3.1). Local conditions do impose the necessity for changes but fewer than is usually thought.

4 SIs should be short, they should not include details about hotels, car parks, meals, etc. Be careful not to impose conditions you will later not to wish to enforce. For example, an SI that regulates tallying out and requires a competitor to hang up the tally on the right hook when re-entering, needs careful thought and wording if you are not to run the risk of having to disqualify the winner of the series for a minor slip which need not have been penalised. As far as possible races should be won or lost and protests based on events on the water – not ashore.

5 The most important and difficult part of SIs is the course, including the starting and finishing lines. Except for a standard Olympic course, courses differ from place to place, and from day to day. When a number of classes start at five-minute intervals and their courses have to be designed in a short time round some of a large number of possible marks (as in Cowes Week) the difficulties and pressures are at a maximum. Having written the course, check it. Take a pencil and follow your instructions round to make sure you have not slipped up. It is impossible to be too careful. When it is intended that yachts should 'loop' a mark this must be specified (RYA 85/4).

6 Instructions to yachts should be mandatory, using the verb 'shall'. ('Shall' is used throughout the IYRR, although 'must' sounds better to many English speakers.) The conditional 'should' or 'ought to', ought not to be used: when a competitor ignores such an instruction the PC has no power to penalise him.

7 While instructions to yachts use the mandatory 'shall', actions of the race committee are described by the present tense or the simple future 'will'. eg 'The Pathfinder shall maintain a close-hauled course...' but, 'The starting line, except for the Pathfinder, will be between ...the mark and... the launch.' Note that the mandatory orders given by the IYRU to race committees in the rules become statements of intent in the sailing instructions eg rule 5.6 'the RC shall notify all yachts ... when a race postponed...will be sailed' become 'A postponed race will be resailed at...on..'. The RC, as the writer of the SIs, cannot give orders to itself, it can only state its intentions. When it does so unclearly, or acts other than in accordance with these proclaimed intentions, it lays itself open to requests for redress under rule 69(a).

Rule 3.2 itself consists of two lists of items to be included in SIs. The first line [3.2(a)] is compulsory and the items are common to all races; the second [3.2(b)] contains items which may or may not be relevant to the race in question. When an item is relevant then it is obligatory to include it. Other matters may, of course, be included in SIs when necessary.

We need look at only two. 3.2(a)(i) underlines the importance of spelling out the rules to be obeyed in the competition. It is essential for entrants to be told for instance what special safety regulations they are to obey. When that essential information has been given in the notice of race, then the notice of race must be mentioned. As the rules are written at the moment it is possible to argue that clauses in the N of R are not binding unless SIs prescribe the N of R among other rules.

3.2(a)(iii) emphasises what was said in para 5 above. It gives a detailed description of how the course is to be explained. A race committee that fails to follow it will be open to claims for redress.

Time bombs lie in wait in even the most tested instructions. The 1984 Cowes Week instructions printed the courses in the same way that they had been printed since at least 1977, but when a rare course was set, because of a rare wind, the two-round courses were found to contain a fundamental ambiguity which had lain dormant all those years and, in spite of the thousands who had read SIs, had never been discovered.

3.3 DISTRIBUTION
The sailing instructions shall be available to each yacht entitled to *race*.

No comment – it is no good writing SIs if they do not reach the competitors. Except for very unimportant local racing there should be one set for each yacht.

3.4 CHANGES
Before a race or during a series, the race committee may change the sailing instructions by timely posting a written notice on the official notice board. On the water, it may make such a change by communicating it to each yacht before her warning signal.

3.5 ORAL INSTRUCTIONS
Oral instructions shall not be given, except in accordance with procedure specifically set out in the sailing instructions.

These two rules need to be look at together because 3.5 qualifies 3.4. Rule 3.4 makes it clear that on shore all changes to SIs are to be in writing. One copy on the notice board will be sufficient, but it is to be hoped that organisations that can, will give copies to each yacht. Although there is no time limit on this it must be presumed that SIs, following rule 3.2(b)(iv), will make a last limit after which they will not be changed, and following rule 4.1'L' signal the posting of the notice of change.

On the water any change must be made before the warning signal and to each competitor. This must be taken to mean written SIs – and it is possible to hand out a sheet of written instructions to every boat in quite a large fleet – because 3.5 states (and here is the qualification) that: 'Oral instructions shall not be given' unless the procedure is in SIs. Therefore if – to invent an example – it is stated that when there is a wind change the magnetic course to the first mark will be announced by hailer, well and good, but if there is nothing in SIs then hailing yachts to tell them, say, that the finishing line has been changed will be quite ineffectual.

Two cases confirm that trying to alter SIs by voice is no good. In IYRU 125 a race officer allowed a boat to tally out late in the first two races in a series, but in the third he refused and the boat was disqualified. She maintained that the RO had set a precedent and effectively altered the SI that required tallying out. Her appeal was refused – 'the RO was not empowered to vary [a sailing instruction] on his own responsibility: rule 3.5 refers. A RC is required to enforce whatever SIs it has seen fit to prescribe.' Again in RYA 1982/7, a hail of 'general recall' was made on the Tannoy and ignored by one yacht. On appeal it was held that she was entitled to disregard the shouted instruction because SIs contained no provision for oral instructions and the hail was therefore without effect. (At first glance this case may seem rather as if it condoned unsporting behaviour, but on consideration it will be seen that it would not be right to expect boats to try to obey possibly semi-inaudible unofficial instructions). US 97 and US 66 deal with similar problems.

Particular care must be taken not to alter SIs orally at a briefing. IYRU 75 states: 'SIs cannot require a competitor to attend a briefing' This is presumably based on an assumption that as oral SIs are void, nothing that is said at a briefing can be taken as binding.

To sum up – avoid oral instructions as far as possible and when essential explain clearly in the written SIs how they are to work.

4 Signals

4.1 VISUAL SIGNALS

Unless otherwise prescribed in the sailing instructions, the following International Code flags (or boards) and other visual signals shall be used as indicated and when displayed alone shall apply to all classes, and when displayed over a class signal they shall apply to the designated class only:

"AP", Answering Pendant — Postponement Signal

Means:

(a) "All races not started are *postponed*. The warning signal will be made one minute after this signal is lowered."
(One sound signal shall be made with the lowering of the "AP".)

(b) Over one ball or shape.
"The scheduled starting times of all races not started are *postponed* fifteen minutes."
(This *postponement* can be extended indefinitely by the addition of one ball or shape for *every* fifteen minutes.)

(c) Over one of the numeral pendants 1 to 9.
"All races not started are *postponed* one hour, two hours, etc."

(d) Over Code flag "A".
"All races not started are *postponed* to a later day."

"B" — Protest signal.

When displayed by a yacht.
Means:
"I intend to lodge a protest."

"C" — Change of Course while Racing.

When displayed at or near a rounding *mark*.
Means:
"After rounding this *mark*, the course to the next *mark* has been changed."

"I" — Round the Ends Starting Rule.

Displayed before or with the preparatory signal.
Means:
"Rule 51.1(c) will be in effect for this start."
When lowered, accompanied by one long sound signal, one minute before the starting signal.
Means:
"The one-minute period of rule 51.1(c) has begun."

"L" — Means:

(a) When displayed ashore:
"A notice to competitors has been posted on the notice board."

(b) When displayed afloat:
"Come within hail," or "Follow me."

"M" — Mark Signal.

When displayed on a buoy, vessel, or other object.
Means:
"Round or pass the object displaying this signal instead of the *mark* that it replaces."

"N" — Abandonment Signal.

Means:
"All races are *abandoned*."

"N over X" — Abandonment and Re-sail Signal.

Means:
"All races are *abandoned* and will shortly be re-sailed. The warning signal will be made one minute after this signal is lowered."
(One sound signal shall be made with the lowering of "N over X".)

"N over First Substitute" — Cancellation Signal.

Means:
"All races are *cancelled*."

"P" — Preparatory Signal.

Means:
"The class designated by the warning signal will *start* in five minutes exactly."

"S" — Shorten Course Signal.

Means:

(a) at the starting line:
   "Sail the shortened course prescribed in the sailing instructions."

(b) at the finishing line:
   "*Finish* the race either:
   (i) at the prescribed finishing line at the end of the round still to be completed by the leading yacht, or
   (ii) as prescribed in the sailing instructions."

(c) at a rounding *mark*:
   "*Finish* between the rounding *mark* and the committee boat."

"X" — Individual Recall.

Broken out immediately after the starting signal is made, accompanied by one sound signal, in accordance with rule 8.1(a)(ii), (Recalls).
Means:
"One or more yachts have started prematurely or have infringed the Round the Ends Starting Rule 51.1(c)."

"Y" — Life Jacket Signal.

Means:
"Life jackets or other adequate personal buoyancy shall be worn while *racing* by all helmsmen and crews, unless specifically excepted in the sailing instructions."
When this signal is displayed after the warning signal is made, failure to comply shall not be cause for disqualification.
Notwithstanding anything in this rule, it shall be the individual responsibility of each competitor to wear a life jacket or other adequate personal buoyancy when conditions warrant. A wet suit is not adequate personal buoyancy.

"First Substitute" — General Recall Signal.

Means:
"The class is recalled for a new start as provided in the sailing instructions."
Unless the sailing instructions prescribe some other signal, the warning signal will be made one minute after this signal is lowered. (One sound signal shall be made with the lowering of "First Substitute".)

Red Flag — Displayed by committee boat.

Means:
"Leave all marks to port."

Green Flag — Displayed by committee boat.

Means:
"Leave all marks to starboard."

Blue Flag or Shape — Finishing Signal.

When displayed by a committee boat.
Means:
"The committee boat is on station at the finishing line."

In rule 4.1 the meanings of a number of international code flags are listed; these meanings are different from those in the international code of signals. There are no grounds for redress when they are not understood or even missed by competitors as was made clear in RYA 82/17. 'Although the race committee's decision to cancel the race was improper, the fact remains that its signal was made in accordance with rule 4.1 and most of the competitors complied with it. There is no rule that requires a race committee to ensure that every yacht receives its signals'. When there is no wind some guesswork may be necessary! In US 170 it was held that 'A flag is displayed within the meaning of rule 4 and constitutes proper notice under rule 5 when it is hoisted or otherwise physically placed in a position customarily used for signalling purposes and in which the flag reasonably could be expected to be seen by the contestants. That the flag hangs limp because of lack of wind does not detract from the fact that it is 'displayed''.

We need only look at 'S'. Before the start of a race, rule 5.3(a) governs course shortening, and after the start, rule 5.4(c). Thus 'S'(a) refers to rule 5.3(a) and 'S'(b) and (c) to rule 5.4(c). 'S'(a) refers back to the sailing instructions for some special shortening course arrangements, as does (b)(ii), but (b)(i) and (c) directly instruct competitors what to do when the flag is displayed either at the finishing line (b) or at a rounding mark (c).

There are two points to look out for: (1) 'S' at the finishing line can mean one of two things, so it is essential to be sure that there are no special sailing instructions about it; (2) at the risk of repeating myself, 'S' is the fount of endless mistakes about the direction in which to cross the finishing line. *Daisy* may only finish 'in the direction from the last mark'.

This sometimes means that, when a course is shortened, a buoy that has served as a rounding mark being left to port (and which would have remained so had the course not been shortened) suddenly changes its nature and becomes a finishing mark to be left to starboard, this causes confusion (see Fig. 98).

Sailing instructions can and often do alter these rules and use other flags to impart information. For the most part, clauses in this rule cannot be infringed, 'Y' is an exception, but if *Daisy* disregards some of the others ('S', 'Red' and 'Green' for example) she will infringe rule 51 by failing to sail the course correctly.

4.2   SIGNALS FOR STARTING A RACE

(a) Unless otherwise prescribed in the sailing instructions, the signals for starting a race shall be made at five-minute intervals exactly, and shall be either:

System 1   Warning Signal   — Class flag broken out or distinctive signal displayed.

Preparatory Signal   — Code flag "P" broken out or distinctive signal displayed.

Starting Signal   — Both warning and preparatory signals lowered.

In System 1, when classes are started:

(i)   at ten-minute intervals—
the warning signal for each succeeding class shall be broken. out or displayed at the starting signal of the preceding class.

(ii)   at five-minute intervals—
the preparatory signal for the first class to start shall be left displayed until the last class starts. The warning signal for each succeeding class shall be broken out or displayed at the preparatory signal of the preceding class.

or

System 2   Warning Signal   — White or yellow shape.

Preparatory Signal   — Blue shape.

Starting Signal for   — Red shape.
first class to start

In System 2, each signal shall be lowered one minute before the next is made.
Class flags when used shall be broken out not later than the preparatory signal for each class.
In starting a series of classes:

(i)   at ten-minute intervals—
the starting signal for each class shall be the warning signal for the next.

(ii)   at five-minute intervals—
the preparatory signal for each class shall be the the the warning signal for the next.

(b) Although rules 4.1 "P" and 4.2(a) specify five-minute intervals between signals, the sailing instructions may prescribe any intervals.

(c) A warning signal shall not be made before its scheduled time, except with the consent of all yachts entitled to *race*.

(d) When a significant error is made in the timing of the interval between any of the signals for starting a race, the recommended procedure is to signal a general recall, *postponement* or *abandonment* of the race whose start is directly affected by the error and a corresponding *postponement* of succeeding races. Unless otherwise prescribed in the sailing instructions, a new warning signal shall be made. When the race is not recalled, *postponed* or *abandoned* after an error in the timing of the interval, each succeeding signal shall be made at the correct interval from the preceding signal.

Sailing Instructions may prescribe any sort of start the race organisers demand, but the two systems described in this rule (System 1 used mostly in Europe and System 2 in America) satisfy most requirements and are well and truly tried through the long years they have been used. The possible exception to this is 4.2 System 1 (ii). It leaves the preparatory flag 'P' flying throughout the long starting sequence and is frequently replaced by another system.

(b) permits time gaps other than five minutes for the intervals and three minutes is commonly used for small dinghies and sailboards.

(c) states that the warning signal may not be made before the scheduled time unless all the yachts entitled to race have agreed. I take this to mean that the start of the race cannot be advanced by, say, half an hour before that scheduled. Presumably it does not mean that if the race committee's watch is one second fast on GMT redress can be claimed. I suspect it was written before the days of universally correct watches.

(d) instructs the race committee to restart the race when there is a mistake in the timing sequence. However when for some reason this is not done, 'each succeeding signal shall be made at the correct interval from the preceeding signal' This means that when the preparatory signal is given four minutes after the warning signal, the starting signal should be given five minutes later; ie nine minutes after the warning signal not 10 minutes after. This does not mean that a boat prejudiced by such an error cannot claim redress.

In US 244 the starting signal was made four minutes after the preparatory signal instead of five minutes as was intended. As a result about half the yachts were not in normal starting positions when the starting signal was made. The race was abandoned but the winner appealed this decision on the grounds that the starting signal was made at the correct interval (one minute) from the lowering of the preparatory signal (System 2) thus fulfilling the requirement that 'each succeeding signal. . .'etc. The US Appeals Committee dismissed the appeal. It remarked about System 2 'the lowering of a signal is not a separate signal but an act of preparing for the next signal'. The time intervals are measured between the making of each signal when they are raised. The fact that some yachts noted the error, adjusted to it and accordingly were not prejudiced, in no way made the race a fair one for those who were prejudiced.' Thus an action of the RC which was the same for everyone was, nevertheless, prejudicial to some. A recent international jury has held that when an incorrect interval between the warning and 'P' is followed by a correct interval between 'P' and the start, a yacht that has been materially prejudiced by this is eligible for redress.

Remember that errors in the starting sequence, either because of timing, or of incorrect visual or sound signals are pretty common. Whenever possible a race committee which is aware of an error would be silly not to start the sequence over again (by means of postponment, abandonment or general recall. But if this is not done the start is valid until one or more yachts can show that their finishing position has been materially prejudiced, and redress is granted (see rule 69).

4.3   OTHER SIGNALS
The sailing instructions shall designate any other special signals and shall explain their meaning.

These few words cover all the infinite possibilities of communicating with competitors by means of flags, or boards. The flags will be other than, or have other meanings than those in 4.1. The boards will be course boards, either displaying the whole course or the magnetic course to the first mark. But whatever they are it is essential that their form and meanings are described in SIs without any possibility of mistake for the competitors. Woe betide a RC what gets it wrong; it will be handing out redress to all and sundry.

4.4   CALLING ATTENTION TO SIGNALS
Whenever the race committee makes a signal, except "S" before the warning signal or a blue flag or shape when on station at the finishing line, it shall call attention to its action as follows:

(a) Three guns or other sound signals when displaying:

    (i)   "N";
    (ii)   "N over X";
    (iii)   "N over First Substitute".

(b) Two guns or other sound signals when displaying:

    (i)   "AP";
    (ii)   "S";
    (iii)   "First Substitute".

(c) Repetitive sound signals while displaying Code flag "C".

(d) One gun or other sound signal when making any other signal, including the lowering of:

    (i)   "AP" when the length of the postponement is not signalled;
    (ii)   "N over X";
    (iii)   "First Substitute".

A helmsman cannot keep his eyes fixed on the committee boat, so his attention is drawn to the display of any visual signal by a noise. Noises will do, a hooter, a whistle, a gun, but probably a voice will not. There must be some reasonable probability of its being heard within a reasonable distance on an average day. What a lot of averages – but while a small hooter will suffice for a committee boat on a short starting line a loud cannon will be required to carry across a line suitable for 100 large offshore racers. Errors in sound signals are dealt with in 4.5.

4.5   VISUAL STARTING SIGNALS TO GOVERN
Times shall be taken from the visual starting signals, and a failure or mistiming of a gun or other sound signal calling attention to starting signals shall be disregarded.

It is the flags (or shapes) that count, not the time of the sound signals. Misfires, or the mistiming of other sound signals are to be disregarded. 'Shall be disregarded' are the words used. Thus redress will not be available on the grounds of the omission of the RC to do something it ought to have done. But note that this only applies to starting signals. It does *not* apply to others, such as recall signals.

5   Designating the Course, Altering the Course or Race

5.1   Before or with the warning signal for a class that has not *started*, the race committee:

(a) shall either signal or otherwise designate the course.

(b) may remove and substitute a new course signal.

5.2   Before the preparatory signal, the race committee may shift a starting *mark*.

5.3   Before the starting signal, the race committee may:

(a) shorten the course to one prescribed in the sailing instructions.

(b) *postpone* to designate a new course before or with the new warning signal, or for any other reason.

(c) *postpone* to a later day.

(d) *cancel* the race for any reason.

5.4   After the starting signal, the race committee may:

(a) *abandon* and resail the race when there is an error in starting procedure.

(b) change the course at any rounding *mark* subject to proper notice being given to each yacht as prescribed in the sailing instructions.

(c) shorten the course by finishing a race at any rounding *mark* or as prescribed in the sailing instructions, or *abandon* or *cancel* the race:

    (i)   because of foul weather endangering the yachts, or

    (ii)   because of insufficient wind making it improbable that the race will finish within the time limit, or

    (iii) because a *mark* is missing or has shifted, or

    (iv) for any other reasons (other than changes in the weather conditions) directly affecting the safety or fairness of the competition.

This rule contains instructions for race committees and race officers, setting out their powers, and the time limitations on these powers.
5.1. Sometimes a number of courses are given in sailing instructions and a flag or numeral pennant indicates which is to be used, sometimes course boards list the marks to be rounded, but whatever method is chosen, it must be communicated to the competitors before the warning signal. If that is impossible the race must be postponed until it is done, when a new starting sequence can begin. The only exceptions are to be found in rule 5.2 –

shifting a starting mark – and rule 5.3(a) – shortening course. RYA 83/7 confirms this saying: 'Physical limitations on signalling the course before or with the warning signal cannot justify non-compliance with rule 5.1. A race must be postponed until the course can be displayed correctly and in time.'

5.2. The starting line must be fixed before the preparatory signal. Any starting mark can be relaid until then but after there must be a postponement. This is a recurrent pitfall for race committees in shifting winds and strong tides.

5.3. At any time before the starting signal, the race committee may act as listed. Note that a postponement may be made 'for any reason'. This presumably includes waiting for boats that come late to the start. It is a practice that often infuriates those who have arrived punctually, but seems within the competence of the race officer. The race may also be cancelled for any reason. But the reason would, I believe, have to be reasonable.

5.4. After the start the picture changes and the race officer has much less choice. In addition to all the things listed, he may, when it is correct to do so, signal an individual or a general recall (see rule 8). Let us look at what rule 5.4 allows him to do. When there is a mistake in the starting procedure he may abandon the race and restart it. Abandoning immediately after the starting signal because, say, a gun is fired 30 seconds early, may be preferable to a general recall because sailing instructions may require a change in starting procedures after a general recall (5.4(a)). He may change the course according to procedure laid down in the sailing instructions, provided the change is made at a rounding mark. This refers mainly to Olympic type courses (5.4(b)).

Finally he may shorten the course (in one of two ways) or abandon or cancel the race. His discretion to shorten, abandon or cancel is not unlimited. Permissible reasons are: bad weather (i), calms (ii), a missing mark (iii), for any other reason directly affecting the safety or fairness of the competition (iv). However there is one thing he is not allowed to do – that is abandon or cancel because of changes in wind direction (unless written into the SIs).

IYRU 110 states: 'The race committee was wrong in abandoning the race. Windshifts are a common occurrence in yacht racing. Anticipating predictable windshifts is a part of the art of sailing. Unpredictable windshifts sometimes introduce a 'lottery' element into a race, but they cannot be said to affect the fairness of the competition with the meaning of rule 5.4'.

The race officer must act reasonably. In IYRU 85, 15 classes sailed the same course. At a certain moment a mark went missing and some boats claimed redress. The race committee cancelled all classes, including two that had had no problems. Reinstating the races for these classes the US Appeals Committee stated that since no claims had come from the two classes appealing and no evidence had been forthcoming of any adverse effect on their competition resulting from the shifted mark, the race committee were not entitled to cancel those two races.

RYA 82/17 emphasises that rule 54.(d)(ii) depends on there being a time limit. When there is none, 'insufficient wind' does not constitute grounds for cancelling a race, because when there is no time limit there must be an intention to continue the race until it is completed, no matter how long that will take.

RYA 85/1 deals with the situation where a race is half completed. After three boats finished, the race was abandoned because of bad weather, and no results were posted. On appeal the decision stated: 'The protest committee was correct in holding that it was empowered by rule 5.4(c) to abandon the race for reasons of safety. However, when there are no handicaps, a yacht that finishes before the abandonment signal is given, is entitled to a result. At that point the race committee become bound by rule 5.5, and those yachts that were unable to finish because of the abandonment, are entitled to consideration of redress.' (Redress might have been a resail for third and subsequent places.)

5.5   After a race has been completed, the race committee shall not *abandon* or *cancel* it without taking the appropriate action under rule 74.2(b), (Consideration of Redress).

The race committee's powers to abandon (and try to resail) or cancel. This rule's restrictions on the race committee's powers to abandon or cancel are often necessary. If only one or two boats out of a large fleet have been prejudiced it is unfair to the rest to scrub the race for all the others. There are numerous forms of redress available which are discussed under rule 74.2(b).

5.6   The race committee shall notify all yachts concerned by signal or otherwise when and where a race *postponed* to a later day or *abandoned* will be sailed.

6   Starting and Finishing Lines

The starting and finishing lines shall be either:

(a) a line between a *mark* and a mast or staff on the committee boat or station clearly identified in the sailing instructions; or

(b) a line between two *marks*; or

(c) the extension of a line through two stationary posts, with or without a *mark* at or near its outer limit, inside which the yachts shall pass.

For types (a) and (c) of starting or finishing lines the sailing instructions may also prescribe that a *mark* will be laid at or near the inner end of the line, in which case yachts shall pass between it and the outer *mark*.

The rule prescribes three methods of establishing a line, whether for starting or finishing. In spite of the mandatory form in which it is written, it does not exclude other lines when correctly prescribed in sailing instructions. For instance US 86 makes it clear that it is perfectly legitimate to use a gate start. Similarly, for a long race, an adequate finishing line can be established by yachts taking their own times when (say) a lightship vessel bears due north. However, the three systems in the rule probably cover 99% of the starts and finishes in the world.

It is not within the scope of this book to discuss the infinite problems of race management and the various methods individual race officers have of solving them, sufficient to note a few points.

When there are no limit (or distance) marks, systems (a) and (b) are simple. An IDM complicates the start because it must be made clear whether, after contact, any rerounding is to be round the IDM only or round the committee boat as well. Sailing instructions should leave competitors in no doubt as to what is intended. System (c) is commonly known as a transit

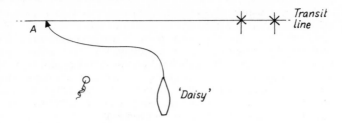

Fig. 17 Daisy *does not infringe 51.2. The string rule only begins as she starts at position* A .

line (although 'transit' really means a passage). When such a line is used it is normal to limit its length. Sometimes the further bank of a river limits it naturally, but it is more common to lay an ODM. The ODM should be on the line or on the course side of it; when it is not, and has been laid or has drifted to the pre-start side of the starting line, a 'Corinthian start' is possible – so called from an RYA case in 1933 – (Fig. 17). Since the Piece-of-String rule 51.2 does not begin until *Daisy* starts, then if the mark is more than a boat's length away from the line it is irrelevant, and she infringes no rule when she goes beyond it. Efforts to rectify this unsatisfactory situation by changing rule 51.3 have failed.

Equally it has been held in IYRU 124 (Fig.102) that a buoy, or other object, on the post-finish side of a finishing line is not a mark and can be disregarded (see rule 51.3).

7 Start of a Race

7.1 STARTING AREA
The sailing instructions may define a starting area that may be bounded by buoys; if so, they shall not rank as *marks*.

7.2 TIMING THE START
The *start* of a yacht shall be timed from her starting signal.

No comment is needed except to emphasize rule 7.2. If the starting gun is fired at 1100 then every yacht is presumed to have started at that instant. It would be palpably absurd to knock 20 seconds off the time of a yacht that has started, badly, 20 seconds late. However like all rules this may be altered by SIs when desired. In long-distance races with a number of legs yachts may be required to take their own starting times.

8 Recalls

8.1 INDIVIDUAL RECALL
When, at her starting signal, any part of a yacht's hull, crew or equipment is on the course side of the starting line or its extensions, or she is subject to rule 51.1(c), (Sailing the Course), the race committee shall:

either

(a) make a suitable sound signal and either:

      (i)   lower the class warning signal to "the dip"; or

(ii)　display Code flag "X"

until all such yachts are wholly on the pre-start side of the starting line or its extensions, or for four minutes after the starting signal, whichever is the earlier; or

(iii)　hail her sail number.

The sailing instructions shall prescribe which of these options will apply.

or

(b) follow such other procedure as may be prescribed in the sailing instructions.

Good starts are the hall-mark of good race management, and must include quick accurate intelligible recall signals. Every experienced competitor and race officer will know how difficult satisfactory recalls are to achieve. The rule requires a sound signal (see rule 4.4) and one of three systems: the class warning signal lowered to 'the dip', the displaying of Code flag 'X' or a simple hail, (which is fine when you can be sure that the hail can be heard right down the line). When the RC fails to fulfil the requirements of the system chosen and prescribed in the SIs then the boat will, if her finishing position has been prejudiced, have grounds for seeking redress, (see 69(a)). But first of all it needs to be made clear that when a yacht is aware that she is over the line, – not just wonders or thinks 'perhaps' but *knows* – then she is obliged to return and start correctly whatever errors the RC has perpetrated. It would be cheating not to do so.

This was originally stated in an old case; (RYA 1954/5) 'If however a yacht is aware that she was over the line at the start, and is aware that she has not returned across it, she is not justified in continuing the race.' This has been confirmed in RYA 1984/5 which states that when a yacht realises she is a premature starter she is bound by rule 33.1 to retire or start correctly.

US 208 tells the story of a premature starter that did not return. When disqualified she sought redress because the RC had failed to hoist the prescribed recall signal, Code Flag 'X'. Reinstating her, the US Appeals Committee said: 'The obligations of the RC to make the designated sound and flag signals to recall a premature starter are mandatory under rule 8.1. The RC cannot escape these obligations by taking refuge in the provision of rule 51.1 that failure of a yacht to see or hear her recall notification shall not relieve her of her obligation to start correctly. These provisions presuppose that the RC has made the required recall signals, and if it fails to do so a yacht may interpret the absence of recall signals as confirmation that she has made a proper start'.

Nor is it enough to make the visual signal and not the sound signal, IYRU 70 ruled: 'When a visual signal is not accompanied by the prescribed sound signal a premature starter is not required when in doubt to respond to a recall'. This interpretation is repeated in RYA 84/5.

In IYRU 111, at the starting signal, some competitors were coming to the line from the course side, the nearest, A, was about 20 yards from the line. No recall signals were made. A hardened her sheets and set off to sail the course taking the absence of recall signals as confirmation that she had started correctly. The fact that A never reached the pre-start side of the line did not nullify rule 8.1, or rules 51.1(a) or (b). A yacht that manoeuvres in the vicinity of the starting line ranks as a starter, even though she never reaches the pre-start side of the line. At her starting signal, she becomes a premature starter, but when the RC fails to make any recall signal, the yacht may be justified in believing that she started correctly.'

Note in rule 8.1(a)(ii) that there is a time limit set for leaving the 'X' flag hoisted or the warning flag at the dip. When a yacht fails to return she must be given the benefit of the doubt for four minutes – a chance to look back through glasses etc – before the signal is removed. The removal of the signal normally means that the yacht has wholly returned and can therefore turn and start; but I imagine (there is no case law at the time of writing) that if a signal is removed at four minutes a yacht will not be justified in taking it as an 'all clear' signal. She will have to judge that for herself.

Note: this rule is addressed to RCs. The yacht's obligation to return and start correctly when she has crossed the line prematurely is to be found in rule 51.

Note: the recall signal is given immediately after the starting signal. When the Round-the-Ends rule (51.1(c)) is in force it may refer to an infringement of that rule in the minute before the starting gun. For instance if *Daisy* has crossed the line that minute and dipped back without going round outside the CV or the ODM (across an extension of the line) she is in breach of the Round-the-Ends rule and must be recalled, as if she were an ordinary premature starter.

Note: radio recalls are excellent when suitable frequencies can be found, but must be used with care. If a mistake such as transmitting the wrong sail number, misleads a competitor there will be grounds for redress, whatever the provisions of the SIs.

8.2   GENERAL RECALL

(a) When there is either a number of unidentified premature starters or an error in starting procedure, the race committee may make a general recall signal in accordance with rules 4.1, ("First Substitute"), and 4.4, (Calling Attention to Signals). Unless otherwise prescribed in the sailing instructions, new warning and preparatory signals shall be made.

(b) Except as provided in rule 31.2, (Disqualification), rule infringements before the preparatory signal for the new start shall be disregarded for the purpose of competing in the race to be re-started.

The two permissible reasons for a general recall are:
1 the existence of a number of *unidentified* premature starters. When the race officer can identify all the boats over the line, he is not justified in signalling a general recall. A famous incident some years ago illustrated this. In a fleet of forty-odd boats, after a series of mis-starts caused by the misbehaviour of the competitors, all except three boats started prematurely. These, none of whom returned, were identified by elimination, and the race was allowed to continue. The goodies were placed 1,2,3 while the baddies, much to their indignation, were disqualified. There was no redress.
2 an error in the starting procedure. Such an error affects the fairness of the competition and can therefore also be remedied under rule 5.4(c)(iv) by abandonment and resail. Unless otherwise written into the SIs, the starting sequence begins again at the warning signal, thus giving the fleet at least 10 minutes to resettle itself.

There may have been infringments of the rules after the first preparatory signal and before the general recall signal but these are to be disregarded 'for the purpose of competing in the race to be re-started'. I take this to mean that if, in that five-minute period, there is an incident between A and B, and B is disabled, and in the subsequent protest A is found to be at fault, A cannot be disqualified from the re-started race but B is still eligible for redress under rule 69(c). Between the recall signal and the new preparatory signal yachts are not *racing* (see the definition of *racing*) and their liability under rule 31.2 not to hinder yachts that are racing in other classes, remains. Rule 8.2(b) will not restrict a race committee's powers to act under rule 75, (Gross Infringement of Rules, or Misconduct).

9   Marks

9.1   MARK MISSING

(a) When any *mark* either is missing or has shifted, the race committee shall, when possible, replace it in its stated position, or substitute a new one with similar characteristics or a buoy or vessel displaying Code flag "M"— the *mark* signal.

(b) When it is impossible either to replace the *mark* or to substitute a new one in time for the yachts to round or pass it, the race committee may, at its discretion, act in accordance with rule 5.4(c)(iii), (Designating the Course, Altering the Course or Race).

9.2   MARK UNSEEN

When races are sailed in fog or at night, dead reckoning alone need not necessarily be accepted as evidence that a *mark* has been rounded or passed.

No marks – no race! Rule 9 requires RCs to remedy the situation when marks go missing, if possible by substitution. When it is impossible to replace the mark the RC can shorten the course, if there is still time, or abandon or cancel the race. However they do not have to do so. In a very odd case, US 230, in a long race a mark disappeared and the yachts turned 'in the area'. All the yachts that took part accepted the results and when an appeal arose from the race (on another matter) the US Appeals Committee, rather reluctantly, accepted the situation. In other circumstances redress might be given to those badly affected.

An interesting Soviet case, now IYRU 56, arose from an incident when one boat's keel pulled the starting mark under the water. When the buoy came free it sprang back and touched another boat. Among other rules cited the protestor asked for the race to be abandoned under rule 9.1 because the mark had shifted but in vain: 'Rule 9.1 applies only to a mark that has shifted so that it is nowhere near its designated position. It does not apply to a mark that moves as the result of another yacht touching it. Therefore abandonment is not an option open to the committee.'

9.2. Few things are more difficult for the poor race committee or jury than when it is faced by the information that thick fog has enshrouded a turning mark for some or all of the boats. When the race cannot for one reason or another easily be abandoned, hours will be spent looking at charts and coming to difficult decisions. I think what this rule does is to permit a protest committee to disbelieve the evidence from a chart and log without implying that the navigator is lying.

10   Finishing Within a Time Limit

Unless otherwise prescribed in the sailing instructions, in races where there is a time limit, one yacht *finishing* within the prescribed limit shall make the race valid for all other yachts in that race.

Unless SIs prescribe a time limit there will be none; if they do, and lay down no other rules, once one yacht has finished in time the rest of the fleet have the opportunity to finish if it takes till next morning. Often SIs state that once one yacht has finished the rest have an hour before the axe falls. Those that have not finished by that time being retired. When SIs state that there is to be no time limit it is clear that the intention is to sail the race to its bitter end and the RC cannot abandon it because of calm weather (RYA 82/17).

In US 199 the race committee got itself into a proper muddle. The Lahaina/Honolulu race consisted of six classes with class trophies and several over-all prizes and trophies. Leading yachts in the larger classes finished within the time limit but none from the smaller. Sorting the muddle out the Appeals Committee held that the first yacht had made the overall trophies available to all yachts, including those in the smaller classes, but that the trophies for the smaller classes, whose leaders had not finished in time could not be won. The decision noted that there could have been incongruous results where a class D yacht could conceivably have won BCT honours yet not have participated in a valid race in her own class.

11   Ties

When there is a tie at the finish of a race, either actual or on corrected times, the points for the place for which the yachts have tied and for the place immediately below shall be added together and divided equally. When two or more yachts tie for a trophy or prize in either a single race or a series, the yachts so tied shall, when practicable, sail a deciding race; if not, either the tie shall be broken by a method established under rule 3.2(a)(viii), (The Sailing Instructions), or the yachts so tied shall either receive equal prizes or share the prize.

The rule lays down clearly what shall happen if there is a tie unless SIs say otherwise. It is very important for any series that the scoring makes it absolutely clear how points are to be awarded and how ties are going to be resolved. The problems, remember, never arise between the yachts placed 13th and 14th, only between 1st and 2nd and are proportionately important.

US 247 illustrates the fate of committees not prepared. A and B finished in a tie

A   1,DNS,1,2,2,1, = 6¼ points
B   3,1,2,1,1,2   = 6¼ points

The race committee broke the tie in favour of B, using all the races to do so. A requested redress on the grounds that the throw-out races should not be counted. The PC sustained this position and awarded the first place to A. On appeal the District Appeals Committee upheld this decision and B appealed again. The USYRU Appeals Committee dismissing the appeal and giving the decision finally in favour of A stated: '...it is the usual practice to eliminate the throw-out race for all scoring purposes including tie-breaking...This is not to say that throw-out races may not be used for tie-breaking but if they are to be so used, the tie-breaking sailing instruction must explicitly say so.' What a lot of trouble could have been saved by one timely sentence in the SIs.

12   **Races to be Re-sailed**

When a race is to be re-sailed:

(a) All yachts entered in the original race shall be eligible to *start* in the race to be re-sailed.

(b) Subject to the entry requirements of the original race, and at the discretion of the race committee, new entries may be accepted.

(c) Rule infringements in the original race shall be disregarded for the purpose of competing in the race to be re-sailed.

(d) The race committee shall notify the yachts concerned when and where the race will be re-sailed.

A race can be re-sailed after it has been postponed before or abandoned after the start. Not only starters in the original race may start in the re-sailed race but those that were entered and indeed others that had not entered, but enter for the 'new' race – provided of course they conform to entry requirements and pay their entry fee! It is very important for the RC to do everything possible to ensure that the time and place for the re-sail is known to those concerned. US 146 upheld the right of four yachts to enter in a re-sail. Two of them had registered for the series, two had not registered in the abandoned race. The RC wrongly decided that only those yachts which had started in the original race would be rescored in the re-sailed race and did not record the finishes of these four yachts. Remember that if it were desired SIs could alter rule 12 and restrict entries in any race re-sailed to starters in the original race.

13   **Award of Prizes**

Before awarding the prizes, the race committee shall be satisfied that all yachts whose finishing positions affect the awards have observed the racing rules, the prescriptions of the national authority when they apply, the sailing instructions and the class rules.

Rule 70.2, which entitles a race or protest committee to protest a yacht with a hearing, is discretionary. The committee *'may* call a hearing'. The natural presumption is a race committee will administer races correctly and try to penalise yachts that infringe rules, but there may be occasions when this seems unnecessary, or inadvisable – for instance for a very minor infringement of the safety regulations such as a whistle being lost overboard – but rule 13 makes it mandatory for the race committee to proceed against a yacht that stands to win a prize. It would not be fair for a yacht that has infringed any of the rules to walk off with the cup.

It cannot be said that IYRU 88 illuminates the rule greatly. Throughout a five-race series, A competed with a crew of three. After the last race B protested A for infringing a class rule that limited the crew to two. This was the first protest relating to the matter. The protest was refused because no protest flag was displayed. B appealed this decision on the grounds that the race committee ought, on its own initiative, to have disqualified A in each race and that its omission to do so permitted it to grant redress under rule 70.3. B also relied on rule 13. Dealing with this last point the Canadian Appeals Committee said: 'The second argument of the protestor [B] requests the race committee to invoke rule 13 and refuse to award the prize to A because, in the circumstances, it cannot be satisfied that she observed a class rule. Rule 13 may be invoked only at the instance of the race committee and cannot be used by a competitor to accomplish indirectly what he should have done but failed to do directly. The race committee chose not to invoke this rule, and its decisions may not be questioned on appeal.'

So it appears that the rule may or may not be mandatory, and even if it is, if a competitor cannot compel a race committee to use it, it becomes, in fact, discretionary.

(Numbers 14, 15, 16 and 17 are spare numbers)

Part III—General Requirements

Owner's Responsibilities for Qualifying his Yacht

*A yacht intending to **race** shall, to avoid subsequent disqualification, comply with the rules of Part III before her preparatory signal and, when applicable, while **racing**.*

Up to now there has been no rule that a yacht could infringe (except Fundamental rules and 4.1 'Y'). In the next three Parts we shall find all the rules that can be broken. I believe that rule 75 is not an exception to this. It is a rule applied by race committees (or juries) when someone misbehaves – but is not really 'infringed'. There is only an unspoken requirement for a competitor to comport himself decently.

18 Entries

Unless otherwise prescribed either in the notice of race or regatta or in the sailing instructions, entries shall be made in the following form:

FORM OF ENTRY

To the Secretary .... Club
Please enter the yacht .... for
the .... race, on the...
her national letters and sail number are ....
her rig is ....
the colour of her hull is ....
and her rating or class is ....

I agree to be bound by the racing rules of the I.Y.R.U., by the prescriptions of the national authority under which this race is sailed, by the sailing instructions and by the class rules.

> *Name ....*
> *Address ....*
> *Telephone No ....*
> *Club ....*
> *Address during event ....*
> *Telephone No ....*

Signed... Date.....................................
(Owner or owner's representative)
Entrance fee enclosed

The comprehensive entry form is presumably printed as a guide to clubs. Note that the competitor is required to sign that he (or she) agrees to be bound by the rules, and we shall see that ignorance of the law is no excuse. He is presumed to have read and understood all the rules – just as when driving a car we are presumed to know the Highway Code.

Of course practically no entry form is exactly in this form, each is adjusted to the individual requirements of the organising authority. The N of R will probably lay down a closing date for entries and many clubs require double entry fees when boats enter late.

19   Measurement or Rating Certificates

19.1   Every yacht entering a race shall hold such valid measurement or rating certificate as required by the national authority or other duly authorised body, by her class rules, by the notice of race or regatta, or by the sailing instructions.

19.2   An owner shall be responsible for maintaining his yacht in accordance with her class rules and for ensuring that her certificate is not invalidated by alterations. Deviations in excess of tolerances specified in the class rules caused by normal wear or damage and that do not affect the performance of the yacht shall not invalidate the measurement or rating certificate of the yacht for a particular race, but shall be rectified before she *races* again, unless in the opinion of the race committee there has been no practicable opportunity to rectify the wear or damage.

19.3   (a) The owner of a yacht who cannot produce such a certificate when required, may be permitted to sign and lodge with the race committee, before she *starts*, a statement in the following form:

To the Secretary .... *Club*

UNDERTAKING TO PRODUCE CERTIFICATE

The yacht .... *competes in the* ....
race on condition that a valid certificate previously issued by the authorised administrative body, or a true copy of it, is submitted to the race committee before the end of the series, and that she competes in the race(s) on the measurement or rating of that certificate.

> *Signed* ....
> *(Owner or his representative)*
> *Date* ....

(b) In this event the sailing instructions may require that the owner shall lodge such a deposit as may be required by the organising authority, which may be forfeited when such certificate or true copy is not submitted to the race committee within the prescribed period.

Had *Liberty* protested *Australia II* about her winged keel, she would have alleged infringement of rule 19 for not being in accordance with her class rules. Then, perhaps, the jury would have opened a hearing, governed by rule 74.3 (Measurement Protests), and, since it would have been unable to reach a decision by itself, would have referred the case to 'an authority qualified to resolve the questions'. This authority would presumably have been the IYRU Chief Measurer. As all the parties had been pestering the Chief Measurer for an opinion on this very subject for weeks, if not for years, no doubt the *Liberty* syndicate thought it knew what the answer would be and did not protest.

'Measurement protests', says Mark Baxter in an article, 'are no different from any other protest under the racing rules. They are emotion charged partly because they somehow seem to imply cheating rather than innocent mistake or error and, partly because we don't know much about them and have little experience of them. There is little evidence that measurement error or non-conformance is usually, a matter of cheating. More often a measurement error is just that, a simple error or misunderstanding about the interpretation or application of a rule. Sometimes a rule is not absolutely clear; sometimes there is a grey area between clearly OK and clearly no good; and sometimes there is misunderstanding coupled with a loophole or ambiguity in the rule which allows considerable variation'.

There is very little case law; most of the bitterly-fought cases happen at international meetings with an international jury and no appeal. It is easy to understand why cheating comes to mind – when an owner fails to 'maintain his yacht in accordance with her class rules' it will be because of some item that makes her faster, not one that makes her slower. Perhaps for this reason people are often unwilling to bring measurement protests against fellow competitors but it is a rule that needs to be very strictly applied. There is no point in racing at all if the boats are not to class or not handicapped as they should be. The boat with the unfair advantage might just as well pull out a pair of oars, or motor.

Daisy cannot be protested for simply being 'too fast'. The protest must allege some specific point or points for examination: for example, that the propellor installation has been altered contrary to IOR 609, or that the rudder of a Laser is larger than that permitted.

How far can a boat discovered not to measure be disqualified retrospectively? If cheating can be proved, probably as far as anyone wants to (last year? the year before last? the probabilities of proof get very slim). Otherwise, with no evidence of cheating, not once a series, prize-giving and all, is over. IYRU 123 states: 'An in-date, authorised certificate, presented in good faith, by an owner who has complied with the requirements of rule 19.2, cannot be retrospectively invalidated after a race or series is completed.'

20 Ownership of Yachts

20.1 Unless otherwise prescribed in the conditions of entry, a yacht shall be eligible to compete only when she is either owned by or on charter to and has been entered by a yacht or sailing club recognised by its national authority or a member or members thereof.

20.2 Two or more yachts owned or chartered wholly or in part by the same body or person shall not compete in the same race without the previous consent of the race committee.

20.3 An owner shall not steer any yacht other than his own in a race wherein his own yacht competes without the previous consent of the race committee.

Not any old yacht can enter a race, *Daisy* must be owned by (on charter to) and entered by either a club or the member (or members) of the club, and this club must be recognised by or affiliated to a national authority which in its turn forms part of the IYRU itself. I suspect that money is at the bottom of this rule. Many national authorities expect every crew member to have a card showing him to subscribe to it directly himself, or to be a member of an affiliated club. In spite of what some people believe, racing at national and international level takes quite a bit of organisation and therefore money, and why should one pay and others contribute nothing?

The rest of the rule (20.2 and 20.3) makes committee consent necessary before either one owner has two boats in the same race, or the owner of one boat steers another in the same race. Both clauses are aimed at preventing collusion between two boats. Note that in 20.3 the owner of A may sail in B, navigate B – do what he will provided he does not set hand to the tiller.

The rule is narrowly interpreted. In IYRU 90 in a Mirror Class series A was entered by the owner, Smith, who steered her in race 1. In races 2 and 3, however, she was steered by Jones (the crew), from whom no entry had been received. The race committee considered Jones to be a non-entrant and non-starter, altered the results and awarded non-starters's points to A in races 2 and 3. The relevant Mirror Class Association rule reads: 'Distribution of duties between helmsman and crew shall be entirely at the discretion of the helmsman, unless otherwise stipulated in the SIs.'

The RC held that this regulation did not allow permanent substitution at the helm by the crew for an entire race or races, since the purpose of that could be to improve a yacht's chances of winning a series. A appealed. The appeal was upheld. The entry was made in respect of the yacht and the owner of a yacht might appoint whomsoever he chose to steer his yacht in a race. The class rule did not affect the position. However the decision made it clear that when organisers want only one helmsman per yacht throughout a series then it must be the subject of a SI.

21   Member on Board

Every yacht shall have on board a member of a yacht or sailing club recognised by its national authority to be in charge of the yacht as owner or owner's representative.

A long time ago this rule had the word 'amateur' before 'member'. It then made good sense. The amateur was either the owner or the owner's representative (for protests etc) but not the paid hand. By 1961 the word amateur had disappeared and the rule has stuck there collecting dust and being used as and when it could serve.

Look at IYRU 1. A dinghy crossed the finishing line, bottom up, with her crew swimming alongside. She was held to have finished and not infringed rule 21 – provided the complete crew remains with a capsized yacht they are considered to be on board for the purposes of rule 21 (and rule 59). Here rule 21 is used as a rule requiring a human being to be on board. There is nothing else in the rules to stop a modern dinghy being radio and computer controlled like model yachts.

In RYA 65/14 when a 14-ft dinghy crossed the line steered by the crew with the helmsman following in the water, the helmsman was held to have been separated from his boat and not effectively in charge when the boat finished. The yacht infringed rule 21. But had the crew been a club member why could he not act as owner's representative?

The rule does not appear to have been used for the last 20 years. However some such rule is necessary. It is essential for organisers to know who speaks for the yacht (owner, owner's representative, which of two joint owners, skipper etc) otherwise a declaration made by one person could be disowned by another.

22   Shifting Ballast

22.1   GENERAL RESTRICTIONS

Floorboards shall be kept down; bulkheads and doors left standing; ladders, stairways and water tanks left in place; all cabin, galley and forecastle fixtures and fittings kept on board; all movable ballast shall be properly stowed under the floorboards or in lockers and no dead weight shall be shifted.

22.2   SHIPPING, UNSHIPPING OR SHIFTING BALLAST; WATER

From 2100 on the day before the race until she is no longer *racing*, a yacht shall not ship, unship or shift ballast, whether movable or fixed, or take in or discharge water, except for ordinary ship's use and the removal of bilge water.

There is no need for comment on this rule except perhaps to say that it is surprising that more protests are not brought under it. Rule 22.1 would probably catch quite a number of boats in popular club racing. The rule recognises the enormous part played in boat speed by weight.

23   Anchor

Unless otherwise prescribed by her class rules, every yacht shall carry on board an anchor and chain or rope of suitable size.

24   Life-Saving Equipment

Unless otherwise prescribed by her class rules, every yacht, except one that has sufficient buoyancy to support the crew in case of accident, shall carry adequate life-saving equipment for all persons on board, one item of which shall be ready for immediate use.

25   Class Insignia, National Letters and Sail Numbers

25.1   Every yacht of an international class recognised by the I.Y.R.U. shall carry on her mainsail, and as provided in rule 25.1(d)(iii) on her spinnaker:

(a) The insignia denoting the class to which she belongs.

(b) A letter or letters showing her nationality, thus:

A	Argentina	D	Denmark	H	Holland
AE	Dubai	DDR	German	I	Italy
AN	Angola		Democratic	IL	Iceland
ANU	Antigua		Republic	IND	India
AR	Egypt	DK	Democratic	IR	Ireland
B	Belgium		People's Republic	IS	Israel
BA	Bahamas		of Korea	J	Japan
BL	Brazil	DR	Dominican	K	United
BN	Brunei		Republic		Kingdom
BR	Burma	E	Spain	KA	Australia
BU	Bulgaria	EC	Ecuador	KB	Bermuda
CB	Colombia	F	France	KBA	Barbados
CH	China	FL	Liechtenstein	KC	Canada
CI	Grand Cayman	G	Federal	KF	Fiji
CP	Cyprus		Republic of	KH	Hong Kong
CR	Costa Rica		Germany	KJ	Jamaica
CY	Sri Lanka	GR	Greece	KK	Kenya
CZ	Czechoslovakia	GU	Guatemala		

KP	Papua New	OM	Oman	SM	San Marino
	Guinea	P	Portugal	SR	Union of
KS	Singapore	PH	Philippines		Soviet Socialist
KT	Trinidad	PK	Pakistan		Republics
	and Tobago	PR	Puerto Rico	TA	Taipei
KV	British	PU	Peru	TH	Thailand
	Virgin Is.	PY	Paraguay	TK	Turkey
KZ	New Zealand	PZ	Poland	U	Uruguay
L	Finland	Q	Kuwait	US	United States
LX	Luxembourg	RB	Botswana		of America
M	Hungary	RC	Cuba	V	Venezuela
MA	Morocco	RI	Indonesia	VI	U.S. Virgin Is.
MO	Monaco	RM	Roumania	X	Chile
MT	Malta	S	Sweden	Y	Yugoslavia
MX	Mexico	SA	South Africa	Z	Switzerland
MY	Malaysia	SE	Senegal	ZB	Zimbabwe
N	Norway	SK	Republic of		
OE	Austria		Korea		

(c) A sail number allotted to her by her national authority. In the case of a self-administered international class, the number may be allotted by the class owners' association.

National letters shall be placed in front of or above the sail numbers. When the national letters end in "I" (e.g. Italy, U.S. Virgin Islands) and are placed in front of the numbers, they shall be separated from them by a horizontal line approximately 50 mm long.

(d)   (i)   Unless otherwise prescribed in the class rules, the class insignia, national letter(s) and sail numbers shall be above an imaginary line projecting at right angles to the luff from a point one-third of the distance, measured from the tack, to the head of the sail; shall be clearly visible; and shall be placed at different heights on the two sides of the sail, those on the starboard side being uppermost.

    (ii)   Where the class insignia is of such a design that, when placed back to back on the two sides of the sail, they coincide, they may be so placed.

    (iii)   The national letters and sail numbers only shall be similarly placed on both sides of the spinnaker, but at approximately half-height.

(e) National letters need not be carried in home waters, except in an international championship.

(f) The following minimum sizes for national letters and sail numbers are prescribed:

Height: one-tenth of the measurement of the foot of the mainsail rounded up to the nearest 50 mm.

Width: (excluding number 1 and letter I) 66% of the height.

Thickness: 15% of the height.

Space between adjoining letters and numbers: 20% of the height.

Classes that have a variable sail plan shall specify in their class rules the sizes of letters and numbers, which shall, when practicable, conform to the above requirements.

25.2 Other yachts shall comply with the rules of their national authority or class in regard to the allottment, carrying and size of insignia, letters and numbers, which rules shall, when practicable, conform to the above requirements.

25.3 When so prescribed in the notice of race or regatta or the sailing instructions, a yacht chartered or loaned for an event may carry national letters or sail numbers in contravention of her class rules. In all other respects the sails shall comply with the class rules.

25.4 A yacht shall not be disqualified for infringing the provisions of rule 25 without prior warning and adequate opportunity to make correction.

An unidentified yacht might as well not be in a race. She cannot be recalled if she is a premature starter, she cannot be finished, she cannot be protested by her competitors. This appears to be well-known to some competitors who do their best to cover their sails with illegible numbers, knowing that 25.4 will allow them time to put it right if someone objects. In the meantime there is always a chance the RO may not identify them, or confuse them with someone else or otherwise be conned into giving them a place when they ought not to have one, or a competitor will not protest them because she cannot identify them.

A typical example of confusion appears in US 110, where *Windsock* was disqualified for not having '49' on her spinnaker as required by SIs. Her own spinnaker had failed to arrive and she borrowed another with the number 44 and tried unsuccessfully to turn the second 4 into a 9. She was then disqualified, but without a hearing or a warning. The upshot was that she was reinstated on appeal because she had had no warning. *Windsock* made a conscientious, if ambiguous attempt to comply with the identification requirements and, accordingly she was entitled by rule 25.4 to notification and given adequate opportunity to make correction, (as well as being entitled to a hearing). So early action by the RC with a hearing and a warning (or a warning and a hearing – but in this case the warning should be in writing) is to be expected before any penalisation. Some SIs carry a paragraph stating that 'this is the warning prescribed by rule 25.4', but I do not believe this would always hold water on appeal or before an international jury, the rule is to help those in trouble with a minor point that cannot affect the speed of the yacht. To refuse the competitor the benefit of the rule would be contrary to its intention.

There is another view of rule 25.4, however. RYA 77/3 deals with GP6677 which lost the first '6' and last '7' on both sides of her main, and the ghost markings from the glue were not in a contrasting colour with the dirty white sail. In RYA 81/13, a Fireball used a spinnaker with no number on it. Both cases state that it is the owner's responsibility to maintain his yacht in the condition upon which her certificate was based and that includes the requirement to carry on her sails the appropriate sail numbers and when she knowingly invalidates her certificate she cannot rely on rule 25.4. A sailing instruction that requires yachts to fulfil this requirement (carry the right numbers in the right way) constitutes prior warning under rule 25.4. It seems harsh to give the right to a warning and then take it away, but at championship meetings, frequented by experienced crews who know the IYRR and their class rules back to front, will necessarily be administered more sternly than local club racing.

26 **Advertising**

Rule 26 shall apply when *racing* and, in addition, unless otherwise prescribed in the notice of race or regatta, from 0700 on the first race day of a regatta or series until the expiry of the time limit for lodging protests following the last race of the regatta or series.

26.1 BASIC RULE
Unless permitted in accordance with rules 26.2 or 26.3, no advertising shall be displayed on the hull, spars, sails and equipment of a yacht while rule 26 is in effect, or on the clothing and equipment worn by the crew when the yacht is under way, except that:

(a) one sailmaker's mark (which may include the name or mark of the manufacturer of the sail cloth and pattern or model description of the sail) may be displayed on each side of any sail. The whole of such a mark shall be placed not more than 15% of the length of the foot of the sail or 300 mm from its tack, whichever is the greater. This latter limitation shall not apply to the position of marks on spinnakers.

(b) one builder's mark (which may include the name or mark of the designer) may be placed on the hull, and one maker's mark may be displayed on spars and equipment.

(c) such marks (or plates) shall fit within a square not exceeding 150 mm x 150 mm.

(d) one maker's mark may be displayed on each item of clothing and equipment worn by the crew, provided that the mark fits within a square not exceeding 100 mm x 100 mm.

(e) the yacht's type may be displayed once on each side of the hull, provided that the lettering shall not exceed 1% in height and 5% in length of the overall length of the yacht, but not exceeding a maximum height of 100 mm and a maximum length of 700 mm.

(f) a sailboard's type may be displayed on the hull in two places. The lettering shall not exceed 200 mm in height.

26.2 EXEMPTION FOR YACHTS
When a national authority wishes to permit further limited advertising, it shall prescribe that this exemption may be used, except that it shall not be granted to yachts in world and continental events and, unless so prescribed by the class rules, in the events of international classes.

(a) When the national authority gives written consent to a yacht, and when the yacht is sailing in its home waters:

(i) her name may be the name, product name or logo of a company or other organisation. The name shall not be displayed more than once on each side of the hull and on the transom, and shall not exceed in height 1½% and in length 10% of the overall length of the yacht, but not exceeding a maximum height of 300 mm and a maximum length of 2100 mm;

(ii) the name, product name or logo of the company or other organisation may be displayed on the clothing and equipment worn by the crew of the yacht.

(b) In giving such consent, the national authority:

(i) may limit the consent to one event or a series of events,

(ii) may limit the duration of its validity,

(iii) shall reserve the right to withdraw such consent, and

(iv) may impose such other terms as it sees fit.

(c) The letter of consent shall be displayed for the duration of an event on the official regatta notice board. When the letter of consent is not displayed, the consent shall be invalid.

(d) When a yacht is granted the exemption in rule 26.2 by her national authority, another national authority may also give consent in accordance with rule 26.2 to the yacht when she is sailing in its waters.

26.3 **EXEMPTION FOR EVENTS**
When authorised by a national authority for an event in its home waters for which all yachts will be supplied by a company or other organisation, the organising authority may permit advertising on the hull of the yachts within the dimensional limitations of rule 26.2(a)(i), and in two places on one boom. However, a competitor shall not be required or induced to display advertising on his clothing or equipment.

26.4 **DISPENSATION**
When a national authority is satisfied, before an event begins, that yachts *raced* with advertising in the same event prior to 16th November, 1983, it may consent to dispensation from part or all of rule 26. In such case, the organising authority shall obtain written approval from the national authority, and that approval shall be announced in the notice of race or regatta and in the sailing instructions.

26.5 **WARNING AND PENALTIES**
As an alternative from or in addition to the penalties prescribed by rule 74.4, (Penalties), the race committee may:

(a) warn the infringing yacht that a further infringement will result in action under rule 70.2, (Action by Race or Protest Committee).

(b) when the infringement occurs when the yacht is not *racing*, disqualify the yacht from the race most recently sailed or from the next race sailed after the infringement.

(c) when it decides there was a gross breach of this rule, disqualify the yacht from more than one race or from the whole series.

A rule that expressed IYRU policy, an old rule in a new form. It does not give much more right to advertise than before unless the National Authority so desires. We shall watch what happens with interest. (see notes on p. 218)

27 Forestays and Jib Tacks

Unless otherwise prescribed by the class rules, forestays and jib tacks (not including spinnaker staysails when not *close-hauled*) shall be fixed approximately in the centre-line of the yacht.

This rule was inserted after 1930 to stop a loophole at the KSSS centenary race in Stockholm when a Six-Metre arrived with double headstays and with the jibs tacked to a curved track on deck. Whether this rule prevents any such 'rule-cheating' nowadays is not known. Probably most classes deal with the problem in their own class rules.

(Numbers 28, 29 and 30 are spare numbers)

Part IV—**Right of Way Rules**

Rights and Obligations when Yachts Meet

*The rules of Part IV do not apply in any way to a vessel that is neither intending to **race** nor **racing**; such vessel shall be treated in accordance with the International Regulations for Preventing Collisions at Sea or Government Right of Way Rules applicable to the area concerned. The rules of Part IV apply only between yachts that either are intending to **race** or are **racing** in the same or different races, and, except when rule 3.2(b)(xxviii), (Race Continues After Sunset), applies, replace the International Regulations for Preventing Collisions at Sea or Government Right of Way Rules applicable to the area concerned, from the time a yacht intending to **race** begins to sail about in the vicinity of the starting line until she has either **finished** or retired and has left the vicinity of the course. (See Appendix 9).*

This preamble establishes which right-of-way rules are to be used when:
1 A, in a race, meets C, a cruiser with no intention of racing. IRPCAS (see Appendix 9) or other Governmental Rules govern the encounter between them. If there is a collision and A is at fault, she is liable in law but she will probably not be disqualified by a protest committee unless she has acted badly. Look at KNVW 2/1982. Two boats were overlapped, W was racing, L not. W wished to sail a lower course to a mark and hailed L, who refused to get out of the way. W then intentionally hit L by bumping her boom several times, thereby causing some damage. The appeal comittee dismissed W's appeal against her disqualification under rule 75.1 because, while not subject to the rules of Part IV, she had committed a gross breach of good manners.

It is an interesting point that the preamble makes: 'such vessel [in this case, C] shall be treated in accordance with IRPCAS ...' and so, since rule 68.1 does not state that a protesting yacht must be racing, in theory C could protest A in the normal way and A could be penalised for infringing the relevant rules even when she had done so by mistake.
2 A and B, yachts in the same series, meet when they are not racing far from the course area. As they are not 'in the vicinity of the starting line' they are not subject to the rules of Part IV and are governed by IRPCAS, but both could nevertheless be disciplined under rule 75.
3 before the preparatory signal, A meets B again, but in the vicinity of the starting line. Neither is racing, but both are intending to do so. The situation is now governed by the rules of Part IV although as yet neither can be disqualified (subject always to rule 75). This is logical; helmsmen cannot swop rules between the five and 10 minute guns and even when not racing they may be mixing with other classes that are. All boats in one area should sail to one set of rules, preferably IYRR as they are specifically designed for groups of small boats milling around a starting line.
4 before A's preparatory signal (ie before she is racing), she meets B, already racing in a different class. The encounter is governed by the rules of

Part IV and each boat may protest the other. Not only B could be disqualified, A too, if she was hindering B could be penalised. This is discussed under rule 31.2.

5 when so prescribed in SIs the relevant parts of Part IV are replaced at night by IRPCAS (Appendix. 9). It is not mandatory to change rules at sunset and may be advisable not to do so in the northern latitudes at midsummer, or when racing in confined waters.

IV

SECTION A—Obligations and Penalties

31   Disqualification

31.1   A yacht may be disqualified or otherwise penalised for infringing a rule of Part IV only when the infringement occurs while she is *racing*, whether or not a collision results.

31.2   A yacht may be disqualified or otherwise penalised, before or after she is *racing*, for seriously hindering a yacht that is *racing* or for infringing the sailing instructions.

Rule 31.1 cannot be infringed, it limits the powers of the protest committee and gives an assurance to a yacht that she can only be penalised (disqualification or such other penalty as the SIs prescribe) while she is racing, in the defined sense of the word. Before her preparatory signal and after she has finished and cleared the finishing line and marks, she is safe. (This assurance is immediately gainsaid by rule 31.2 discussed below).

As well as setting limits for penalisation rule 31.1 explains that it makes no difference whether there is a collision or not. The use of the word 'may' does not give a discretion to a protest committee to disqualify or not. Rule 74.4 (Penalties) makes it clear that when, after a hearing, a yacht is found to have infringed a rule she must be penalised.

Rule 31.2 alone among the rules, contains the word 'hindering'. Although there is no case law, I take it to mean that not only an obligated yacht that has infringed a rule of Part IV when not racing, but even a right-of-way yacht can be protested and penalised for hindering. For instance A has finished and is no longer racing, so she turns back and sets out on starboard tack to get in the way of B, on port tack. She thus succeeds in making B 3rd instead of 2nd. Now if this was deliberate A would be subject to rule 75, but if it was only carelessness then she could be caught by rule 31.2. At the end of this rule, rather unsuitably because it has nothing to do with Part IV, is a phrase stating that a yacht can be penalised for infringing a SI when not racing: for example failing to tally-out before going afloat, or sailing back across the line after finishing when expressly forbidden.

32   Avoiding Collisions

A right-of-way yacht that fails to make a reasonable attempt to avoid a collision resulting in serious damage may be disqualified as well as the other yacht.

The right-of-way rules are framed to avoid collision, but nevertheless collisions happen. After a collision, when the infringing yacht has been duly disqualified, the right-of-way yacht may, or may not, be also penalised dependent on her behaviour and on the type of damage sustained. The rule is not mandatory but restrictive: it permits a protest committee to absolve the right-of-way yacht however bad the collision but it does not allow her to be penalised unless two conditions have been fulfilled, first that she has not made a reasonable attempt to avoid the collision and secondly that the damage has, in fact, been serious.

'Serious' is defined in IYRU 36, or rather not defined. 'It is impossible generally to define the term "serious damage" as used in rule 32. In determining whether or not the damage resulting from a collision is serious, consideration must be given to: its extent and cost of repair relative to the size and value of the yacht concerned; whether or not it was feasible or prudent for her to continue to race; and whether the damage markedly affected her speed and materially prejudiced her finishing position'. This is all right as far as it goes, but some avoidable collisions, in open waters in bad weather, have not caused serious damage but could have easily have done so. The difference between slightly bending a stanchion and bringing down a mast may be only an inch but that inch will be enough to save the right-of-way yacht from rule 32.

Even when there is serious damage it must still be proved that the right-of-way yacht failed to make a reasonable attempt to avoid the collision. In IYRU 53 P, travelling at 10 knots, holed S which had tacked immediately in front of her. In the resulting protest S was held to have infringed rule 41 and P, as right-of-way yacht, to have made herself liable to penalisation under rule 32. She appealed and won her appeal. 'P took no action to avoid a collision, but what could she have done? Given her speed and the distance involved, she had perhaps one or two seconds to decide what to do and then to do it. It is a long-established underlying principle of the right-of-way rules that a yacht becoming burdened by an action of another yacht is entitled to sufficient time for response'.

However the right-of-way yacht cannot always invoke the unexpectedness of the event. In IYRU 51 (Fig. 25) two yachts in different classes were rounding the same mark in opposite directions. P's claim to room under rule 42 was dismissed and she was disqualified under rule 36, but S was also thrown out for failing to make a reasonable attempt to avoid a collision. A similar case is illustrated in IYRU 37 (Fig. 50).

Finally look at RYA 85/7. B forced a passage between A and the shore. Despite A's hail to keep clear and to pull in her boom B did not do so. The boom end touched A's backstay and the mast came down. The committee used their discretion under rule 33.2 (unreasonably as I believe) to disqualify A for failing to take avoiding action. A appealed. The RYA reinstating her, held that A had no reason to anticipate that serious damage would result and therefore her action in hailing B to pull in her boom was adequate to fulfil the requirements of rule 32.

33   Rule Infringement

33.1   ACCEPTING PENALTY

A yacht that realises she has infringed a racing rule or a sailing instruction is under an obligation either to retire promptly or to exonerate herself by accepting an alternative penalty when so prescribed in the sailing instructions, but when she does not retire or exonerate herself and persists in *racing*, other yachts shall continue to accord her such rights as she has under the rules of Part IV.

First of all this rule applies not only to infringements of Part IV but, in spite of its location, to all those of other rules listed in the definition of rules at the beginning of Part VI. Its message is of the greatest importance, for nowhere else is it stated that when you know you have broken a rule you must exonerate yourself, when possible, or retire. When the referee fails to see a foul by a footballer there is no obligation on the player to penalise himself, nor is there in many games, but in sailing, as for instance in golf, where much of the game is played out of sight of others, it is essential for the competitor to be 'honour bound' to keep the rules. In RYA 1984/5 a Laser was granted redress and reinstated when no sound signal had accompanied her recall signal. The decision stated: 'There is no onus on a yacht to respond when a sound signal is not made, unless she realises that she is a premature starter, when she is bound by rule 33.1 to retire or start correctly'.

Secondly the choice given in the rule between retiring or accepting an alternative penalty 'when so prescribed in the sailing instructions' does not exclude the three methods of exoneration provided for in the IYRR themselves: in 51.1 (b) for premature starters, in 51.4 for passing the wrong side of a mark and in 52.2 for touching a mark. Each of these is discussed under its own rule.

The systems of exoneration prescribed by sailing instructions are usually those found in Appendix 3 – either 720° turns or the percentage penalty (flag '1') – but may be other methods or variations as laid down by the organising authorities. It is important for competitors to study what system is in use; it is sad to see a boat retire and go home when she could have exonerated herself.

Most commonly A infringes a rule but genuinely believes that she has not done so, either because she is not fully conversant with the rules or because she has mistaken the facts. She naturally continues to race and then, whatever the rights or wrongs, other yachts must accord her her rights under Part IV. Nor does she lose her right to protest. In IYRU 2 A protested B and B was disqualified, nevertheless B's protest against C, although the incident took place later, is valid. The fact that B has infringed a rule does not allow C to do so.

The substance of this rule is illustrated by an interesting case that never came to appeal and so has no formal seal of approval. Yacht A hit a mark, her helmsman knew it and knew of his obligation to retire promptly (there was no re-rounding permitted). He did not retire and finished third getting a sound signal from the race committee. He did not inform the race officer afloat or the regatta office ashore that he had hit the mark. Finally, when another yacht protested him he retired. The protest committee decided that the action was a gross breach of good sportsmanship and excluded him from the remainder of the regatta under rule 75.1.

33.2   CONTACT BETWEEN YACHTS RACING

When there is contact that is not both minor and unavoidable between the hulls, equipment or crew of two yachts, both shall be disqualified or otherwise penalised unless:

IV

either

(a) one of the yachts retires in acknowledgement of the infringement, or exonerates herself by accepting an alternative penalty when so prescribed in the sailing instructions,

or

(b) one or both of these yachts acts in accordance with rule 68, (Protests by Yachts).

It was held in IYRU 77 that when two yachts collide there must have been an infringement of a rule. It is therefore only fair to other competitors that the infringement should be dealt with. Hence this rule compelling one or both yachts to protest after touching. There is one exception; when the contact was minor and unavoidable, otherwise A and B cannot laugh off a collision, however slight, and sail on as if nothing had happened. When A knows she is at fault she must retire (rule 33.1) unless she can exonerate herself by doing turns etc. When B knows she is at fault – likewise. But when they both think they were in the right at least one of them must protest or risk both boats being disqualified.

IYRU 89 deals with the various situations that can arise and is worth quoting at length. It has been, temporarily I believe, withdrawn, because it has been partially outdated by the 1985–88 rules. I have adapted what follows. The question was asked: 'When a valid protest is lodged concerning an incident in which contact between two yachts is alleged to have occurred, or a penalty hearing is called by the race committee under rule 70.2 regarding such an incident, what procedure should the race committee follow with reference to rule 33.2?'

The IYRU answered:

1 When one yacht involved in the incident protests the other for infringing any rule of Part IV, other than rule 33.2, the protest will be decided in the normal way, it is not open to the PC to find that contact was minor and unavoidable and the infringing yacht will be penalised.

2 When one of the yachts protests under a rule of Part IV, other than rule 3.2, she may state that the protest is lodged solely to comply with rule 33.2 and ask the protest committee to find that the contact was minor and unavoidable. When the protest committee so concludes, it will permit the protest to be withdrawn under rule 68.9, but when it finds that the contact was *not* minor and unavoidable, the protest will be heard and the infringing yacht penalised.

3 When a third yacht protests in accordance with rule 68.2 under a rule of Part IV other than rule 33.2, the infringing yacht will be penalized. Moreover, when it is determined that neither yacht lodged a valid protest or retired or accepted an alternative penalty, the right-of-way yacht is also subject to penalty under rule 33.2

4 When a third yacht protests both yachts in accordance with rule 68.2 for an infringement of rule 33.2 and it is determined that there was contact (that was not both minor and unavoidable) and that neither yacht lodged a valid protest or retired or accepted an alternative penalty, both will be penalised.

5 When a third yacht sees that one of the yachts has displayed a protest flag and therefore does not display a protest flag herself, but after the race finds that no protest has been lodged and then protests under rule 33.2 (but not under another rule), she is relieved by rule 68.3 of the necessity to display a protest flag. In such an event, both yachts will be disqualified unless the protest committee determines that contact was minor and unavoidable.

6 The race committee may call a hearing in accordance with rule 70.2 for an infringement of rule 33.2 and when neither yacht lodged a valid protest, or retired or accepted an alternative penalty, both will be disqualified unless the protest committee determines that contact was minor and inavoidable. *Note:* Under paragraphs 4; 5 and 6, the race committee is required only to find as facts that:

a) contact occurred and

b) whether or not the contact was minor and unavoidable. The protest committee is not required to establish which yacht was at fault.

Now let us look at the way some of these terms are to be interpreted. Minor and unavoidable. In RYA 1977/4, when the words used were 'minor contact', but the intention was the same, it was stated: 'The words "minor contact" envisage collisions such as might occur in drifting conditions at the start or when rounding marks – certainly not in winds gusting force 3 to 4 when yachts should be under full control.' A more recent US case (US 240) in 1981 reiterates this: 'The words minor and unavoidable are intended to be applied to such contacts as occur at starts and mark roundings when there is very little wind and a concentration of yachts. It is not intended as a reason for exonerating poor seamanship or failure on the part of the burdened yacht to keep clear when there is reasonable good steerage way. If the yachts had steerage way, even a minor contact would have been avoidable.'

'The test of avoidability is not to be applied at the instant before contact. In almost all cases a collision is unavoidable at that time. It applies to the event leading up to the contact. When yachts can manoeuvre, even though the wind is light and variable, they have steerage way and contact is not to be considered unavoidable.' Finally US 240 states: 'The "minor and unavoidable" test applies only in a rule 33.2 situation; it does not apply with respect to any other rule of part IV.' It goes without saying that contact will not be considered minor when damage results. All this goes to show that the 'minor and unavoidable' plea is not to be accepted lightly by PCs.

However in US 232 A rounded ahead of B, A's spinnaker got out of control, streamed astern and touched B's headstay, the contact was allowed to be considered minor and unavoidable.

In an unpublished International Jury decision at an Admiral's Cup race contact was held to be minor etc, when two kedged yachts in open Channel came together as they untangled their kedge lines, entwined by the tidal currents.

In RYA 1982/13 *Sue* and *Jessie* collided at the start. *Sue*, on port tack, realised she was at fault and attempted to do her 720° turns, so *Jessie* did not protest, *Marjorie*, a third yacht, protested the other two under rule 33.2 for not bringing a valid protest. At the subsequent hearing it was found that *Sue* had failed to do her turns correctly and she was disqualified. *Jessie* however was not penalised for failing to protest under rule 33.2 as she had not known of the facts until after the protest itself. 'A yacht – said the RYA – is relieved of her duty to protest after a collision when the infringing yacht performs her 720° turns, albeit incorrectly.'

Finally look at a very complicated case: RYA 1983/4. The incident occurred at the gybe mark, when A and B collided. The collision was seen by C and D who hailed that one yacht must protest or retire. A replied that she would protest. C and D planed off to the leeward mark, many lengths ahead of A and B, and, after rounding the mark, saw that A had a flag flying. As a result neither C nor D displayed a flag, but after the race they checked that A had lodged a protest concerning the incident and they had no reason to doubt its validity.

The protest was considered late at night, when the PC found that A had not displayed her flag 'at the first reasonable opportunity' and refused the protest as invalid. The decision was posted the next morning. As soon as they saw it C and D lodged a joint protest against A and B under rule 33.2. A and B were disqualified. The second protest (by C and D) was held to have been lodged in accordance with rule 68.3 because the protestors had seen every indication that a protest would be lodged and could not know that the protest was invalid until the PC's decision was posted.

Retiring. Note that in order for B's retirement to absolve A from protest under rule 33.2, the retirement must result from B's acknowledgement of her infringement. In US 210 the port-tack boat suffered severe damage and retired. S took it for granted that P had retired in acknowledgement of the infringement and did not put up her protest flag. Later she found that this was not so. Confirming the PC's disqualification of both boats the US Appeal Committee said: 'Retirement by itself does not necessarily indicate acknowledgement of an infringement, especially when serious damage has occurred.' Without evidence of such acknowledgement the other yacht is obligated to protest under rule 33.2 and may claim lack of knowledge of the facts justifying a protest under rule 68.3 as grounds for being excused for failure to display a protest flag. If she is in doubt regarding the significance of a yacht's retiring, she always has the option of displaying a flag and filing a protest.

Rule 33.2 therefore is a basically simple rule with complicated ramifications. There is only one absolutely safe road to follow. When you make contact with another yacht and the incident is not your fault, get your protest flag up at the first reasonable opportunity and then proceed to lodge your protest in the ordinary way. It may turn out not to have been necessary – but never mind.

34 Hailing

34.1 Except when *luffing* under rule 38.1, (Luffing and Sailing above a Proper Course after Starting), a right-of-way yacht that does not hail before or when making an alteration of course that may not be foreseen by the other yacht may be disqualified as well as the yacht required to keep clear when a collision resulting in serious damage occurs.

34.2 A yacht that hails when claiming the establishment or termination of an *overlap* or insufficiency of room at a *mark* or *obstruction* thereby helps to support her claim for the purposes of rule 42, (Rounding or Passing Marks and Obstructions).

When a right-of-way yacht alters course unexpectedly, in such a way that the other yacht may not be able to foresee the manoeuvre, she should hail. It is not obligatory for her to do so, but if, having right-of-way, she fails to hail and a collision results in serious damage she may be disqualified as well as the burdened yacht. In such circumstances hailing is an obvious and greatly -to-be-recommended precaution. It may only be ignored when the leeward or clear-ahead yacht of two has luffing rights under rule 38.1.

Rule 34.2 recommends hailing at a mark to help substantiate the evidence at any subsequent protest hearing. Rule 34 cannot be infringed but there are other rules where hails are essential if certain objectives are to be obtained: rule 38.4 – a hail to prevent or curtail another yacht's luff; rule 42.1 (d) – a hail to legitimise taking an inside yacht to the wrong side of a mark and rule 43 – a hail to compel the windward yacht of two at an obstruction to tack or keep clear. Each of these is discussed under its own rule number. Note that there is no requirement, or even recommendation for a starboard-tack yacht (not altering course) to hail a port-tack yacht. Only a good lookout and rule 32 saves P from being sunk with impunity!!

IYRU 130 is interesting about misleading hails. At the two-length circle O hailed 'no overlap'. The hailee, I, believed her, bore away and hit O's rudder. O was disqualified and appealed. 'O's hail is not to be assumed to be a bluff', said the US Appeals Committee, 'but simply a mistake in judgement, and its clear implication is that in O's opinion I had no right to room and was expected to round astern or outside. I, if she acted immediately, as she did, was entitled to rely on such a hail and if it was incorrect O must accept responsibility for the resulting contact.' In IYRU 130 the misleading hail was made in good faith, but in IYRU 107 it was not. 'A yacht deliberately hailing "starboard" when she is on port tack is liable to disqualification under the Fundamental Rule C, Fair Sailing.' So no 'funny' hails and take great care when you are not just giving warning of your own intentions but expecting the hailee to act.

Whether a hail was made or not, and when made, was made loudly enough, and when loud enough was heard (there are none so deaf . . .) and when heard was understood are matters of fact for protest committees to determine case by case.

SECTION B—Principal Right of Way Rules and their Limitations

These rules apply except when over-ridden by a rule in Section C.

The basic rules of encounters between yachts are to be found in this section. They apply unless a rule of Section C governs the situation. Thus when, perhaps surprisingly, no rule of Section C fits, the basic rules govern.

35   Limitations on Altering Course

When one yacht is required to keep clear of another, the right-of-way yacht shall not alter course so as to prevent the other yacht from keeping clear; or so as to obstruct her while she is keeping clear, except:

(a) to the extent permitted by rule 38.1, (Same Tack, Luffing and Sailing above a Proper Course after Starting), and

(b) when assuming a *proper course*:
   either

   (i)   to *start*, unless subject to rule 40, (Same Tack, Luffing before Starting), or to the second part of rule 44.1(b), (Returning to Start),

   or

   (ii)   when rounding a *mark*.

There are two qualifications to be fulfilled before a yacht is capable of infringing rule 35: first she must be the right-of-way yacht and secondly she must alter course. An alteration of course by a burdened yacht will not bring the rule into effect, nor will a right-of-way yacht sailing a steady, straight course. The object of rule 35 is safety. When a burdened yacht, be she P, W or other, is doing her duty and either keeping clear or attempting to keep clear she must not be obstructed by unexpected and unpredictable alterations of course by the right-of-way yacht. When such an alteration results in a collision it is usually pretty obvious that the burdened yacht has been prevented from keeping clear, but when there is no collision the line between obstructing and not obstructing may be fine and difficult to draw. A workable definition of obstruction is propounded in RYA 1972/2: 'Obstruct, in the context of rule 35, means putting the burdened yacht at a disadvantage greater than that which she would have suffered in complying with her obligations if the right-of-way yacht had held her course.'

There is a great deal of case law which, in view of the importance of this rule, is worth looking at in some detail. Let us start with US 186 (Fig. 18) which is an excellent example of the kind of incident rule 35 is designed to avoid. It was blowing 35 and gusting to 45 knots when T, a 42-ft cutter under headsail only, reached the mark with R, a Cal 29 with small jib and reefed main, about 3–6 lengths astern. When T tacked she bore away to gain speed and then hardened up to a course to clear the mark. Meantime R, which had seen T bearing down on her, tacked and T struck her full amidships. R sustained major hull damage. When T's tack was completed she became the right-of-way starboard-tack yacht and entitled to sail any course she liked, but she could not then alter that course and thereby defeat R's efforts to keep clear. T was disqualified for having infringed rule 35. In US 166 there was no collision but S was again held to have infringed rule

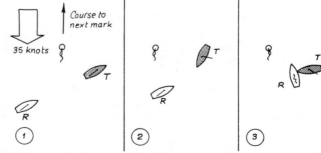

Fig. 18

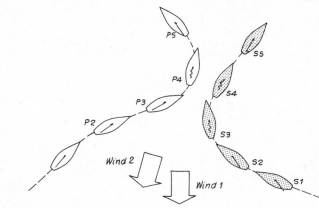

Fig. 19

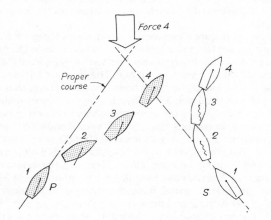

Fig. 20

35. From Fig. 19 it is apparent that after S was lifted and P was headed (position 2) P was clearing S with room to spare. S's alteration of course above close-hauled, preparatory to tacking, was in clear violation of rule 35 since it forced P to tack to avoid collision.

The distance between the boats is important. In IYRU 10 (Fig. 20) P and S were close-hauled on converging courses. P bore away to pass astern of S and a moment later S elected to tack. P resumed her close-hauled course and passed S about a length to windward of her. P protested S under rule 35 for having obstructed her while she was keeping clear. S was disqualified under rule 35 and appealed. The decision, upholding the appeal, ran as follows: 'The facts found give no indication that rule 35 was infringed. Had P remained on her new course and S remained on starboard, P would have passed astern safely. When S tacked, however, she did so at a sufficient distance from P to enable her to keep clear, which P demonstrated by actual

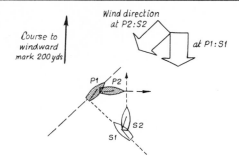

Fig. 21

performance. The action of P, in altering course, did not of itself require S to maintain her course. To rule that the right-of-way yacht must do so for this reason alone would seriously and unnecessarily limit her rights under basic rule 36.'

While the distance between the boats was too great for invoking rule 35 in the case we have just looked at, it was not so in US 157. In this case S luffed on a windshift when less than two lengths from P and then at the last minute fell off and went astern of P. The PC decided that if S had not altered course to windward she could have claimed right-of-way under rule 36. By luffing she violated rule 35. 'When S is within close proximity to P, S should hold her course until it becomes necessary to alter it to avoid a collision that might result in serious damage.' S was disqualified and appealed. The interpretation of the rule was accepted but S's appeal was upheld because the facts did not support the conclusion that S's alteration of course had prevented P from keeping clear. 'The original alteration of course to windward by S could have resulted in a violation of rule 35 if it had not been for the fact that S almost immediately bore off to allow P to cross safely ahead of her without an alteration of course on her part.' S asked when she might alter her course to windward in response to a windshift and answer came: 'She may do at any time unless she is so close to a burdened yacht in the act of keeping clear that her course change would prevent the burdened yacht from keeping clear, or obstruct her while so doing. Such a course change less than two boat lengths from the burdened yacht is too close.'

Windshifts often lead to protests under rule 35 and IYRU 52 (Fig. 21) illustrates another such case. Here S, suddenly freed by a windshift, headed up and found herself on a collision course with P. P had previously been on a course that would have passed ahead of S. S bore away at the last moment and avoided hitting P. The appeals committee absolved both yachts as neither had infringed any rule, but S, while entitled to take advantage of the windshift was also bound by rule 35 which she would have infringed had she not altered course again.

RYA 1967/5 reinforces the lesson of IYRU 10, that the right-of-way yacht may alter course without infringing rule 35 provided she is far enough away. Fig. 22 shows P, close-hauled, during pre-start manoeuvres (team-racing) trying to cross ahead of a reaching starboard-tack yacht. S luffed to a

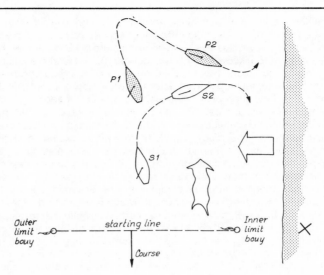

Fig. 22

close-hauled course and P failed to keep clear. P protested S under rule 35. The PC found that P had had ample time to keep clear after S was close hauled and disqualified P under rule 36. On appeal the decision was confirmed. Because changes of course are frequent, and sometimes continuous, before the start of a race, when there is no proper course, rule 35 protests arise mostly from incidents in that period.

IYRU 115 is an old US case recently incorporated in the IYRU interpretations. It traces the fortunes of two boats. A is attempting to drive the other, B, away from the starting line in the pre-start manoevres just before the starting gun. Each yacht protested the other but after going to appeal the outcome was that neither yacht was held to have infringed a rule and both protests were dismissed. It is worth looking at in detail, Fig. 23.

Before the starting signal, the two yachts reached away from the starting line. A, moving faster, passed and was clear ahead of B at position 3. At

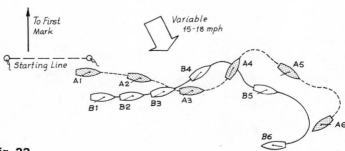

Fig. 23

position 4, A luffed up to close-hauled, intending to tack back to the line, but she found that B also had luffed and worked into a position where, had A tacked, there would have been an immediate collision. A then bore away to gybe, only to discover that B had now borne away into a position where a gybe would again cause a collision. Finally, B gybed and headed for the starting line, leaving A well astern. A protested B under rule 35, claiming that she had been obstructed while in the act of keeping clear. The race committee disqualified B, which appealed, holding that her disputed manoeuvres were legitimate means of driving a competitor away from the starting line. The district appeals committee agreed and reversed her disqualification. A appealed that decision. Dismissing it, the USYRU Appeals Committee decision went as follows 'B's actions describe a classic manoeuvre in match and team racing, used to gain a favourable starting position ahead of another competitor. The essential point is that rule 35 applies only to a right-of-way yacht, which B, at positions 3 and 4, was not'.

At position 4, B, as a windward yacht, was obligated to keep clear under rule 37.1, but A could not tack without certain infringement of rule 41.1. At position 5, B became the leeward yacht, she began to hold rights under rules 37.1 and 40, and A could not then have gybed without infringing rule 41.1 there as well. The facts show that neither yacht infringed any rule.

US 172 answers questions about match-racing starts, when yachts circle continuously. It was stated in answer to a question that the failure of a right-of-way yacht to settle onto a compass course could be a violation of rule 35. When a circling yacht does not alter her helm and bring it amidships she is altering course. She must settle on a compass course as soon as she gains right of way or risk infringing rule 35. The circling yacht is not required to sail a straight course once she becomes right-of-way yacht; she may continue to circle or otherwise alter course as long as she 'does not thereby prevent the burdened yacht from keeping clear or obstruct her while she is keeping clear'. Pre-start manoeuvres in high-class match-racing is a subject on its own, where the right-of-way rules, including rule 35, are stretched to their limits to accommodate situations not envisaged when they were written. IYRU Cases 35 and 36 deal with the relationship between rules 35 and 36.

IYRU 35 (Fig. 24) shows us two boats running on opposite tacks. About two minutes after she had gybed onto starboard, S hailed P and began to luff. The boats touched. Did rule 36 apply or rule 35? The answer of the USSRYRF was as follows: 'S, having completed her gybe in accordance with rule 41.1 was the starboard-tack right-of-way yacht under rule 36, and

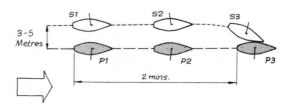

Fig. 24

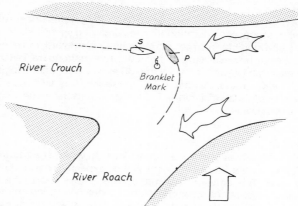

Fig. 25

P, as the port-tack burdened yacht was bound to keep clear. Because the yachts were not subject to rule 37 (Same-Tack Yachts) any alteration of course by S was governed by rule 35, and she was entitled to luff provided she satisfied its requirements. In this case she hailed, (as provided for in rule 34.1) and informed P of her intention to luff, thus giving P time and opportunity to keep clear.' IYRU 36 also deals with the relationship between rules 35 and 36. In answer to a question it was stated that rule 36 does not over-ride rule 35, it always applied.

IYRU 51 (Fig. 25) illustrates the relationship between rules 32 and 35. When S met P, each rounding the same mark but in different directions (as per SIs!) S held her course and made no attempt to avoid the resulting collision. She pleaded that she thought she would have infringed rule 35 had she done so. Although the damage was serious P was disqualified under rule 36 and S exonerated. P appealed on the grounds that even when the RC set courses which rounded marks in opposite directions, rule 32 and the ordinary rules of seamanship prevailed. The appeals committee, while dismissing P's appeal against her own disqualification under rule 36, also disqualified S under rule 32. This case is also discussed under rule 32.

Finally US 98 looks at the relationship between rules 35 and 44 (Premature Starter returning to Start). It held that although a premature starter, whilst returning, was obliged to keep clear of all other yachts that had started or were starting correctly, nevertheless those yachts were still subject to rule 35. This case is discussed more fully under rule 44.

Exceptions to rule 35

The exceptions to rule 35 have one thing in common; they all permit the rule to be waived in situations in which the burdened yacht can expect the right-of-way yacht to alter course and can therefore anticipate her manoeuvre.

35 (a)

The right-of-way yacht, when she has luffing rights under rule 38.1, may luff without any consideration for the windward yacht. W will be expecting L to try and stop her from getting through to windward and should be ready to keep clear however sudden her defensive manoeuvre. IYRU 3, citing US 20, states that W cannot invoke rule 35 even when, after a legitimate luff, L bears away so sharply that the boats touch. It is W's own fault for not keeping a reasonable distance. US 42 deals with the same subject which is further illustrated under rule 38.

35 (b)(i)

The right-of-way yacht may ignore rule 35 when she assumes a proper course to start; a burdened yacht will be expecting her to do so and must keep clear. The time for this manoeuvre is very short. The definition of 'proper course' states categorically that there is no such animal before the starting signal, so presumably a yacht cannot assume a proper course before the gun. The rule itself makes it clear that the exception ends when the yacht starts. Even during this brief period yachts are subject to rule 40 (Luffing before Starting), which includes, as we shall see, a sort of amplification of rule 35. In addition there is nothing here to affect rule 41 (Tacking and Gybing). However two cases IYRU 86 and US 150 appear to extend the scope of the exception to include a few seconds before the starting signal. IYRU 86 (Fig. 26) deals with pre-start manoeuvring. As A nears the starting line, but before the starting signal, timing her start, B closes in from astern, sailing faster, and tries to establish an overlap to leeward. A bears away to keep B directly astern of her. Finally A luffs abruptly and heads for the line. At this point B is so close astern that she hits A's stern quarter as it swings round.

The question was then asked: 'Does such a manoeuvre by A constitute obstruction within the terms of rule 35?' The answer was as follows: 'Before the starting signal, there is no proper course, and A, so long as she holds right of way by staying clear ahead, is free to manoeuvre as she wishes to protect her position and give herself a good start. Bearing away to prevent an overlap is consistent with that tactic. B, on the other hand, is

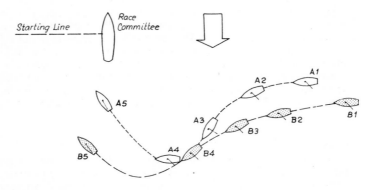

Fig. 26

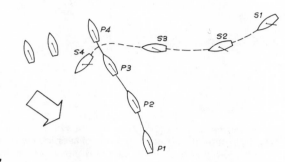

Fig. 27

burdened throughout as a yacht clear astern, and A is doing nothing B could not anticipate, including the abrupt alteration of course to head for the line. B is in error by not keeping sufficiently clear to fulfil her obligations under rule 37.2.'

US 150 (Fig. 27) is another pre-start case where S slowly altered course to windward in a long sweeping curve of about 25°. At a point half way along this curve P saw S coming at her. P made little effort to keep clear . . . and S was forced to bear off to avoid a collision. P was disqualified under rule 36, but appealed arguing that rule 35 should have been applied.

In its decision the US Appeals Committee stated: '. . . the alteration of course by S was clearly consistent with making a proper approach to the starting line. P had ample time to avoid her yet made little attempt to do so.' The decisions in these two cases, while not falling within the scope of 35 (b) (i), treat the situations as if P should within reason, anticipate the right-of-way yacht's alterations of course.

35 (b) (ii)

It would be surprising if the right-of-way yacht did *not* turn onto a proper course when rounding a mark, and therefore she may do so without regard to rule 35. US 167 illustrates the workings of the rule very well. Answering a question on the situation shown in Fig. 28 the Appeals Committee stated: 'The purpose of rule 35 is to protect a burdened yacht from unpredictable

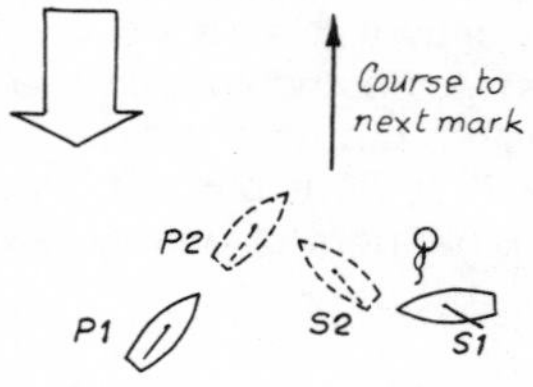

Course to next mark

Fig. 28

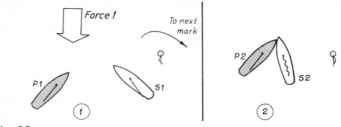

Fig. 29

alterations of course by the right-of-way yacht which prevent or obstruct the burdened yacht fulfilling her obligations of keeping clear.' Rule 35 does not shift the basic rights and obligations of the two yachts. In the incident illustrated, S altered course to a new proper course when rounding the mark as expressly permitted by rule 35 (b) (ii). The course alteration was precisely predictable both as to time (at the mark) and to extent (to close-hauled – S's new proper course). Accordingly P had ample time to keep clear in anticipation of S's alteration of course.'

US 231 understandably interprets the rule to mean not only rounding a mark but also altering course to reach the finishing line. In the case of a starboard-tack yacht approaching a mark to be left to starboard, she will be protected from infringing rule 35 by the exception in 35 (b) (ii) until she passes beyond head to wind and begins to tack and therefore ceases to be the right-of-way yacht. Fig. 29 shows the situation in RYA 1982/8 where S luffed as part of her rounding manoeuvre and was entitled 'to alter course to windward until she was head to wind...' Finally in RYA 1984/9 Fig. 30 we see a case where yachts on opposite courses met at a mark. S altered course, but instead of luffing to round the mark as might have been expected she bore away in her effort to avoid P. Both yachts were disqualified. P, which had not been keeping a good look out, under rule 36 and S under rule 35. US 98, which would nowadays give rise to a consideration of 35 (b) (ii) is discussed under rule 44 (Returning to Start).

Rule 35. Summary

Rule 35 protects the burdened yacht from unexpected and unpredictable alterations of course by the right-of-way yacht. It is for this reason that so many of the incidents we have looked at took place before the start when it was anyone's guess which way a yacht might turn. The exceptions to the rule cover those occasions when the burdened yacht can predict, and so anticipate, the manoeuvre. It is a question of degree when the right-of-way yacht must ignore rule 35 and alter course to avoid what she believes will be a serious collision, but, in the final resort, alter course she must to minimise damage. Rule 35 is one of the most important rules in the book and as we look at other right-of-way rules we shall often have to hark back to these pages.

IV

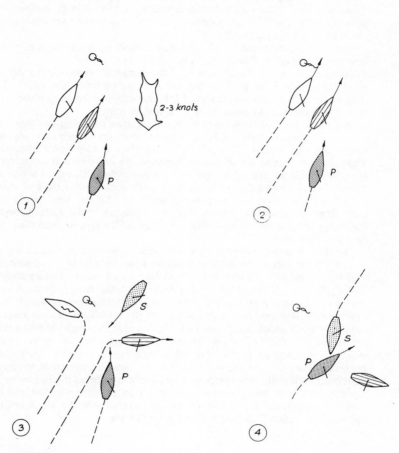

Fig. 30

36   Opposite Tacks—Basic Rule

A *port-tack* yacht shall keep clear of a *starboard-tack* yacht.

Rule 36 generates more protests than any other, and this is not surprising. A reach or a run may involve a yacht in incidents with one or two others on the same tack, overtaking or converging, but a beat to windward opens up the possibility of a direct encounter with every boat in the fleet. The principle of rule 36 is simple and unequivocal, but there is a considerable amount of case law to be looked at and a few exceptions to the basic rule.

The exceptions are listed here, but each is discussed in full under its own rule number:

1 at marks and obstructions: while rule 42 does not apply between opposite tacks on a beat, it does apply to opposite tacks running when – subject to the provisions of rule 42 – an outside starboard-tack yacht may have to give room to an inside port tack one.

2 at marks or obstructions: 42.1 (e) may compel S when inside to gybe to assume a proper course to the next mark.

3 at marks or obstructions: rule 42.2 (a) obliges S, when clear astern, to keep clear even if the yacht ahead is on, or gybes onto, port tack.

4 at the end of a tack under rule 43, P can expect S to keep clear.

5 at the start: rule 44 governs S returning to start.

6 at a mark: rule 45 governs S re-rounding after touching the mark.

Let us start by looking at a straight 'port and starboard' incident, uncomplicated by rules 35 or 41. P believes she can safely pass ahead of S and holds her course, S bears away because she believes she would hit P if she did not do so. US 32 draws a very clear picture. S, when about 20ft distant from P (both Eight-Metres), bore away about one point and passed astern of P, clearing her by approximately five feet or less. The protest committee deduced that had the yachts continued at the same speed on their original courses P would have cleared S. S's protest was dismissed and she appealed.

The US Appeals Committee's remarks, reversing the decision and upholding the appeal, have never been bettered. 'Had S held her course and had P crossed her, an incontrovertible fact would have been established and a protest by S would have been disallowed. But S actually bore away, and the prognostication that P would have crossed her was based (**1**) on an estimate of clearance by inches, and (**2**) on the constancy of the speed and course of each yacht, two factors which, owing to the vagaries of the wind, are subject to rapid changes. Reasonable doubt exists as to whether P would have cleared S had the latter held her course. When there is reasonable doubt as to the ability of the port-tack yacht to cross ahead of a starboard-tack yacht, the starboard-tack yacht is entitled to bear away and protest, and need for adequate evidence rests on the obligated port-tack yacht to support her claim that she would have cleared the starboard-tack yacht.' RYA 1981/9 closely follows this US case.

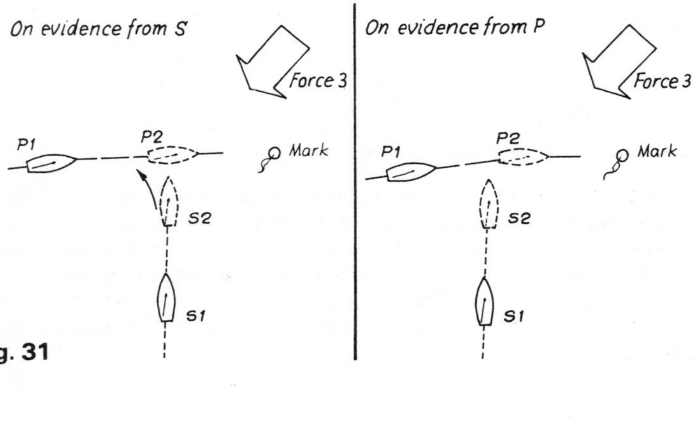

Fig. 31

The situation is further illustrated by IYRU 113 (Fig. 31). In a similar case P did not deny or admit that S bore away but said that, if she did, it was unnecessary. This was the most favourable picture P could present. Drawing heavily on US 32 (quoted in full above) the CYA stated that: 'when a protest committee found that S did not alter course or that there was not a genuine and reasonable apprehension of collision on the part of S, it should disallow the protest. When satisfied that S did alter course and that there was reasonable doubt that P could have crossed ahead of S, if S had not so altered course, then P should be disqualified.' The case goes on to discuss rule 36 as follows:

'Rule 36 protests in which no contact occurred are common. Protest committees tend to handle them in a very disparate manner. Some place the onus on the port-tack yacht to prove conclusively that she would have cleared the starboard-tack yacht even when the latter's evidence is barely worthy of credibility. No such onus appears in rule 36 (unlike rules 41.3, and 42.3 (d) and (e)).

'Other protest committees appear reluctant to allow any rule 36 protests in the absence of contact and place the onus on the starboard-tack yacht to prove conclusively that contact would have occurred had she not altered course. Both of these approaches are incorrect – the first places an improper and undue onus on a port-tack yacht, and the second places too high an onus on the starboard-tack yacht and encourages collisions which the rules are intended to prevent.'

When, instead of trying to cross ahead of S, P passes astern, it has been held (RYA 1981/2) that a port-tack yacht may steer a course to pass close astern of a starboard-tack yacht without infringing rule 36. This is logical for it should not be difficult for P to control her bearing away very accurately.

Rule 36 applies when running or reaching as well as when beating, and IYRU 35 illustrates this, it is quoted and discussed under rule 35. IYRU 45 is similar. Fig. 32 shows three yachts, one on starboard tack and two on port, running for a mark. S established an overlap on PL when PL and PW were within two boat-lengths of each other but PW was clear ahead; shortly afterwards PL established an overlap on PW. The three yachts continued on slightly converging courses, without altering course, until S touched first PW and then PL. PW protested S alleging that she had infringed rule 42.3 (a), because PL constituted an obstruction to PW and S had no right to come

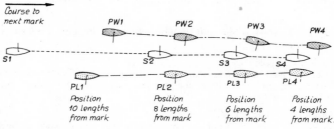

Fig. 32

between. The protest committee disqualified PL and PW under rule 36 and PW appealed.

The appeals committee dismissed the appeal, saying: 'Under rule 36, S held right of way over both port-tack yachts, PL and PW. Consequently, the appellant, PW, did not rank as an obstruction to S and rule 42.3 (a) did not apply between S and PL.'

IYRU 36 states, in answer to a question, that rule 36 does not over-ride rule 35 and does not entitle a starboard-tack yacht to steer any course deliberately to hit a port-tack yacht by luffing or bearing away. Whether S has prevented P from keeping clear, or has obstructed her thus infringing rule 35 will depend on the facts found in each individual case. The relationship between rules 35 and 36 is further discussed in IYRU 52, where S luffed to take advantage of a wind shift. This has been discussed under rule 35 (see Fig. 21).

Hails are frequently exchanged between P and S, but are not required by the rule. RYA 1982/8 carries a dreadful warning for P. P hailed S to 'hold her course', but S ignored the hails and luffed almost head to wind to nullify the effects of the collision she foresaw. In the resulting protest and appeal P lost out: 'Hails such as "hold your course" are not provided for in the racing rules and do not affect the operation of rule 36', stated the appeals committee. This decision is backed by US 137. S hailed 'starboard tack' and P, believing she could cross S responded, 'Hold your course'. S, however, tacked short and protested. In reply to questions about P's hail it was said: '. . . it is permissible to hail but the rules do not recognise such a hail as binding on the other yacht. S can tack (or bear away) at any time she is satisfied that an alteration of course will be necessary to avoid a collision'.

Finally, Rule 42 (Rounding or Passing Marks and Obstructions) does not apply between two yachts on a beat, or when one of them will have to tack either to round a mark or to avoid the obstruction. This is discussed under rule 42, but IYRU 17, 37, 51, 68 and 93 and RYA 1981/3 refer.

37   Same Tack—Basic Rules

37.1   WHEN OVERLAPPED
A *windward yacht* shall keep clear of a *leeward yacht*.

37.2   WHEN NOT OVERLAPPED
A yacht *clear astern* shall keep clear of a yacht *clear ahead*.

37.3   TRANSITIONAL
A yacht that establishes an *overlap* to *leeward* from *clear astern* shall allow the *windward yacht* ample room and opportunity to keep clear.

38   Same Tack—Luffing and Sailing above a Proper Course after Starting

38.1   LUFFING RIGHTS
After she has *started* and cleared the starting line, a yacht *clear ahead* or a *leeward yacht* may *luff* as she pleases, subject to the *proper course* limitations of this rule.

38.2   PROPER COURSE LIMITATIONS
A *leeward yacht* shall not sail above her *proper course* while an *overlap* exists, if when the *overlap* began or at any time during its existence, the

helmsman of the *windward yacht* (when sighting abeam from his normal station and sailing no higher than the *leeward yacht*) has been abreast or forward of the mainmast of the *leeward yacht*.

38.3 OVERLAP LIMITATIONS

For the purpose of rule 38 only: An *overlap* does not exist unless the yachts are clearly within two overall lengths of the longer yacht; and an *overlap* that exists between two yachts when the leading yacht *starts*, or when one or both of them completes a *tack* or *gybe*, shall be regarded as a new *overlap* beginning at that time.

38.4 HAILING TO STOP OR PREVENT A LUFF

When there is doubt, the *leeward yacht* may assume that she has the right to *luff* unless the helmsman of the *windward yacht* has hailed "Mast Abeam", or words to that effect. The *leeward yacht* shall be governed by such hail, and, when she deems it improper, her only remedy is to protest.

38.5 CURTAILING A LUFF

The *windward yacht* shall not cause a *luff* to be curtailed because of her proximity to the *leeward yacht* unless an *obstruction*, a third yacht or other object restricts her ability to respond.

38.6 LUFFING TWO OR MORE YACHTS

A yacht shall not *luff* unless she has the right to *luff* all yachts that would be affected by her *luff*, in which case they shall all respond, even when an intervening yacht or yachts would not otherwise have the right to *luff*.

Two yachts must, by definition, be either clear ahead and clear astern of each other, or overlapped, although rule 38.3 limits the definition for same-tack yachts in respect of luffing rights. Overlapped or not, two same-tack boats may be on converging or on parallel courses, the two may converge on steady courses or they may converge because one or both of them alters course: L by luffing, W by bearing away. L may or may not have luffing rights. A faster yacht may establish an overlap from astern either to windward or to leeward. Either yacht may or may not be on a proper course. All these variables make it difficult to determine which part of the rules should be applied. Once the facts are distinguished and clear the application of the rules becomes simple.

Rule 37, qualified when appropriate by 38.2, applies at all times except when specifically overridden by a rule of Section C (see rules 42, 44 and 45). Rule 38 applies after a yacht starts and has cleared the starting line. Rule 40 provides a modified version of rule 38 (and uses some of rule 38's provisions) suitable to the confused melée before the yachts start and clear the starting line. This distinction is very important and the timing of the incident is an essential factor. There is no proper course until the starting signal (see definition), so there is a time, however short, between the starting signal and when a yacht starts and clears the starting line when she has a proper course but is not subject to rule 38.2, ie she may sail above her proper course although even then she may be subject to rule 42.4 – anti-barging. When L chooses not to assume a proper course after the starting signal but before she started there is no obligation on her to do so (US 227).

1 Yachts overlapped on steady converging courses before they become subject to rule 38.2. Here rule 37.1 is unqualified. W must keep clear of L, although 37.3 may give her some protection at the very beginning of the overlap. When there is an incident, W often protests under rule 40, but rule

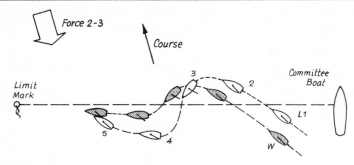

Fig. 33

40 deals with luffing and 'a leeward yacht sailing a steady converging course towards the windward yacht is not luffing. By definition luffing involves an alteration of course' (RYA 67/6).

Fig. 33 (IYRU 24), shows that before the start L passed astern of W at position 3, overtook her to leeward and sailed a steady course without luffing until her shroud touched W's boom end. W protested, invoking rule 40, but was disqualified because 'a leeward yacht, before she has started and cleared the starting line, does not infringe rule 40 (or 37.1) by steering a steady converging course towards a windward yacht'.

2 Yachts on steady converging courses subject to rule 38.2. Once the yachts have started and cleared the starting line, (unless she has luffing rights under rule 38.1 and we shall come that shortly) L must not sail above a proper course but as long as she does so W must keep clear. (Some believe that even when L does sail above a proper course, W is still bound to keep clear, so that in the event of a collision both would be disqualified, L for infringing rule 38.2 and W, rule 37.1). We saw what is or is not a proper course in the definition, and we have said that when both boats are on a proper course it is L's that must prevail (see Fig. 12). It is well illustrated by an unpublished case that stays vividly in my mind (Fig. 34). *Tomboy*, a large slowish handicap cruiser, was broad-reaching up the river Crouch with the wind on her starboard quarter, two Squibs, also on starboard tack, chose for perfectly legitimate reasons of wind and tide, to cross the river from the south to the north shore. While doing so, their courses converged with that

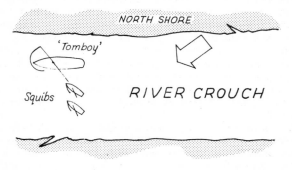

Fig. 34

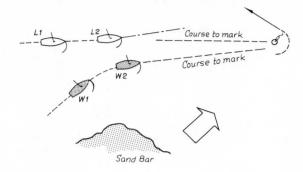

Fig. 35

of *Tomboy* which made no attempt to get out of their way. One of the Squibs protested her and, she was disqualified under rules 37.1 and 38.2 for failing to keep clear.

There are innumerable cases on the subject but one must suffice – US 127 (Fig. 35). Both yachts were under spinnakers in a light and shifting wind. L hailed W to keep clear, and W failed to respond, L bore off and protested. W was sailing the most direct route to the mark but L was also sailing a proper course, one of the number of proper courses that may exist at any given moment depending on the circumstances. W was disqualified under rule 37.1.

RYA 73/2 ruled that a leeward yacht must gybe when this is the only means of fulfilling her obligation not to sail above her proper course. We shall see that this obligation is written into rule 42.1 (d) when the situation occurs at a mark or obstruction.

37.2

Yachts clear astern and clear ahead. Remember that this rule is for same-tack yachts only. In open waters S, astern, will have rights over P, ahead; at marks and obstructions this will not be so (see rule 42, Fig. 77). On a free leg of the course the leading boat's freedom to manoeuvre may be curtailed by rule 39, otherwise she may do what she likes.

37.3

A yacht clear astern becomes overlapped. Rather misleadingly, this rule is headed 'transitional', but it can be considered as a part of rule 37.1. As one inch of *Daisy's* bow crosses the 'imaginary line projected abeam from the aftermost point of the other's hull and equipment in normal position', she becomes overlapped. When this overlap is established to leeward, *Daisy*, in an instant, ceases to be the burdened yacht and becomes the right-of-way yacht (subject to 38.2). It would be manifestly unfair if W could be disqualified for failing to keep clear in an instant, since she could not do so. So *Daisy* (L) must allow W 'ample room and opportunity to keep clear'. Firstly W must be able to keep clear. L must not creep in so close that W cannot luff away without hitting her. When W has something to weather of her, preventing her from getting away, she will usually be protected by rule 42.1 (a) which requires L to give room at obstructions.

The room must be taken at the first opportunity. The opportunity, as has

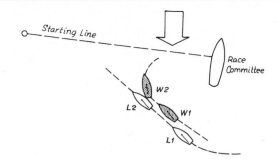

Fig. 36

often been said, is not a continuing one. In US 233 (Fig. 36) after the overlap had been established, the two yachts continued sailing for a few lengths on parallel courses with L moving somewhat faster. When the boats were overlapped eight to 10 feet, L, by hail, indicated her intention to luff. W responded by luffing and tacking, her port counter hitting L amidships. From the time of the overlap until after the contact, L held a steady course and did not luff.

W was disqualified under rule 37.1. The few lengths that the two had sailed overlapped had been adequate to meet the requirements of rule 37.3. W in the course of her appeal contended that: 'The leeward yacht has the obligation to leave more than adequate room, and room that is sufficient to satisfy the windward yacht'; and maintained that the rules do not place any obligation on W during a transitional period to hold her course or luff slowly, and that rule 37.3 explicitly places all the burdens on L. This argument was rejected: 'Ample', in rule 37.3, 'means adequate, or only that which is required for W to keep clear and not that required to satisfy her with respect to anything she desires to do'.

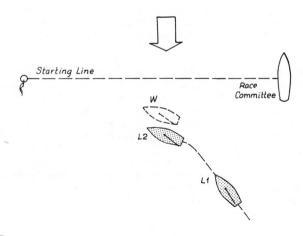

Fig. 37

IV

In IYRU 116 (Fig. 37) the situation was similar except that W had no way on. In spite of L's hails, W did nothing until the overlap was established, then she started to trim her sails and head up. L had to bear away to avoid contact. L protested W under rule 37.1 but the protest was dismissed. L appealed, but her appeal failed too. The decision went as follows: 'Adequate time for response, when rights and obligations change between two yachts, has been written explicitly into rule 37.3, among others, by its requirement to allow the windward yacht "ample room and opportunity to keep clear". Under this provision, a yacht clear ahead need not anticipate her requirement to keep clear as a windward yacht before the yacht clear astern establishes an overlap to leeward. If L, which established an overlap so close that W was not able to keep clear, had not borne away immediately, she would have infringed rule 37.3. Since W at once trimmed sails, headed up, and therefore kept clear, she fulfilled her obligations under rule 37.1. Neither yacht infringed any rule.' Remember that in all these cases, L has sailed a steady course without luffing.

38.1 Luffing Rights

This rule gives permission to a yacht after she has started and cleared the starting line (otherwise she would be subject to rule 40) to 'luff as she pleases' whether she is clear-ahead or to leeward but only in circumscribed circumstances – subject to rule 38.2. In the old days the rule explained itself as well '... she may luff as she pleases to prevent a yacht on the same tack from passing her to windward ...'

Before looking at the limitations on when and how such freedom is available to her or not, let us consider what she may do when there is no doubt about her rights. L need give no warning to W at all. If W is so rash as to put herself in a position where L can hit her, she has only herself to blame. Rule 35, that shield of the burdened yacht, is lifted (see rule 35(a)) and we shall see that not only must W give L all this room to luff she must allow enough room for L to bear away as she likes even when her luffing rights end. The only exception is that provided in rule 42 for rounding marks and those other two rules of Section C, 44 and 45 which remove all rights from yachts exonerating themselves. Remember that these are luffing rights – they give L no right to tack; the moment she passes head to wind she infringes rule 41.

38.2 The limitations on luffing

Rule 38.2 limits L's right to 'luff as she pleases', but not the action of a clear-ahead yacht, only being effective while there is an overlap (and as we shall see in 38.3 the term 'overlap' is less extensive than it has so far been). The rule goes on looking at the situations from L's point of view. How does it look from that of John, W's helmsman. John is sailing faster than L and is establishing an overlap from astern. He knows that L may luff suddenly and mercilessly, regardless of her proper course. However all goes well, L is thinking of other things and decides not to luff. At a certain moment, John, sailing no higher than L (the boats must be parallel – or even converging) sitting in his normal station, sees that he is abreast of L's mast. As soon as he sees this – but NOT before – he hails 'mast abeam' and L's rights are over. She must straightway swing back onto a proper course (or below it if she wishes) and John can relax. He can relax for the duration of the overlap,

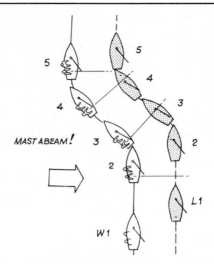

Fig. 38 *At position 3, W hails 'mast abeam'; now L must not sail above a proper course.*

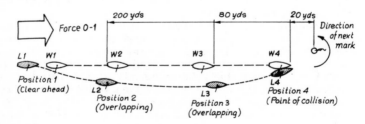

Fig. 39

even if he drops back; unless he goes clear astern L will not recover her rights. The rule also covers the point that L will have no rights when John was ahead or abreast of her mainmast when the overlap began. When L does decide to luff, the situation is the same but if she leaves her luff too late, or is too far away, the very act of luffing will bring John abreast of her mast and so lose her her rights. Fig. 38 shows the positions.

Before going on to look at the intricacies of luffing overlaps – rule 38 overlaps – look at one case that shows L's right to luff when she has not got luffing rights. IYRU 11 (Fig. 39). About 200 yards from the mark L established a leeward overlap on W from clear astern and the two yachts then sailed alongside each other, about one-and-a-half lengths apart, until they were 80 yards from the mark. At this point L began to luff up slightly to lay the mark. W, not sailing below her proper course, maintained a steady course. L never became clear ahead. W's boom touched L's shroud and L protested under rule 37.1. L's protest was dismissed and she was disqualified on the grounds that she had not allowed W ample room and opportunity to fulfil her obligation to keep clear as required by rule 37.3. L appealed.

Upholding the appeal the RYA stated: 'It was clear from the protest committee's findings and diagram that W was bound by, but did not infringe, rule 39, which required her not to sail below her proper course. When L established a leeward overlap from clear astern W became bound by rule 37.1 to keep clear of L. At the same time L was bound by rule 37.3 to allow W ample room and opportunity to keep clear but this obligation was not a continuing one and in this case the overlap had been in existence for a considerable period during which nothing had obstructed W's room. Although W did not infringe rule 39 by sailing below her proper course L was justified in altering course slightly to close the mark, provided that she did not sail above her proper course; it is L's proper course that is the criterion for deciding whether rules 37.1 and 38.2 have been infringed. L at no time sailed above her proper course'.

IYRU 101 provides an interpretation of normal position: 'The helmsman's normal position may vary in yachts of the same class, depending on the strength of the wind, sea conditions and other factors, provided always that he does not move to a position in order to justify a mast-abeam hail.'

38.3 Overlaps

Rule 38.3 sets limits to overlaps in so far as they relate to the proper course limitations of the preceding rule. It has two provisions:

1 An overlap, does not exist unless the yachts are clearly within two overall lengths of the longer yacht. Thus L can sail where she likes, above her proper course if she so thinks fit, until less than two lengths of open water lies between the two yachts at which point the overlap begins.

2 A *new* overlap is considered to begin when a yacht (or both of them) tacks or gybes or when the leading yacht of two overlapped yachts starts. So even if W has reached the mast-abeam position when both yachts, say, gybe and W finds herself once again astern of that position she must keep clear of any luffing L may choose to indulge in now that a new overlap has begun. This is illustrated in RYA 68/7 (Fig. 40), where L and W round a mark, L simply bearing away while W took a wider sweep, tacked and thus overlapped to

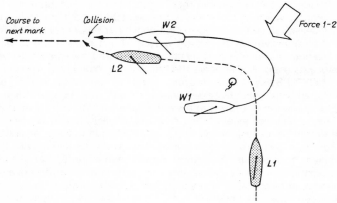

Course to next mark   *Collision*   W2   *Force 1-2*

L2

W1

L1

Fig. 40

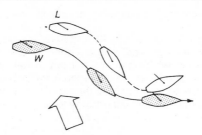

Fig. 41

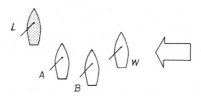

Fig. 42 *L may luff: she has luffing rights on A, B and W. So W must keep clear of A and B even though they have no luffing rights on her.*

windward. The protest committee disqualified L for sailing above her proper course under rule 38.2. On appeal however it was held that by tacking W began a new overlap which from that moment determined their new rights and obligations, and that since W's helmsman was astern of L's mast, L had the right to luff and W had infringed rule 37.1.

The second phrase in the rule quite clearly states that even when L believes W has hailed too early, she, L, may not continue to luff as she pleases nor sail above her proper course. Her only recourse is to protest. (It is worth reminding the reader at this point that we are not dealing here with a ladylike luff by L to a course 'not above her proper course' after fulfilling the requirements of rule 35 and maybe 37.3. It is confusing because in this case she has no luffing rights and yet may luff! However while L must bear away as soon as she hears the hail she must be given room to do so.

In IYRU 3 (Fig. 41) L luffed and, when W hailed 'mast abeam', bore away so sharply that her tiller extension touched W. The appeal decision in favour of L quoted the decision in a similar case (USYRU 20) viz, that a leeward yacht which has legally luffed a windward yacht may bear away suddenly and that W, in responding to L's luff, is obliged to keep far enough away from L to give L room to bear away both suddenly and rapidly upon being hailed 'mast abeam' (or before). So we have a pretty clear picture; a clear astern yacht decides to pass another yacht to windward. While she is still astern, or as she starts to establish an overlap, L luffs sharply, W luffing up to keep clear. However W is the faster boat and in spite of the luffing overtakes L until W's helmsman sighting abeam and sailing parallel is level with L's mast. 'Mast abeam' he cries and hearing his loud hail L bears sharply away, regretfully allowing W to get through.

38.4 Hailing to stop or prevent a luff.

'When there is doubt' the rule begins 'L may assume she has the right to luff unless W has hailed 'mast-abeam'. IYRU 48 (Fig. 43) illustrated this by accepting that L had the right to sail above a proper course when W failed to hail at all and while the situation was still in doubt. However IYRU 99 makes it quite clear that when there is *no* doubt, then the first part of rule 38.4 does not become operative. In this case L's pulpit struck near the forward end of W's cockpit near her helmsman's normal station and it was clear that W had reached a position well ahead of mast abeam prior to the time of contact. There thus being no doubt that L's luffing rights had terminated under rule 38.2 she infringed that rule by failing to bear away to a proper course. So, while W can occasionally get away with it without hailing, she will undoubtedly be in a far stronger position in the protest room if she has hailed as she came mast abeam: and in her turn L cannot go on luffing after she *knows* beyond doubt that the mast-abeam position has been reached just because W has failed to hail.

The general position is set out in US 78. The hailing provisions in rule 38.4 were included in the "luffing rule" to reduce arguments and protests and they should be so interpreted. The helmsman of a windward yacht who fails to protect his rights by hailing in proper time is entitled to little consideration. It is easy for him to see when he attains the "mast abeam" position. On the other hand, the helmsman of the leeward yacht is, as a rule, in no position to determine "mast abeam". Hence he must rely on, and be governed by, a hail to know when he has lost his luffing rights.

'A hail should, as a rule, be unnecessary when the leeward yacht established her overlap from clear astern. But when an overlap results from convergence, or the completion of a tack or gybe, the leeward yacht should be held blameless if the helmsman of the windward yacht:

a) that attains the "mast abeam" position fails to hail either before the leeward yacht begins to luff or the instant she begins to luff. Failure to notice a luff is no excuse for not responding to it or for not hailing.

b) that attains the "mast abeam" position during a luff, fails to hail in time to enable the leeward yacht to bear away before contact.

'Since the helmsman of W, in the case before us, failed to hail in time to enable L to bear away before contact, the decision of the Race Committee is

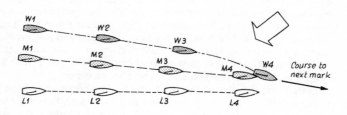

Fig. 43

reversed, and L is absolved from blame, and W is disqualified for infringing rule 38.5 in not keeping sufficiently clear of L to enable her to avoid contact by curtailing her luff as soon as she was obligated to begin doing so by the hail of "mast abeam".'

IYRU101 comments: 'Rule 38.4 is not satisfied by a hail that is not loud enough to be heard. In this case, while L is still in doubt, she has a right to luff until W succeeds in informing her that she has attained mast-abeam. If W's first hail was inadequate, a second louder hail was required. The deciding factor is not the positions of the yachts at the moment of contact, although these positions are important evidence for arriving at the facts.'

38.5

The closely regulated battle between L and W ends with a warning to W not to try to curtail L's luff just because the two boats are very close together. W may only curtail her luff because she has reached mast-abeam position or because of an 'obstruction or a third yacht or other object'. On the face of it, this is a belt and braces phrase, another yacht is either an obstruction, governed by rule 42, or is controlled by rule 38.6, and it is difficult to understand what an object can be that is not an obstruction. When she meets such an impediment, which prevents her responding further, W should hail, indeed RYA 84/15 holds that 'it is implicit in rule 38.5 that a hail is required to curtail a luff when curtailment is necessitated by an obstruction'.

38.6

Until now we have looked two yachts overlapped under rule 38, but often a number of boats are involved and then *Daisy*, wishing to luff as she pleases, must be in such a position that she can, in fact and by right, luff *all* yachts which could be affected. When she can do so they must all respond and keep clear. In Fig. 42 L has the right to luff A, B and W, and A and B must respond although they themselves do not have the right to luff W. The rule may be clear but it is extremely difficult sometimes to establish the position of the other yachts mixed up in the incident. Fortunately L, with a lot of boats up to windward, and perhaps with some shouting, is unlikely to risk a luff because she will be unable to see whether or not she has luffing rights over the most windward of the bunch.

IYRU 48 looks at a three-boat situation, (Fig. 43). At position 1 the three yachts were overlapped, M with luffing rights over W, L with luffing rights over both. All three were sailing somewhat above their proper course. By position 3 W had gained sufficiently on M to be 'mast abeam' although she did not hail. Next, W bore away slightly toward the mark and her stern quarter contacted M's bow. W continued to gain and presumably, at some point, attained 'mast abeam' on L but she unfortunately was not included in the hearing. The protest committee disqualified W under rule 37.1 for not keeping clear of a leeward yacht and she appealed.

Dismissing the appeal the US Appeals Committee said: 'Had L not been present in this situation the answer would be straightforward. Undoubtedly, given the points of contact between W and M, W's helmsman came abreast of M's mast sufficiently prior to contact that M clearly had lost her luffing rights and, in the absence of L, would have been sailing above her proper course in contravention of rule 38.2. M, however, had obligations to L as well since L's bow was ahead of hers at all times. L also retained her luffing rights over W longer than did M but whether she lost them prior to W's bearing away is not made clear either by the stated facts or the diagram. Since there was doubt, L was within her rights in the absence of a hail from W, in continuing to sail above her proper course. Meanwhile M observed her obligations to L under rule 38.6 by responding and under rule 37.1 by keeping clear of a leeward yacht. W, on the other hand, failed to observe rule 38.6 for her helmsman either had not come abreast of L's mast or, if she had, failed to hail to that effect. As a result, W infringed both rules 38.6 and 37.1.'

39   Same Tack—Sailing below a Proper Course after Starting

A yacht that is on a free leg of the course shall not sail below her *proper course* when she is clearly within three of her overall lengths of either a *leeward yacht* or a yacht *clear astern* that is steering a course to pass to leeward.

It would not be right for a slow boat to be able to prevent a faster one from passing her (cf running and motor racing). As it is, the faster boat may be luffed when she tries to pass to windward and blanketed when she tries to pass to leeward. This rule prevents the situation being made worse by a clear-ahead yacht bearing down on the one trying to pass. Rule 39 has a limited scope because it only applied on 'a free leg of the course'. This does not mean a leg planned by the RC to be a reaching or running leg but one that actually is so. Given the inconsistency of the wind even the 'windward' leg can be a free leg of the course. Rule 39 applies on any leg where the proper course for the next mark requires an off-wind point of sailing.

Rule 39 cannot apply until the starting signal, because as the definition says there is no proper course until then. The rule is often spoken of as if it forbade W to bear away, but this is not so. It forbids W to sail below a proper course. US 79 (Fig. 14). W, because of a strong current and a light wind, headed to leeward of the direct line mark, a course which in fact brought her directly to the mark. L protested W under rules 37.1 and 39. 'The diagram shows', said the Appeals Committee, 'that after W had crossed L's bow at position 3, she sailed the shortest course to the mark and therefore did not sail below her proper course. Therefore she could not be construed as

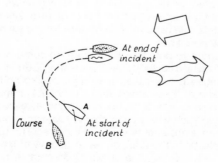

Fig. 44

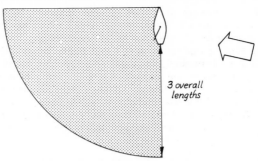

3 *overall lengths*

Fig. 45 Daisy *cannot bear away while another boat is in the shaded areas* and *steering a course to pass to leeward.*

having infringed rule 39'. (She was held not to have infringed rule 37.1 either as she kept clear of L as required by that rule).

The rule is illustrated in IYRU 108 (Fig. 44). Laser (A) and Javelin (B) were reaching on starboard tack. B, with her spinnaker set, was rapidly closing A. While B was within three of her overall lengths of A, A altered course and sailed below a proper course to take station immediately ahead and to leeward of B. In so doing she infringed rule 39. Fig. 45 shows the area affected by rule 39.

40   Same Tack—Luffing before Starting

Before a right-of-way yacht has *started* and cleared the starting line, any *luff* on her part that causes another yacht to have to alter course to avoid a collision shall be carried out slowly and initially in such a way as to give a *windward yacht* room and opportunity to keep clear. However, the *leeward yacht* shall not so *luff* above a *close-hauled* course, unless the helmsman of the *windward yacht* (sighting abeam from his normal station) is abaft the mainmast of the *leeward yacht*. Rules 38.4, (Hailing to Stop or Prevent a Luff); 38.5, (Curtailing a Luff); and 38.6, (Luffing Two or more Yachts), also apply.

Rule 38 is unsuitable for pre-start manoeuvring because it relies on L, at a certain moment, sailing a proper course, and according to the definition there is no such thing as a proper course before the starting signal. Also before the start boats are sailing all which ways and W needs to be protected to a certain extent from her perilous position under rule 37.1 vis-à-vis L. So this rule governs a same-tack luffing yacht until she starts and clears the starting line.

It is important to note that L must luff to come within reach of rule 40. Many of the quoted cases show W protesting L under rule 40 but losing her protest because L has sailed a straight course and not luffed, we have already looked at these cases under rule 37.1. L may luff whenever she likes, W being bound by 37.1, but not 'as she pleases', she must luff 'slowly' and initially in such a way as to give W room and opportunity to keep clear (the obligation is not a continuing one as we saw in rule 37.1, but this time it appears explicitly in the rule), but keep clear W must. Hence all the cries of 'up, up, up' as L luffs slowly and W tries desperately not to be pushed across the line. An echo of rule 38.2 appears in the second sentence, where we

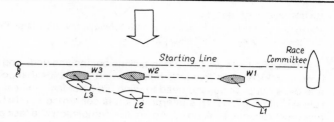

Fig. 46

see that W may not luff above close-hauled unless W's helmsman is aft of her (L's) mast. (See rule 38.2 for details which are the same). The distance or time from the starting line makes no difference, the rule applies equally four minutes before the starting signal 500 yards from the line and as the boats start.

US 204 shows a very typical case. Fig. 46 shows L and W some minutes before the start, W to weather with sails well out and L, overtaking to leeward, with sails sheeted in rather more. After the overlap had been established from astern, the separation between the yachts was about one boat length. The two sailed along on a somewhat converging course for at least five lengths at which point the separation was down to half a length or less. At about one minute before the start, a collision occurred. W protested L under rule 40 for luffing rapidly and L protested W under rule 37.1. As is so often the case, once the facts were established the application of the rules was easy. Did L luff? If she luffed did she luff slowly? Did she give W room and opportunity *initially* to keep clear? How far did L luff? The appeals committee, settling what had to a large extent been a disagreement about facts stated: '... the overlap had existed over a period of time during which there was a gradual convergence of the two yachts until there was a half a length or less between them. Absent any indication of an attempt on the part of W to keep clear and of the luff by L having been executed other than slowly, there are no grounds for inferring that the luff was improper under rule 40.' W was disqualified under rule 37.1.

41 Changing Tacks—Tacking and Gybing

41.1 BASIC RULE

A yacht that is either *tacking* or *gybing* shall keep clear of a yacht *on a tack*.

41.2 TRANSITIONAL

A yacht shall neither *tack* nor *gybe* into a position that will give her right of way, unless she does so far enough from a yacht *on a tack* to enable this yacht to keep clear without having to begin to alter her course until after the *tack* or *gybe* has been completed.

41.3 ONUS

A yacht that *tacks* or *gybes* has the onus of satisfying the race committee that she completed her *tack* or *gybe* in accordance with rule 41.2.

41.4   WHEN SIMULTANEOUS
When two yachts are both *tacking* or both *gybing* at the same time, the one on the other's port side shall keep clear.

In the definitions we saw when tacking begins and ends and when *Daisy* is on a tack. 'A yacht that luffs head to wind and holds that point of sailing and does not pass beyond head to wind does not tack and cannot infringe rule 41' (RYA 67/1). This interpretation is confirmed in IYRU 58, US 138 and most recently RYA 85/6. Again, the completion of a tack onto a close-hauled course is discussed in IYRU 32: 'When beating, a yacht has completed her tack when she is heading on a close-hauled course regardless of her movement through the water or the sheeting of her sails'. All these cases deal with tacking too close (or not as the case may be) – in common parlance, 'he tacked in my water' (never, 'I tacked in his water'!).

As usual there are exceptions. A premature starter returning to start (rule 44.1) and a yacht exonerating herself under rule 52 and therefore subject to rule 45, are both outlaws, and there is no obligation on a yacht tacking or gybing to keep clear of them. (Their position is not entirely desperate, however, they would still be protected by rule 35 from such sudden alterations of course that they could not avoid contact.) In rule 42.2 (a) a yacht clear-ahead has the right to gybe round a mark in peace, and the clear-astern yacht must keep clear. In rule 43, as we shall see, for reasons of safety, *Daisy* can hail for room to tack and when the other boat hails 'you tack', she may do so without bothering about rule 41.

In rule 42.2 (a) only the gybing yacht is protected, not so the tacking yacht. IYRU 26 (Fig. 47) shows how A, although clear ahead of B, can be carried far out of her way. 'In tacking to round a mark, a yacht clear ahead must comply with rule 41, and a close-hauled yacht clear astern is entitled to hold her course to prevent the other from tacking.'

When *Daisy* tacks from starboard onto port tack she becomes the burdened yacht when she tacks, and remains the burdened yacht when she sails off on port tack, and similarly when she tacks into a windward position, relative to another yacht; the only protection she has is under rule 35. But when *Daisy* tacks from port to starboard, or into a leeward position, she changes from being the burdened yacht while subject to rule 41 to right-of-

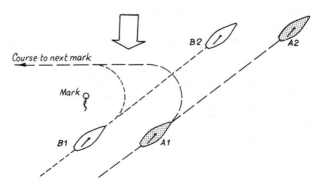

Course to next mark

Mark

Fig. 47

way yacht under rules 36 and 37 respectively. It is therefore essential to pin down as exactly as possible the moment this reversal of roles occurs. Rule 41.2 attempts to do this, and US 50 describes it well: 'Two yachts about 17 feet overall, were beating on opposite tacks. After completing a tack from port to starboard, A was between six and 10 feet directly ahead of B who thereupon gained and narrowed the interval between them to two or three feet. B then tacked and protested A under rule 41.2 for tacking too close. A was disqualified and appealed.'

After quoting rule 41.2 the decision goes on: 'The important consideration here is that the yacht which will have to take steps to keep clear after another yacht's tack has been completed, is not obligated to begin to alter her course prior to the completion of the tack, that is until the other yacht has borne away to a close-hauled course. The facts found ... indicate clearly that B held her course for about three seconds after A's tack had been completed and then was able to tack without interfering with A. This information confirms by actual performance that the requirements of the rule were complied with and that A's tack was made properly and at sufficient distance from B.'

IYRU 10, illustrated and discussed under rule 35 (Fig. 20), confirms the US decision: 'When S tacked she did so at a sufficient distance from P to enable her to keep clear, which P demonstrated by actual performance.' IYRU 53 is similar to IYRU 26 except that the two boats are no longer overlapped, (Fig. 48). 'L a length to leeward and a length ahead of W tacked as soon as she reached the starboard lay line. Almost immediately she was hit and holed by W travelling at about 10 knots. The race committee disqualified L for infringing rule 41.2. It also disqualified W under the Fundamental Rule C – Fair Sailing, pointing out that she knew L was going to tack but did nothing to avoid collision. W appealed asserting that she was not obligated to anticipate an illegal tack.

Upholding the appeal the US Appeals Committee said: 'The Fundamental Rule can be invoked only when no other rule applies. When L began to tack right of way transferred to W which would retain it until L completed her tack in accordance with Rule 41. Therefore rule 32 applied to W. She took no action to avoid collision but what could she have done? Given her speed

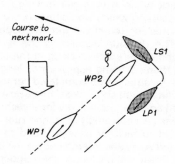

Fig. 48

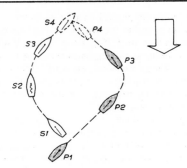

Fig. 49

and the distance involved she had perhaps one to two seconds to decide what to do and then to do it. It is a long established underlying principle of the right-of-way rules that a yacht becoming burdened by an action of another yacht is entitled to sufficient time for response. Also, while it was obvious that L would have to tack to round the mark W was under no obligation to anticipate that she would do so in contravention of rule 41.2.'

One situation arises fairly frequently in pre-start match racing manoeuvres. The two boats are close-hauled on the same tack when L, ahead, tacks, hoping to pass ahead of P or to put her about. W does not wait for L to complete her tack but tacks too, and immediately protests L (now S for tacking too close. W maintains that had she waited to tack until S's tack had been completed there would have been no way in which she could have avoided a collision and as the boats were lent it was incumbent on the helmsman to avoid any such thing. These are always difficult cases, the onus clause cannot be applied too rigidly or W in the case above would use it to her advantage. It is one of the instances when match racing stretches the rules to their limits. They were not designed for close in-fighting.

Rule 41.4. Simultaneous tacking. As shown in Fig. 49 US 129, after A's bow passed astern of B, B sailed for about one length and then put her helm down preparatory to tacking. As soon as A saw B alter course to tack, she also tacked. Both yachts were then tacking at the same time about three lengths apart. B started to tack (passed head to wind) before A and completed her tack while A was still tacking (at position 3 both yachts tacked to avoid a collision which would have occurred at position 4). The PC disqualified A for tacking too close and she appealed, claiming that rule 41.1 governed. The decision dismissing the appeal reads: 'During the period when B and A were both tacking at the same time, there was no contact between them, B being approx three lengths from A, so B did not infringe rule 41.4. Inasmuch as B completed her tack onto port while A was still tacking, A, even though she tacked "into a position which gave her right of way" did not do so far enough away for a yacht on a tack to enable this yacht to keep clear.' A accordingly infringed rule 41.2.

'When B started to tack by passing head to wind, she became the obligated yacht, and A, as she altered course, held right of way first briefly under rule 41.1, while still on a tack, then under rule 41.4 when on the starboard side of B while both yachts were tacking – during both of which times B kept clear – and finally under rule 36, after completing her tack. This persistent alteration of course by A in contravention of rule 35, put B in a position from which she was unable to keep clear by her own efforts alone'.

The RYA took a different view when two same-tack boats tacked together: 'If one yacht sees another beginning to tack, and immediately follows suit, rule 41.4 does not apply, because they did not tack at the same time.' (RYA 69/4). I find the RYA version simpler and just; when one boat may follow another and yet come under rule 41.4 a cunning helmsman can use it to his advantage.

IV

SECTION C—Rules that Apply at Marks and Obstructions and other Exceptions to the Rules of Section B

When a rule of this section applies, to the extent to which it explicitly provides rights and obligations, it over-rides any conflicting rule of Section B, Principal Right of Way Rules and their Limitations, except rule 35, (Limitations on Altering Course).

Fairness and safety dictate the need for special rules when rounding marks or passing obstructions (it is usually that way). What would happen without them?

1 The windward of two port-tack boats nearing a mark to be left to port, would always have to slow down and drop back to keep out of L's way or be pushed to the wrong side of the mark. (see Fig. 57, IYRU 109, discussed later). This would in theory mean that boats could only round marks in Indian file.

2 When L was inside boat there would not be a great deal of difference because 37.1 then works similarly to rule 42.

3 When two boats were running on different gybes, S would always be able to make it very difficult for P to round the mark (see Fig. 59 US 164, discussed later).

4 The leeward of two same-tack close-hauled boats would not be able to hail to tack as rule 43 now allows her. Without it she would have to slow down and drop back, or bear away and gybe round while she still had room to do so. (It is noteworthy that, while you might expect no provision in the collision regulations (IRPCAS) for rounding marks it would be reasonable to think that some form of rule 43 would exist – but it does not).

5 Without rule 44 and 45 yachts trying to exonerate themselves, sailing in opposite directions to the rest, would be unfairly entitled to rights of way.

These are just some of the problems there would be without Section C. In all cases the risk of collision would be heightened if the basic rules were left unadapted. Note however that only when a rule of Section C explicitly provides a right or an obligation are the basic rules overridden. Rule 35 is never overridden although as we saw when looking at that rule, it incorporates one or two exceptions to itself which apply at marks.

42   **Rounding or Passing Marks and Obstructions**

Rule 42 applies when yachts are about to round or pass a *mark*, other than a starting *mark* surrounded by navigable water, on the same required side or an *obstruction* on the same side, except that:

(a) rule 42 shall not apply between two yachts on opposite *tacks* on a beat or when one of them will have to *tack* either to round the *mark* or to avoid the *obstruction*;

(b) rule 42.4 begins to apply when yachts are approaching the starting line to *start*.

42.1   **WHEN OVERLAPPED**

An Outside Yacht

(a) An outside yacht shall give each inside *overlapping* yacht room to round or pass the *mark* or *obstruction*, except as provided in rule 42.3. Room is the space needed by an inside *overlapping* yacht, which is handled in a seamanlike manner in the prevailing conditions, to pass in safety between an outside yacht and a *mark* or *obstruction*, and includes space to *tack* or *gybe* when either is an integral part of the rounding or passing manoeuvre.

(b) An outside yacht *overlapped* when she comes within two of her overall lengths of a *mark* or *obstruction* shall give room as required, even though the *overlap* may thereafter be broken.

(c) An outside yacht that claims to have broken an *overlap* has the onus of satisfying the race committee that she became *clear ahead* when she was more than two of her overall lengths from the *mark* or *obstruction*.

An Inside Yacht

(d) A yacht that claims an inside *overlap* has the onus of satisfying the race committee that she established the *overlap* in accordance with rule 42.3.

(e) When an inside yacht of two or more *overlapped* yachts, either on opposite *tacks* or on the same *tack* without *luffing* rights, will have to *gybe* in order most directly to assume a *proper course* to the next *mark*, she shall *gybe* at the first reasonable opportunity.

42.2   **WHEN NOT OVERLAPPED**

A Yacht Clear Astern

(a) A yacht *clear astern* when the yacht *clear ahead* comes within two of her overall lengths of a *mark* or *obstruction* shall keep clear in anticipation of and during the rounding or passing manoeuvre, whether the yacht *clear ahead* remains on the same *tack* or *gybes*.

(b) A yacht *clear astern* shall not *luff* above *close-hauled* so as to prevent a yacht *clear ahead* from *tacking* to round a *mark*.

A Yacht Clear Ahead

(c) A yacht *clear ahead* that *tacks* to round a *mark* is subject to rule 41, (Changing Tacks—Tacking and Gybing).

(d) A yacht *clear ahead* shall be under no obligation to give room to a yacht *clear astern* before an *overlap* is established.

42.3   EXCEPTIONS AND LIMITATIONS

(a) Limitation on Establishing an Overlap
A yacht that establishes an inside *overlap* from *clear astern* is entitled to room under rule 42.1(a) only when, at that time, the outside yacht:

   (i)   is able to give room, and

   (ii)   is more than two of her overall lengths from the *mark* or *obstruction*. However, when a yacht completes a *tack* within two of her overall lengths of a *mark* or *obstruction,* she shall give room as required by rule 42.1(a) to a yacht that cannot thereafter avoid establishing a late inside *overlap.*

At a continuing *obstruction,* rule 42.3(b) applies.

(b) Limitation When an Obstruction is a Continuing One.
A yacht *clear astern* may establish an *overlap* between a yacht *clear ahead* and a continuing *obstruction,* such as a shoal or the shore or another vessel, only when, at that time, there is room for her to pass between them in safety.

(c) Taking an Inside Yacht to the Wrong Side of a Mark.
An outside *leeward yacht* with luffing rights may take an inside yacht to windward of a *mark* provided that she:

   (i)   hails to that effect, and

   (ii)   begins to *luff* before she is within two of her overall lengths of the *mark,* and

   (iii)   also passes to windward of it.

42.4   AT A STARTING MARK SURROUNDED BY NAVIGABLE WATER
When approaching the starting line to *start* and after *starting,* a *leeward yacht* shall be under no obligation to give any *windward yacht* room to pass to leeward of a starting *mark* surrounded by navigable water; but, after the starting signal, a *leeward yacht* shall not deprive a *windward yacht* of room at such a *mark* by sailing either:

(a) above the compass bearing of the course to the first *mark,* or

(b) above *close-hauled.*

Rule 42 governs an infinite variety of situations at marks and obstructions when boats crowd together, fighting for the best position. It is therefore long and complicated. The first 15 lines, up to the end of rule 42.1(a) are intricate and covered by a great deal of case law. Many of these cases illustrate more than one point, but I have tried to group them into the following order:
1 Rounding or passing on the same side.
2 About to round.
3 The exceptions in rule 42 (a) and (b).
4 The overlap.
5 Leaving the circle and re-entering.
6 Taking room made available.
7 The mark passed.
8 The definition of 'room'.
9 A third yacht as an obstruction.
After this we can continue from rule 42.1(b) onwards rule by rule.
NOTE: in discussing this rule 'the circle' will mean a circle, centre the mark

IV

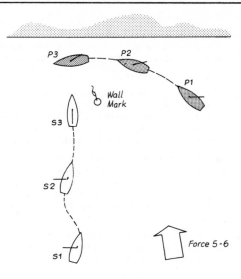

Fig. 50

(or obstruction), radius two overall lengths of the outside yacht. This avoids the necessity of saying 'came within two of her overall lengths of the mark' every time it occurs.

1 Rounding or passing on the same side. In practice there is no difference between rounding and passing as far as concerns the rights and obligations arising out of rule 42. 'Passing', if we were told it included 'rounding', would suffice, since whether a yacht barely alters course when she passes or turns through 180° as she rounds, she will be treated the same. Both a mark and an obstruction are defined in Part I and have been fully discussed there, but it is important to remember that obstructions are often other competing yachts. Before rule 42 can apply the yachts must be about to round a defined mark or a defined obstruction (sometimes both) on the same side, and when it is a mark that we are dealing with 'on the same required side'. This means that when boats are rounding a mark in opposite directions rule 42 does not apply and the basic rules of Section B do – as if the mark had been removed.

IYRU 37 (Fig. 50) shows just such a case. P and S were nearing a mark to be left to port. S mistakenly believed she should leave it to starboard and – to put it briefly – they collided. The protest committee disqualified S under rule 42 but referred the matter to the national authority. The RYA decided otherwise, saying that since the yachts were not 'about to round a mark on the same side' rule 42 did not apply and disqualified P under rule 36. A decision that did not help S though, since she was disqualified too, this time for failing to try to avoid a collision under rule 32. In IYRU 51 (Fig. 25) the two boats meeting at a mark, rounding in opposite directions, were in different classes. Each was sailing her own course correctly. Again because they were not rounding on the same side, the mark could be 'removed' and basic rules applied. Again P was disqualified for infringing rule 36 and S for not

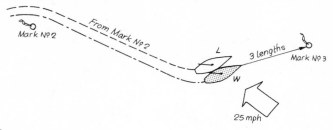

Fig. 51

trying to avoid a collision causing serious damage (rule 32) Council remarked dryly. 'It is most undesirable for a race committee to instruct yachts in different races and on different legs of the course to round the same mark on different required sides'.

As far as marks are concerned the yachts must be passing on the required side. If two yachts are going to the wrong side they are not 'about to round or pass' and basic rules will apply between them.

2 About to round. 'The phrase "about to round" has never been defined precisely nor can it be. In approaching a mark there is no exact point at which a yacht becomes "about to round". Clearly a yacht two lengths from a mark is about to round but this could be so at a somewhat greater distance too. The distance varies with such factors as the conditions of wind and tide, the speed of the yachts, their size and the amount of sail handling required just before or during rounding. The transition moreover is gradual. The nearer a yacht is to a mark the more definitely she is about to round the more she is committed to do so and the more her competitors expect her to do so and plan their own courses accordingly.' Thus the US Appeals Committee gave a decision in IYRU 55.

The rule itself contains in rule 42.3(c) a requirement for action when L, wishing to take W to the wrong side of a mark, must hail and begin to luff before she reaches the circle, but for everyday ordinary purposes the circle is considered the vital moment when the rules change. RYA 68/10 states: 'rule 42.1(a) does not override rules 37.1 and 38.1 until the outside or leading yacht of two overlapped reaches' the circle. This British decision supported an American one of some years before. In US 58, the two Lightnings in Fig. 51 were reaching in a rough sea in a 25-knot wind. At three lengths from the mark, W, who had been sailing a course somewhat to windward of the mark, bore away and collided with L. L had luffing rights on W. The PC disqualified L for not giving room under rule 42 and she appealed. Reversing the decision the Appeals Committee said: 'The facts show that L on starboard tack, had the right to luff W throughout the incident and at this distance from the mark had the right to take W to windward of the mark if she wished under rule 42.3(c). If she did not choose to exercise her right to luff, rule 42.1(a) would begin to apply at two lengths from the mark ...'. W was still subject to rule 37.1 and was disqualified.

Nevertheless it is nowhere written into the rule that rule 42 cannot begin to apply further away than two lengths and if we think of a mark such as the Fastnet Rock, approached in high winds and a big sea, it is easy to understand that the provisions of the rule might have to come into force at a

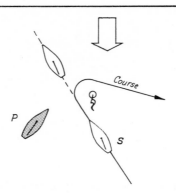

Fig. 52

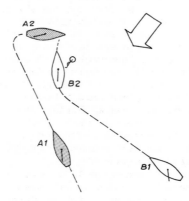

Fig. 53

considerably greater distance than usual for reasons of safety.

3 The exceptions in 42 (a) and (b). Here we deal with the two exceptions that make the whole (or almost) of rule 42 inapplicable. Rule 42.3 – Exceptions and Limitations – which qualify parts of the rule are dealt with later, under that rule number.

(a) Between opposite-tack yachts on a beat. In IYRU 17 (Fig. 52) the question was asked: 'Two close-hauled yachts on opposite tacks meet at a starboard-hand windward mark. P gives S adequate room to round the mark with due allowance for wind, tide, etc. However, S holds her course with the intention of forcing P to tack to keep clear. Can P disregard rule 36 if she considers S to be sailing beyond her proper course and to have sufficient room to round the mark?'

'No', came the answer from the RYA: 'rule 36 applies. When S chooses to hold her course, P must keep clear.' Similarly in RYA 81/3 (Fig. 53); A was disqualified after an appeal by B. The protest committee misdirected itself by applying rule 42.2(a) although A was clear ahead of B two lengths from

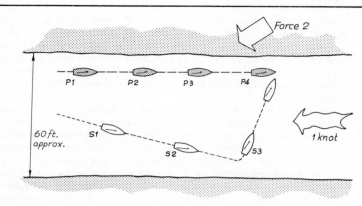

Fig. 54

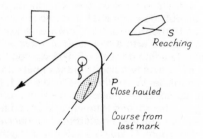

Fig. 55 *P must tack to round mark. 36 applies not 32.*

the mark she could only claim room if she remained on the same tack or gybed. When A tacked onto port she was required to comply with rule 41, and when she tried to cross ahead of B, on starboard, she became subject to rule 36 exactly as she would have been if the mark had not been there.' The alternative is true too: if, when A and B are approaching on opposite tacks one of them tacks they become same-tack yachts and subject to the appropriate part of rule 42.

The exception has its consequences at obstructions as well as at marks, IYRU 93 (Fig. 54) illustrates this. P can just lay along the shore, while S, which for some undisclosed reason has been further offshore, now comes in. P has neither the protection of rule 42, because of the exception we are considering, nor of rule 43, because the two boats are not on the same tack. P *must* keep clear. 'A close-hauled port-tack yacht that is sailing parallel and close to a continuing obstruction must be prepared to keep clear of a yacht that has completed her tack onto starboard and is approaching on a collision course.'

RYA 84/11 shows a similar incident while US 231 illustrates the exception at a finishing line mark. Just occasionally one of the two opposite-tack boats may have overstood so much that she is no longer close-hauled when approaching the mark, but as shown in Fig. 55, P will have to tack to round the mark, so the exception applies. It does not apply when opposite-tack boats are running, when one of them will (probably) have to gybe.

(b) The other total exception is that of starting marks surrounded by navigable water. However it does not make an enormous difference. When L is inside, she has rules 37.1 and 40 on her side, entitling her effectively to room at the mark. When L is outside, the situation at the start is controlled by rule 42.4, the anti-barging rule, which will be looked at in due course.

Yachts nearing a mark (or an obstruction) are either overlapped or not (see definitions clear-astern, clear-ahead, overlap) and the rule has two main sections. 42.1 – when overlapped and 42.2 – when not overlapped. Both aim to make the rounding (or passing) of marks (or obstructions) as fair and safe as possible.

42.1(a).

This is the first command to the competitor – so far there has only been explanation and statements of law. It contains the basic principle of the whole rule: an outside yacht shall give each inside overlapping yacht room to round ... and it then warns that there are – and in what rule are there not? – exceptions. It ends with a definition of 'room'. There is prolific case law.
4 The Overlap. Leading off with US 164 we see that rule 42.1(a) overrides rule 36. Fig. 56 shows two opposite-tack boats arriving at a mark on a run with S on the inside. When they reached pos. 1, IS hailed 'starboard' and continued to do so. Both inside and outside the circle S hailed P several times saying 'starboard' and P finally responded that S was not entitled to rights just because she was on starboard (under rule 36) but asked whether IS had sufficient room. Finally S's spinnaker touched P's backstay and she protested. The PC stated correctly that S's rights as starboard-tack yacht

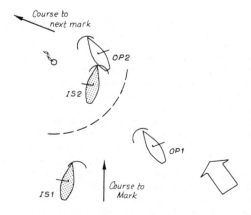

Fig. 56

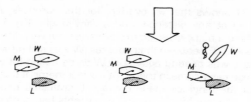

Fig. 57

had been extinguished and replaced by those of rule 42, and that while as inside yacht she was entitled to room to round the mark, she was not entitled to any more room than was necessary. The case ended with the Appeals Committee deciding that, since the room offered her had been adequate for her to gybe round, she infringed rule 42.1(e) by not doing so.

In US 22 (Fig. 57) three overlapped yachts were nearing a mark to be left to port. In position 3, M bore away to avoid W's stern as she luffed to round the mark and collided with her. M, was disqualified and appealed. Reversing the PC decision the Appeals Committee said: 'As the yachts approached the mark, in the circumstances presented, the windward yachts M and W were required to keep clear of L as required by rule 37.1. When L came within two of her overall lengths of the mark, she, as outside yacht, became obligated by rule 42.1(a) to give W and M, overlapping her on the inside, room to round the mark ... While not specifically required by the rules it is customary for a yacht when in doubt as to the sufficiency of the room being accorded to her to hail to that effect as a precaution, as M did. In position 3, only rule 42.1(a) applied ... and rule 42.1(a) overrides rule 37.1 as stated in the Preamble to Section C of Part IV.'

IYRU 109 (Fig. 58) would never have got published had it not been for the procedural query on which it went to appeal. But it shows two overlapped boats arriving at a mark and L, outside, refusing to allow W room to round it. W has to go the wrong side of the mark and then circle round for another try. L maintained that W was not entitled to room on a beat. But as we have seen, the exception on a beat applies only to opposite-tack yachts and L was duly disqualified under rule 42.1(a) for failing to give W room.

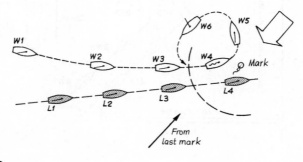

Fig. 58

IYRU 21 shows that an overlap, for the purposes of rule 42, can be established at any distance, and at any angle. Fig. 8 shows L and W approaching a mark to be left to starboard from very different angles, there being about 90° between their courses. W was sailing with the tide almost on a run, L was beating against it. W twice hailed for water, and L twice replied 'you can't come in there'. At the last moment L attempted to give W room but the dinghies made contact. L protested under rule 37.1. The protest committee found that the two yachts had been overlapped, within the definition of the term, 'at all material times', therefore, rule 42.1(a) applied and overrode rule 37.1. It dismissed L's protest, then proceeded against her and disqualified her for failing to give room to an inside yacht that had established her overlap in proper time.

L appealed, asserting that it was illogical and beyond the intention of the definition of overlap and of rule 42 to consider as overlapped two yachts whose headings differed by 90°. Furthermore, W was not an 'inside' yacht until a moment before contact. She also asserted that the purpose of rule 42 is to protect a yacht in danger of hitting the mark that is unable to go astern of the outside yacht. Throughout her approach to the mark until she finally luffed, W was easily able to pass astern of L. The RYA agreed with the protest committee's decision and dismissed the appeal.

Sometimes the act of tacking forms the overlap. Looking at Fig. 59 (IYRU 76) we see that AL could not hail for room to tack under rule 43 because she was still in deep water. When BW tacked (and became BL), A did so too, changing their positions. BL can now just fetch the end of the breakwater close-hauled, but AW has been forced to overstand, she must bear away and needs room to round. The tack has formed an overlap between the two and BL is bound by rule 42.1(a) to give room.

5 Leaving the circle and re-entering. What happens if one boat sails into

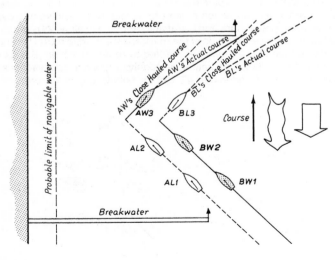

Fig. 59

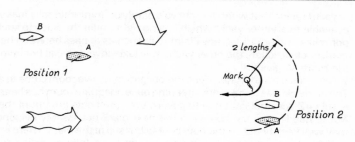

Fig. 60

the circle, sails out of it again and then re-enters? IYRU 71 (Fig. 60) shows A approaching a mark clear ahead of B, however she gets into a muddle at the mark and the tide carries her considerably beyond it and well outside the circle. 'When it is established that A, the yacht clear ahead, was carried by the current outside two of her own overall lengths of the mark, rules 42.2(a) and 42.3(a)(ii) cease to apply to B, the yacht clear astern. If B is within two of her overall lengths of the mark when B returns within that distance and establishes an outside overlap on B, rule 42.1(a) will begin to apply, and B can claim room at the mark. The onus of satisfying the protest committee that A went outside the two-lengths circle will, in accordance with rule 42.1(d), lie on B.'

6 Taking room available. RYA 84/1 (Fig. 61) shows three yachts approaching a mark on a run. The leeward outside boat would dearly have loved to have prevented the inside boat, *Constitution*, passing between her and the mark, but she was unable to head up because of *Hammer and Tongs*. *Constitution* was found to have infringed no rule, she had taken room made available to her and she could, at her own risk, take advantage of it. The principle was stated clearly in US 38: 'It is an established principle

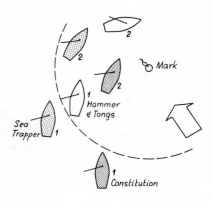

Fig. 61

of yacht racing that when a yacht voluntarily or unintentionally makes room available to another yacht which has no right under the rules to such room nor makes nor indicates any claim to it, such as to pass between her and a mark or obstruction, the other yacht may take advantage, at her own risk, of the room so given'.

7 The mark passed. When does the obligation to give room come to an end? The circle ceases to have any meaning once adequate room has been given, ie rule 42 does not continue to govern until the boats are out of the circle. Nor is heading on the course to the next mark necessarily evidence, tide may well keep boats on the new course but still at the mark. There is no cut-and-dried rule, the burdened yacht must have fully complied with her obligation to keep clear but not one minute longer. At that moment basic rules return with all their force. Or do they? There is an unresolved Catch 22 situation when L, with luffing rights, gives W room to round. At some instant rule 42 stops and rules 37.1 and 38.1 return. Then the relationship between the two changes and L becomes right-of-way yacht. However she is not subject to rule 35 because rule 35(a) makes an exception. So what is to stop L swinging up and hitting W before she has time to respond? I do not know, but I imagine that a protest committee would hold there to be a residual period in rule 42 in this particular case to permit W to get out of the way, otherwise she could be ousted every time.

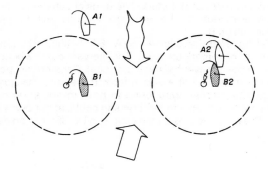

Fig. 62

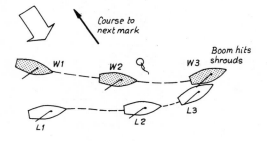

Fig. 63

US 256 shows a case where the boats headed into a very strong current. B was held at the mark and A, which had been clear ahead was carried back on to her (Fig. 62). The protest committee disqualified A for failing to give B room under rule 42.1(a), A appealed and the US Appeals Committee reversed the decision, reinstating A and disqualifying B. The yachts were not overlapped as they approached the mark to round, and B fulfilled her obligation to keep clear of A while A rounded. After A gybed and started on the next leg, rule 42 no longer applied, so that when B also rounded and gybed onto port she became obligated under rule 37.2 as a yacht clear astern to keep clear of A . . . B could and should have kept clear by bearing away . . .

In IYRU 50 (Fig. 63) the incident happened before both boats were out of the circle, but this made no difference to the fact that the mark had been passed, the basic rules applied and W was bound by rule 37.1 to keep clear (it also appears from a reading of the whole case that W had taken more room than she needed at the mark, which as we shall see in the next paragraph is not permitted to her).

8 The definition of 'room'. A discussion of the meaning of room is given in IYRU 40 and can be usefully produced in full.

'Question. What is the maximum amount of room an inside yacht is entitled to take in passing or rounding a mark or obstruction? What is the minimum amount that an outside yacht is required to give? The possible answers vary widely. To suggest the extremes, they might be:

'As a minimum, enough room with sails and spars sheeted inboard, for the hull to clear by centimetres both the mark and the outside yacht;

'As a maximum, all the room the inside yacht takes, setting her course as far abeam of the mark as she wishes.

'Between these extremes are two more moderate possibilities: next to the minimum enough extra clearance to allow for some error of judgement or execution; or, next to the maximum, enough room to make a tactically desirable rounding. Perhaps the most reasonable answer would fall roughly between these two.

'Answer. The word "room" in rule 42.1(a) means the space needed by an inside yacht, which, in the prevailing conditions, is handled in a seamanlike manner, to pass in safety between an outside yacht and a mark or obstruction.

The term "prevailing conditions" deserves some consideration. For example, the inside one of two dinghies approaching a mark on a placid lake in light air will need and can be satisfied with relatively little space beyond her own beam. Contrariwise, when two keel sloops, on open water with steep seas are approaching a mark that is being tossed about widely and unpredictably, the inside yacht may need a full boat-length's room or even more to ensure safety.

The phrase "in a seamanlike manner" applies in two directions. First, it addresses the outside yacht, saying that she must provide enough room that the inside yacht need not make extraordinary or abnormal manoeuvres to keep clear of her and the mark. It also addresses the inside yacht. She is not entitled to complain of insufficient room when she fails to execute with reasonably expected efficiency the handling of her helm, sheets and sails during a rounding. In short, the purpose of rule 42.1(a) is to enable yachts to round and pass marks and obstructions in safety and with equity. When

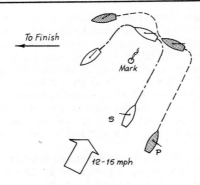

Fig. 64

that principle is observed problems do not arise'.

Little remains to be said. RYA 75/6 interprets 'room' to include the right to shoot a mark: 'The leeward of two close-hauled overlapping yachts which are approaching the finishing line to finish is entitled to luff and shoot to pass on the required side of the limit mark to finish, and W must give her room under rule 42.1(a). US 83 (Fig. 64) shows two yachts at a mark. S inside has to gybe, P, outside merely luffs up. S was entitled to gybe in a seamanlike manner (which she did) and when they touched P infringed rule 42.1(a). Protest committees will often have to find a lot of facts about the type of boats, the weather conditions etc before they can reach a reasonable decision as to whether a yacht had enough room or whether she took more than she should have.

9 A third yacht as an obstruction. We have seen in the definition that a 'vessel' may be an obstruction, and this term includes another yacht in the race. She is usually a right-of-way yacht, but sometimes is one that should give way but cannot do so. Rule 43 deals with hailing to tack at an obstruction, and this includes a yacht obstruction. Rule 42.3(b) governs room at a continuing obstruction, which may also be a yacht. These will be dealt with in due course. Here we will look at the third yacht as an obstruction in regard to rule 42.1(a).

In IYRU 20 (Fig. 65) S was right-of-way yacht in respect of two port-tack yachts PW and PL, she therefore ranked as an obstruction to PW because PW had to make a substantial modification of her course to pass on one side

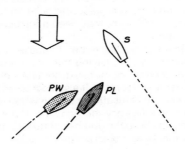

Fig. 65

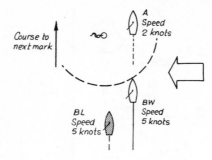

Fig. 66

or another of S. Disqualifying PL under rule 42.1(a) and reinstating PW the RVA stated. 'When two close-hauled port-tack yachts meet a starboard-tack yacht that ranks as an obstruction to either or both, two rules operate to assist the nearer, more vulnerable yacht to keep clear. When PL needs to tack to avoid collision she may, under rule 43, hail PW, whether overlapped or clear astern, to give her room to do so. When it is the windward of two overlapped yachts that is at risk she is entitled, under rule 42.1(a), to room to bear away and clear the obstruction. The latter rule, not rule 43, applied to PW in this case.

'PW could have tacked into the open water to windward to solve her problem, and considerations of strategy in the race might well have made that desirable. This situation, however, hinges on the decision by PL. If she elects not to invoke rule 43 or, as in this case, is not entitled to do so, she is then, as an outside yacht passing an obstruction, bound by rule 42.1(a) to give room to the windward yacht to pass on the same side.'

In IYRU 91 (Fig. 66) it is the yacht clear ahead that forms the obstruction. Answering a question as to the relationship between BL and BW, the RYA stated: 'With respect to A, both yachts astern are subject to rule 37.2. A thus ranks as an obstruction to both. When they come within two lengths of A, still overlapped, rule 42.1(a) will come into effect. If BL then elects to pass A to leeward, rule 42.1(a) will require her to give room to BW, as inside yacht, to do likewise. If, on the other hand, BW elects to luff and pass A to windward, she must, under the same rule, give room to BL, as inside yacht, to pass to windward, should she also elect to do so.'

It was then asked: 'If the answer is that A ranks as an "obstruction" would BW have to claim room to pass to leeward of A, or would BL risk disqualification by not automatically giving room?' 'There is no requirement' went the answer 'in rule 34 to hail for room at a mark or obstruction. The second part of the rule places no obligation on a yacht to take any action; it merely states that a hail will support a yacht's claim for the purposes of rule 42, when a protest hearing ensues.'

It does not ask or answer the question as to what would happen if BL wished to pass to windward of A. She may do so, having rights under rules 37.1 and 42.1(a), but, unless she has luffing rights, she is a right of way yacht altering course subject to rule 35 and rule 34.1, putting herself at risk

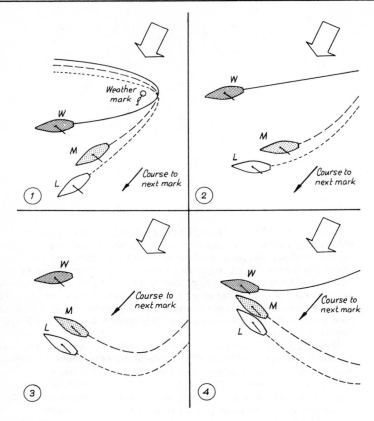

Fig. 67

if she alters course unexpectedly without hailing.

In IYRU 4 (Fig. 67) after the three yachts round the windward mark, W elects to sail high on the course to the next mark and luffs as shown in position 1. L, sailing directly for the mark, is overtaken by M and luffs in defence (Pos. 2), at which point four lengths separate M and W. L continues to luff, and M continues to respond until she fouls W and L fouls M. No hail of any kind is made by M or W during the incident.

Answering a series of questions the RYA says that L is entitled to luff M until position 3, but when they near position 4 M's ability to respond further is restricted by W. Since at this point neither M or L have luffing rights over W, they are required by rule 38.2 not to sail above their proper courses. When asked whether, since L's vision of W is obstructed by M, L can continue to luff until hailed, it then says that M should hail for room to keep clear of W, under rule 42.1(a), since W is an obstruction. This concords with RYA 84/5 where it was stated that it is implicit in rule 38.5 that a hail is required to curtail a luff when curtailment is necessitated by an obstruction.

In IYRU 112 (Fig. 68) S was again the obstruction to two port-tack boats,

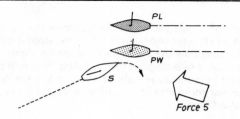

Force 5

Fig. 68

but this time they were sailing almost reciprocal courses. In a moderate to rough sea and a fresh breeze, S, close-hauled, converged with PL and PW broad reaching on a different leg of the course. PW and S's rigging touched, in spite of S luffing sharply in an effort to avoid a collision. PW had been unable to bear away because PL did not give her room to do so and PW should have been exonerated from her infringement of rule 36. There was evidence that PL knew that S was approaching and PW would probably need room. PW claimed to have hailed twice and the yachts were within conversation distance of each other, yet PL did not admit to hearing a hail. Whatever the truth about the hail, PL should have known that under rule 42.1(a) the inside yacht is not required to hail. PL was disqualified.

Finally on this subject look at IYRU 45 (Fig. 32), discussed under rule 36. It was held that neither port-tack boat was an obstruction to S and therefore S could not infringe rule 42. Both port-tack boats were disqualified. This case does not mean that a burdened yacht cannot be an obstruction to a right-of-way yacht, she may well be so if she cannot get out of the way, and the right-of-way yacht can call for room to tack. See IYRU 19 (Fig. 108 under rule 74.4).

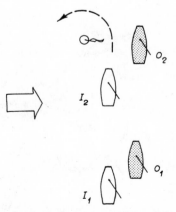

Fig. 69 *The overlap is broken, but I still has right to room.*

42.1(b)

Provided the inside yacht has an overlap at the circle she will carry her right to room on until she rounds the mark, even if the overlap is broken.

Fig. 69 shows how the inside yacht keeps her rights when the overlap is broken at such a late stage in the rounding. This rule makes it quite clear that, at least from this time, rule 42.1(a) is in force; it does not say that rule 42.1(a) cannot come into force earlier in those rare cases which we have already talked about.

42.1(c) (d)

The two onus clauses can be looked at together. In each case the onus is on the boat that must show that there has been some change in the situation. The outside yacht must be able to show that an overlap that has perhaps been in existence since the last mark has been broken before the circle is reached, while the inside yacht must show that, having been clear astern, she has been able to establish an overlap correctly (ie before the circle *and* when the outside yacht is able to give it – see 42.3(a)). Both onuses therefore work towards safety, one makes the would-be inside yacht loth to push in, the other encourages the outside yacht to give room

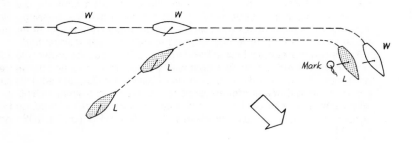

Fig. 70

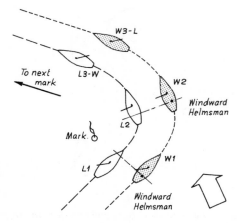

Fig. 71

even if, were it possible to know the facts accurately, she did not strictly need to do so.

In RYA 67/12 (Fig. 70) we see L with what will be an inside overlap at about 12 lengths from the mark. Starting to round the mark L asked for water, but W replied, 'you have lost the overlap', and a collision resulted. On appeal the decision went in favour of L. The RYA said: 'It is agreed that some 10 to 12 lengths from the mark, L established an overlap to leeward on W as a result of their courses converging. Clearly, L discharged the onus laid on her by rule 42.1(d). If the overlap was broken before W came within the two-lengths distance of the mark (rule 42.3(a) (ii)), L became bound by rule 42.2(a). If the overlap continued to exist at the time W came within the two lengths distance of the mark and was broken thereafter, W was bound by rule 42.1(b). In the absence of any corroborative evidence on either side the onus lay on W to satisfy the protest committee that the overlap was broken before she came within two lengths of the mark.'

42.1(e)

The inside yacht also has her obligations to fulfil. We have seen that she may not take more room than necessary, and we know that as leeward yacht rule 38.2 requires her not to sail above a proper course unless she has luffing rights. It is only fair therefore that when an inside, leeward yacht rounds a mark she should assume a proper course as soon as she can, and when the rounding requires a gybe, that she gybe – provided always that she has not got luffing rights under rule 38.1

IN IYRU 62 (Fig. 71) the question was asked: 'The diagram shows L, an inside yacht without luffing rights, claiming room at a mark where the proper course to the next mark involves a gybe. If L were to carry W well beyond the mark and above her proper course when does rule 38.2 replace rule 42.1 (b) and can W force L to gybe and assume a proper course?'

The RYA replied: 'Rule 42.1, as a whole, applies only while overlapping yachts are in the process of rounding or passing a mark or obstruction. However rule 42.1(e) specifically governs an inside yacht after she has passed the mark by requiring her to gybe at the first reasonable opportunity. When rule 42.1 ceases to apply L is then bound by rule 38.2 to gybe onto a proper course. The terms "above" and "below" a proper course are not included in Part 1, Definitions and the phrase "above her proper course" in rule 38.2 is to be interpreted as meaning "on the same side of a yacht's proper course as her windward side". Hence W may require L to gybe and assume a proper course. Should W drop astern of L then her right to force L to gybe, if L has not already done so, would terminate.'

Appendix 4 – Team Racing Rules, para 1.4 gives an excellent description of the inside yacht's rights and obligations, whether she be L or W.

42.2(a) (b)

We have looked at yachts overlapped when they reach the circle, now let us look at those clear astern and clear ahead of each other.

The clear-astern yacht is already obliged to keep clear because she is subject to rule 37.2 but this only covers same-tack boats. In open waters S, when clear astern, has rights over P, clear ahead of her. But not so at the mark (always remembering that yachts on a beat are excluded). This rule enlarges the obligation to include opposite-tack yachts, which, since they

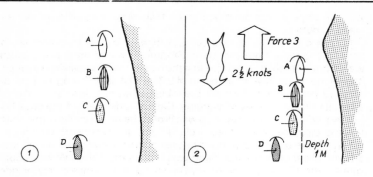

Fig. 72

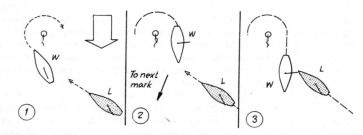

Fig. 73

are not on a beat, must be running, so that S must give way to P.

In IYRU 68 (Fig. 72) two starboard-tack yachts were running along the shore, A clear ahead of B. While on the same tack B kept clear of A as she was required to do under rule 37.2. Then B blanketed A, causing her to gybe unintentionally, onto the port gybe. B hailed 'starboard', a hail that A acknowledged, and B then ran into A's stern. The gybe initiated a new set of conditions under which, in open water, would have given B right-of-way over A under rule 36, but as they were passing an obstruction (the shore) rule 42.2(a) applied and B was still obligated to keep clear of A even though she was now on starboard tack.

RYA 69/6 however shows a case where the clear-ahead yacht could not claim the protection of rule 42.2(a) – she was too far ahead! Fig. 73 shows what happened. W, coming round the mark on a starboard-tack run, met L beating up to the mark. In spite of W's attempts to maintain that she had rights of way under rule 42.2(a) she was disqualified under rule 37.1. As we saw under rule 37.1 this is a particularly dangerous moment because the boats are approaching each other at great speed.

IYRU 26 illustrates how the clear ahead yacht is bound by rule 41 to keep clear while she tacks. In Fig 47 A and B are close-hauled, nearing the mark with A clear ahead and to leeward. A expects B on fetching the mark, to tack to round but instead B holds her course, preventing A from tacking. B is entitled to do this, since rule 42.2(c) only permits A to tack in accordance with rule 41. This is a common team and match-racing manoeuvre known as 'reaching a yacht past a mark'.

But, if A does not tack and remains on the same tack, though head to wind the clear astern boat has to keep clear. In US 138 (Fig. 6) B was disqualified. A was still on a tack (see definition and rule 41) and therefore rule 42.2(a) obliged B to keep clear.

42.3 (a) Exceptions and Limitations

IV

Limitation on establishing an overlap. To be precise this limitation is really limiting the right to room under rule 42.1(a). It is always possible to establish an overlap, but it may be an overlap that does not give the right to room. The second point to be noticed is that this limitation only applies to a clear-astern yacht establishing an inside overlap from clear astern. The overlap will only be 'proper', and by that I mean give a right to room, when the outside yacht is able to give room, and is outside the circle. We saw in 42.1(b) that an outside yacht, overlapped at the circle, must give room; now we see that if she is not overlapped when she reaches the circle she is 'safe' from a boat coming up from clear astern. (There is one exception we will look at in a moment). It would be different if the overlap were formed by tacking.

This limitation has been present in all the cases we have looked at, and is well illustrated by IYRU 127 which shows a complex situation. As we see in Fig. 74 five yachts are approaching a leeward mark, four are in line with A1 (nearest the mark), the fifth, B, is clear astern of all four when A1 and A2 come within two lengths of the mark. When the four front boats reach the mark and turn to round it, the change of bearing of A3 and A4, relative to B, results in B becoming overlapped inside them while each is outside the

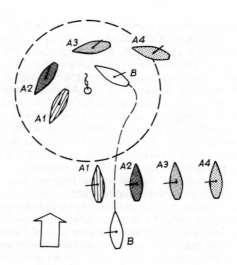

Fig. 74

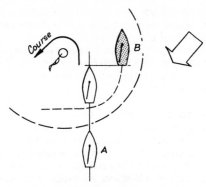

Fig. 75 *A cannot now avoid establishing an overlap and B must give A room.*

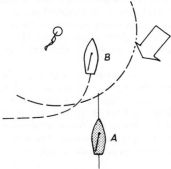

Fig. 76 *A, well astern and slightly to weather can avoid establishing an overlap.*

circle. B rounds behind A1 and A2 but inside A3 and A4 both of which are able to give her room. B is entitled to room under rule 42.3(a). Since B is astern of A1 and A2 when they come to the circle she is required by rule 42.2(a) to keep clear of them 'in anticipation of and during the rounding or passing manoeuvre'. As between B and the two outside yachts, however, a different relationship develops. A3 and A4, in order to leave room for the two inside yachts with their booms fully extended, must approach the mark on courses that bring them abreast of it outside the circle. When they alter course to begin rounding, their sternlines move aft rapidly, so that B obtains an inside overlap before either A3 or A4 comes within two lengths of the mark. If this is so and if the other part of rule 42.3(a) is satisfied, namely that A3 and A4 are able to give room, B is entitled to it.

The exception to the rule is in the last sentence of it which reads: 'However, when a yacht completes a tack within two of her overall lengths of a mark or obstruction, she shall give room as required by rule 42.1(a) to a yacht that cannot thereafter avoid establishing a late inside overlap'. Fig. 75 shows the rule in action. B has crossed ahead of A at the mark and tacked inside the circle, putting herself immediately ahead of and to windward of A. A must now be given room, because there is nothing much else she could do (other than go the wrong side of the mark, and it would be grossly unfair to her to make her do that). The rule includes the word 'however' as it's only available to 'a yacht that cannot avoid establishing and overlap'. If we look at Fig. 76, we see B again tacking in the circle but A is far astern and in a position in which she could easily pass outside B. Now, if B slows down for some reason A cannot claim room.

42.3(b)

At a continuing obstruction. When may *Daisy* sailing faster than the boat ahead of her, come in between this other boat and a continuing obstruction such as the shore or a third yacht sailing a similar course? 'Only when there is room for her to pass between them in safety'. This means at the beginning. Once she has established her overlap safely, thereafter the outside yacht must give her room to pass or keep clear of the obstruction. We see this in IYRU 69 (Fig. 77). Assuming that B establishes her inside overlap in safety, is A when hailed, required to give room? Provided that B had room to pass in safety between A and the shore at the time A established the overlap, yes, she is entitled to room and A may not luff her into the shore. 'In safety' means that B will be in no danger of either touching A or running aground. When A is sailing as close to the shore as is prudent in the prevailing conditions, B is not entitled to establish an overlap and does so at her own risk.

In IYRU 67 (Fig. 78) things happened this way. W established an overlap on L not quite two lengths to windward of her. Subsequently, M established an overlap between them. All three yachts finished with no narrowing of space between L and W and no contact. W protested M for taking room to which she was not entitled, citing rule 42.3(a) (ii). The protest was dismissed on the grounds that L and W had left sufficient room for M between them and W appealed.

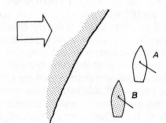

Fig. 77

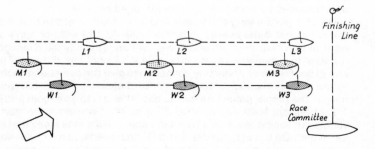

Fig. 78

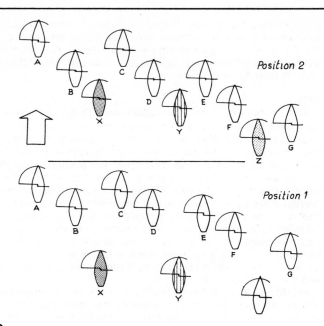

Position 2

Position 1

Fig. 79

Dismissing the appeal the RYA stated: 'W's case is based on the provision, in rule 42.3(a) (ii), that a yacht shall not establish an overlap between another yacht and an obstruction (considering L to be the obstruction) when that other yacht is within two lengths of the obstruction as W was. The relevant exception to that prohibition is rule 42.3(b) which states that a yacht clear astern may establish an overlap between a yacht clear ahead and a continuing obstruction but only when, at that time, there is room for her to pass between them in safety. L clearly was an obstruction to W, as she was to M as well. Was she also a continuing obstruction? Once W overhauled L the two yachts sailed overlapped at least six lengths towards the finishing line. That was easily long enough to qualify L as a continuing obstruction. Since M was able to intervene safely, which she demonstrated by performance, she infringed no rule.'

US 257 gives a long and interesting interpretation of this rule. It clarifies the point that if the overlap is broken, rule 42.1(b) will not apply and the clear-astern boat must establish her overlap 'in safety' all over again and remains the obligated yacht under rule 42.2 until she does so. The clear ahead boat is never under any obligation to give the overtaking yacht room. When there is insufficient room but nevertheless the boat astern pokes her bow in, the proper procedure for the boat ahead is to give room and protest.

Last but not least look at IYRU 27 (Fig. 79). Soon after the start all the yachts are sailing towards a headland about half a mile away that must be left to port. On the way, yachts A and G, each overlapped with the yachts on either side, run into a soft patch of wind. X, Y and Z come roaring up in a vicious little squall and establish overlaps on the yachts ahead. In every case there is room for X, Y and Z to poke their bows into the line without fouling anyone but not room to sail through unless everyone trims their mainsheet.

Questions. Who makes room for X when she makes her first overlap to leeward of B? Who makes room for Y when she makes her overlaps to windward of E and to leeward of D almost simultaneously? Who makes room for Z when she makes her first overlap to windward of G?

Answers. As it is stated that there is not enough room for X, Y and Z to sail between the respective overlapping yachts, rule 42.3(b) applies. X, Y and Z are bound to keep clear because, at the time the overlaps are established, there is not enough room to pass in safety with regard to B and C, D and E, and F and G respectively. C, E and G represent continuing obstructions. In addition, if X were to foul B she would infringe rule 37.3. If she were to foul C she would infringe rule 37.1, and the same principle applies to Y and Z.

42.3(c)

Taking an inside yacht to the wrong side of a mark. When looking at the phrase 'about to round' we saw that rule 42 came into effect before the circle with this particular clause. The inside leeward yacht must begin to luff before she reaches the circle when she wishes to carry W up to windward of a mark. The wrong side has been defined as beyond a line through the mark at right angles to the direct course from the previous mark (US 57). It is

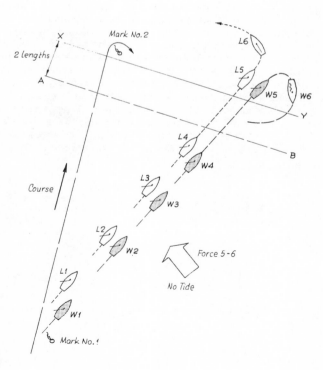

Fig. 80

this point that gives most trouble with the rule. Because rule 38.1 permits a yacht with luffing rights to luff as she pleases without hailing, is any silent luff before the circle legitimate provided L does not intend to take W to the wrong side of the mark, or must all luffs at that period be preceded by a hail?

IYRU 60 (Fig. 80) shows clearly when the boats are too far away for the rule to apply. W protested L because she did not hail but at no time during the manoeuvre did either yacht get closer than approximately 10 lengths from the mark, which means that throughout the manoeuvre the yachts were in open water. 'Rule 42.3(c) begins to apply only when yachts are about to round or pass a mark . . . on the same required side. In open water, a leeward yacht with luffing rights is entitled to exercise them "as she pleases". If however she delays doing so until she is "about to round or pass" a mark rule 42.3(c) then requires her to warn the windward yacht of her late intention and to begin to luff before she is within two lengths of the mark.'

IYRU 55 discussed 'about to round' in relation to this rule. It is worth looking at in detail. It was six lengths from the mark when L luffed prior to bearing away breaking the overlap and rounding the mark. W protested under rule 42.3(c) and when her protest was dismissed, appealed. The US Appeals Committee's interpretation of the meaning of 'about to round' has been quoted under rule 42 (see rule). Dealing specifically with 42.3(c) it dismissed the appeal and said: '. . . a yacht wishing to take a competitor to the wrong side of mark must begin to do so before coming within two lengths of it. The important thing to keep in mind is that the rights and obligations of rule 42 are designed to bring about roundings that are consistent and equitable. When such a rounding is made problems do not arise. In the present case a dinghy six lengths from a mark in a moderate breeze is not about to round and L was within her rights to do what she did which was not to take W "to windward" of the mark but simply to luff as permitted by rule 38 with the intention of breaking an overlap.'

In IYRU 128 (Fig. 81) L luffed sharply at about three boat lengths from the mark. W responded but contact occurred. W protested L and appealed when she lost her case. On appeal it was held that at three lengths W was still obligated to respond to a proper luff and L infringes rule 42 only if she subsequently fails to give W room when required to do so. She lost her appeal.

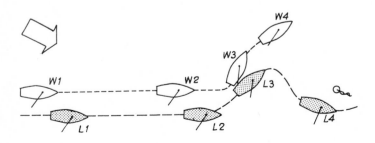

Fig. 81

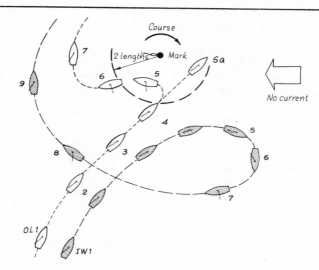

Fig. 82

However this decision was not unanimous. I think there can be little doubt that had L not borne away, and had in fact carried W to the wrong side of the mark, that is across a line perpendicular to the course from the last mark, she would have infringed the rule.

Again in IYRU 61 (Fig. 82) we see L luffing W towards the wrong side of the mark, but at position 3 W decides she has had enough, tacks and gybes round. In answer to questions the RYA stated: 'If W elects to tack before she is taken beyond the mark there is no requirement for L to carry on beyond the mark to position 5a and once W has tacked L infringes no rule by bearing away to round the mark'; the word 'also' is intentionally used in rule 42.3(c) to cover this situation.

This ploy is used mainly in team racing to allow a yacht behind to get through. Since it seems doubtful when luffing under rule 38.1 changes to luffing under rule 42.3(c) the wise helmsman will probably hail when he luffs anywhere between four lengths from the mark until he reaches the circle, when luffing a boat with an inside overlap becomes illegal.

42.4

The Anti-Barging rule. The manoeuvres of yachts at starting marks surrounded by navigable water are governed by basic rules, except for the prescriptions of rule 42.4. When L is the inside boat at the starting mark she will be given room by W not because of rule 42.1(a) but by reason of rule 37.1. In the old days all marks were the same, and it was the thing to make a fan start, overlapped windward yachts sweeping in and rounding up, calling for water and pushing all the leeward boats out of the way in their fight for the windward berth. This rule was changed in 1950 when the anti-barging rule was imported from the USA.

I cannot do better than quote an extract from Harold S Vanderbilt printed in the 1950 rules – with illustrations – to explain the new rule (What a pity our modern rules – are not so helpful!). 'Before the starting signal any leeward yacht may head above the first mark or luff above close-hauled, so as to deprive a windward yacht of room at the mark. If a leeward yacht, by so sailing, has been able to force a windward yacht up into the danger zone, before the starting signal the windward yacht may be compelled to leave the mark on the wrong side and start late. . . . After the starting signal in Fig. 83(a), A, B and C, since they are beating to the first mark, may not luff above a close-hauled course so as to deprive a windward yacht of room at the mark. D, E and F are in the danger zone. E has room to pass between A and the mark, clear ahead of C and, since E is sailing below the course to the first mark, she can freeze out F. C can freeze out D . . .

'Only where a leeward close-hauled yacht is in the position of B, can C pass the mark on the required side, *not because she has an overlap*, but *because there is room for her to do so*, since, after the start, B may not deprive C of room by luffing above her close-hauled course.

'In Fig. 83(b), with a reaching or running start, A, before the start, can luff

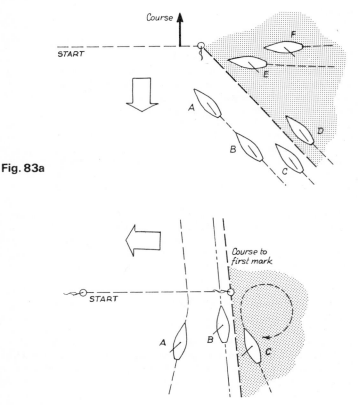

Fig. 83a

Fig. 83b

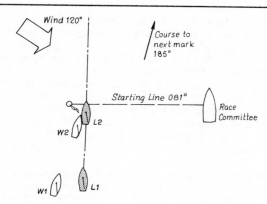

Fig. 84

B gradually into the danger zone, which in this case would be to windward of a line drawn through the line mark and the first mark of the course. Assuming that the boats are in the positions shown after the starting signal, A must not head above her course [compass not proper] to deprive B of room, so B will be able to pass the line mark on the required side. B, however, can freeze out C, because B is already on the compass course for the next mark. Therefore there will not be room for C, and she may be forced to leave the distance mark on the wrong side and start late.'

US 184 (Fig. 84) shows a case where L incorrectly excluded W. L was sailing a proper course to the first mark but the rule clearly requires her not to sail above a compass course to the next mark. A rule-change since this case has made it improbable that such a case would now get to appeal. When the course is a beat L may not sail above close-hauled. These provisions ensure that W can anticipate what L will do and know whether there is room for her at the mark or not.

IYRU 54 (Fig. 85) discusses the relationship between rule 37.1 and 42.4.

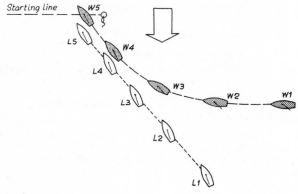

Fig. 85

W was barging and disqualified. 'Whenever two yachts are on the same tack within risk of collision basic rule 37 always applies to a greater or lesser degree. For example, the obligation of a windward yacht to keep clear when rule 38.1, the luffing rule, applies is absolute. At the other end of the scale is rule 40, luffing before starting wherein a leeward yacht's right to manoeuvre is greatly restricted. During an approach to the starting line with the windward yacht sailing below a close-hauled course rules 42.4 and 37.1 apply together, equally and extensively, since they are complementary. The first confirms the right of a leeward yacht at a starting mark, the second imposes obligations on a windward yacht.

'In this case L, sailing no higher than close-hauled, was compelled to bear away to avoid contact. That fact alone, whether or not contact occurred later, is sufficient evidence to justify disqualifying W under rule 37.1. She forced room to which she was not entitled and deprived L of her right under rule 42.4 to sail as close to the starting mark as she wished'.

43 Close-Hauled, Hailing for Room to Tack at Obstructions

43.1 HAILING

When two *close-hauled* yachts are on the same *tack* and safe pilotage requires the yacht *clear ahead* or the *leeward yacht* to make a substantial alteration of course to clear an *obstruction,* and when she intends to *tack,* but cannot *tack* without colliding with the other yacht, she shall hail the other yacht for room to *tack* and clear the other yacht, but she shall not hail and *tack* simultaneously.

43.2 RESPONDING

The hailed yacht at the earliest possible moment after the hail shall: either

(a) *tack,* in which case the hailing yacht shall begin to *tack,* either:

(i) before the hailed yacht has completed her *tack,* or

(ii) when she cannot then *tack* without colliding with the hailed yacht, immediately she is able to *tack* and clear her;

or

(b) reply "You *tack*", or words to that effect, when in her opinion she can keep clear without *tacking* or after postponing her *tack.*
In this case:

(i) the hailing yacht shall immediately *tack* and

(ii) the hailed yacht shall keep clear.

(iii) The onus of satisfying the race committee that she kept clear shall lie on the hailed yacht that replied "You *tack*".

43.3 LIMITATION ON RIGHT TO ROOM TO TACK WHEN THE OBSTRUCTION IS ALSO A MARK

(a) When an *obstruction* is a starting *mark* surrounded by navigable water, or the ground tackle of such a *mark,* and when approaching the starting line to *start* and after *starting,* the yacht *clear ahead* or the *leeward yacht* shall not be entitled to room to *tack.*

(b) At other *obstructions* that are *marks*, when the hailed yacht can fetch
the *obstruction*, the hailing yacht shall not be entitled to room to *tack*
and clear the hailed yacht, and the hailed yacht shall immediately so
inform the hailing yacht. When, thereafter, the hailing yacht again hails
for room to *tack* and clear the hailed yacht, the hailed yacht shall, at the
earliest possible moment after the hail, give the hailing yacht the
required room. After receiving room, the hailing yacht shall either retire
immediately or exonerate herself by accepting an alternative penalty
when so prescribed in the sailing instructions.

(c) When, after having refused to respond to a hail under rule 43.3(b), the
hailed yacht fails to fetch, she shall retire immediately, or exonerate
herself by accepting an alternative penalty when so prescribed in the
sailing instructions.

This is primarily a safety rule to permit a close-hauled yacht, caught
between another close-hauled yacht and an obstruction to avoid the latter
without substantial loss of distance. It is a complicated rule and needs
looking at in detail.

43.1

1 'Hailing'. To initiate the rule the two yachts must be on the same tack. In
IYRU 93 (Fig. 57 under rule 42) P cannot avail herself of the rule because
she and S are on opposite tacks. RYA 84/11 shows a similar case. In what
follows the boats are called W and L but they need not be overlapped, the
hailing boat may in fact be the leeward boat or she may be clear ahead but
down to leeward. (Strictly speaking the terms L and W apply only when the
two are overlapped).

2 '... safe pilotage requires ... [her] ... to make a substantial alteration of
course to clear an *obstruction*.' When the leeward yacht can avoid the
obstruction by altering course – in this case bearing away – very slightly she
will be required to do so and will not be entitled to the protection of rule 43.

US 116 (Fig. 86) shows us PL calling for room to tack from PW to avoid an
obstruction caused by the starboard tack yacht S. PW failed to tack and S
had to tack back onto port to avoid a collision. S protested PL and PW under
rule 36 and PL protested PW under rule 43. 'Inasmuch as PL would have
had to make a substantial alteration of course – stated the decision – to pass
astern of S, even if she had borne off instantly as S tacked to starboard, she

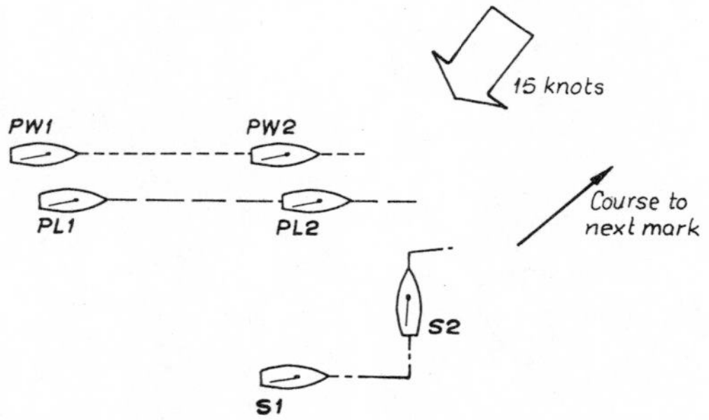

Fig. 86

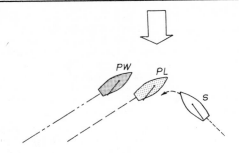

Fig. 87

had the right to hail PW as she did'. PW was disqualified under rule 43 and PL exonerated.

On the same subject IYRU 6 is shown in Fig. 87. 'S hailed PL as the two dinghies approached each other on collision courses. PL in turn twice hailed "water for starboard boat", but PW did not respond. PL hailed a third time, and PW then began to tack but S, now within three feet of PL, had to bear away sharply to avoid collision. PW retired and S protested PL under rule 36. The race committee disqualified PL observing that, not having had a timely response from PW, she ought to have used her right to luff and forced PW to tack.

PL appealed, asserting that:

a) she had no right to luff PW onto the opposite tack;

b) PW would have had mast abeam before they came head to wind;

c) even with both of them head to wind, S would still have had to alter course to avoid collision.

Further, she had foreseen the development and had initially hailed PW in ample time.'

Upholding the appeal the RYA stated: 'Having hailed three times, PL was entitled to expect that PW would respond and give her room to tack. She was not obliged either to anticipate PW's failure to comply with rule 43.2(a) or to bear away astern of S. PL is exonerated as the innocent victim of

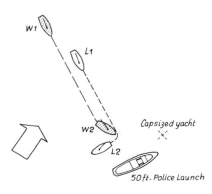

Fig. 88

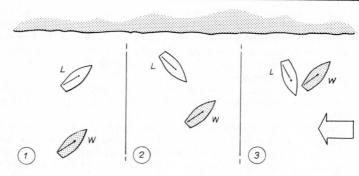

Fig. 89

another yacht's infringement of a rule, under the provisions of rule 74.4(b).'

US 81 (Fig. 88) shows L and W approaching a large police launch which was rescuing another yacht, L hailed for room to tack and tacked, but W bore away under her stern and protested her for infringing rule 41 – tacking too close. 'L, she said, could have avoided the obstruction by bearing off. There was open water all round the obstruction'. The appeals committee disagreed: 'If L had approached the launch sufficiently close to its leeward end so that, with only a slight alteration of course when near it, she could safely have passed to leeward of it, she should have done so. This situation did not prevail in this case. L's course brought her close to the windward end of the police launch and she not only had to tack in order to pass it to windward but would have had to bear away substantially below her actual course to pass it to leeward. . . . she had a right under rule 43.1 to hail W for room to tack'.

3 '. . . she intends to *tack* but cannot *tack* without colliding . . .'. If L tacks and avoids W she cannot then protest W under this rule.

IRYU 80 illustrates this. (Fig 89). As the two yachts approached the shore L hailed W for room to tack whereupon W replied, 'take my stern'. L interpreted that to mean 'you tack' and tacked immediately. After tacking she had to bear away to pass under W's stern which she cleared by three feet. She protested W under rule 43. The race committee decided that W failed to meet the onus of rule 43.2(b) (iii) and disqualified her. She appealed. The district appeals committee reversed the decision, quoting from US 108. 'The important question is whether the hailing yacht is able to tack without colliding with the other yacht.' From the facts found, it is clear that L was able to tack promptly, did so, and was able to keep clear of W by taking her stern. Thus, rule 43 was entirely satisfied. L appealed this reversal.

Dismissing the appeal it was said: 'In her statement L argued that she was entitled to sufficient room to tack, to fill her sails and to get under way on port tack without interference and that, as in the decision of US 108, she should have been allowed room to tack without "loss of distance" and without the necessity of taking violent action to avoid collision. The reference in US 108 to the purpose of rule 43 does not support L's argument. The "loss of distance" referred to there means the loss incurred from the substantial alteration of course necessary if the leeward yacht had to go around the obstruction rather than hailing for sea room. Nothing in rule 43 is intended to protect the hailing yacht from a "loss of distance" incurred by bearing away astern of the hailed yacht. The district committee was correct in concluding that the established actions of both L and W proved that L had adequate room to keep clear.'

4 '... she shall hail ...'. Note the imperative *shall*. No hail, no rights under rule 43. What happens if the hail is not heard is discussed in IYRU 117 and RYA 80/6.

In IYRU 117, L hailed for room to tack and after a short interval, of time, during which there was no reply from W, tacked. The boats collided. W, it turned out, had not heard the hail. The US Appeals Committee, upholding W's appeal against disqualification stated: 'The failure of a hailed yacht to hear an adequate hail does not exonerate her from her obligations under rule 43. On the basis of the facts presented, however, it is necessary to question whether the hail for room in this instance was adequate. Rule 43.1 provides that the hailing yacht shall not hail and tack simultaneously. The purpose of that is to provide time for the specific response called for under rule 43.2 (to tack or reply "you tack"). In either case, the hailing yacht shall tack *after* the appropriate response from the windward yacht. Therefore, the leeward yacht must not sail into a position, before hailing, where she cannot allow sufficient time for a response.'

'Failure of a windward yacht to hear a properly made hail would not necessarily relieve her of her obligations to a leeward yacht. Where, however, the leeward yacht, as in this case, observed no response after her hail, a second and more vigorous hail would be required to constitute proper notice of her intention to tack. L's hail was inadequate for the purpose of involving rule 43, and she was properly disqualified under rule 36'.

In the second case RYA80/6 L's hail was heard by W's crew but not by her helmsman so she did not respond. L hailed again, W then tacked and L tacked so quickly that she just touched W's rudder. The PC disqualified W but referred the matter to the RYA. Upholding the decision it was stated: 'Although it is well established that W is not required to take any action before L hails, W must be on the alert for a hail and, when it is given, respond promptly to it.' Moral: hail loudly.

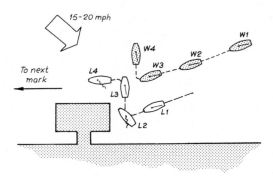

Fig. 90

5 '. . . room to *tack* and clear. . .'. In US 108 (Fig. 90) L hailed at position I, tacked at position 2 and at position 3 forced the other yacht WS to tack to avoid hitting her amidships. At the same time L tried unsuccessfully to tack back. L protested W under rule 43.1. W contended that rule 36 applied and that rule 43 could only be used when both boats were on the same tack and one of them cannot tack without colliding. She lost the protest and took it to appeal.

Dismissing W's appeal the US Appeals Committee said: 'The safety objective of the rule would be nullified if it applied only while the first yacht was in the act of tacking, since the position of the yacht often leaves her still unable either to cross ahead of the other yacht or to bear away and pass astern, as in this case. However, if L's course is sufficiently to leeward so that after tacking onto the starboard tack she has room to bear away and pass astern, she is required to do so, since she is then able to "tack without colliding with the other yacht".'

The case establishes L's right to tack and get safely clear of the obstruction even though she is a port-tack boat meeting a starboard tack one. It is worth noticing that only very rarely does a problem arise from a rule 43 incident when L tacks onto starboard. Looking at all the cases through the books we see that the problems arise mostly on a 'left-hand' shore.

In RYA 77/8 poor L, having tacked on to port then had to tack back again, because S did not keep clear, and ran aground. The RYA stated, reaffirming the US statement: 'On a course approaching an obstruction, a close-hauled starboard-tack yacht, with another yacht clear astern or to windward of her is the sole judge of her own peril, and when she hails for room to tack to clear the obstruction she is entitled to be given room not only to tack to port, away from the obstruction, but also safely to clear the hailed yacht.

'The hailing yacht is the sole judge as to whether or not it is safe for her to bear away so as to pass astern of the hailed yacht and the latter must give her room; if she deems the hail to have been improper her only remedy is to protest'.

6 '. . . she shall not hail and *tack* simultaneously . . .' The tacking yacht must not hail and put her helm down as she does so. (As we saw in IYRU 117 and RYA 80/6 under 4 above, there is a certain amount of disagreement when she has to hail a second time – but she should certainly not tack immediately unless absolutely driven to). However there is no doubt when she hails for the first time. US 131 makes it quite clear. L 'hailed for room to tack and put her helm down'. W protested L for infringing rule 43.1 and L was disqualified. The Appeals Committee confirmed L's disqualification saying: 'it was L's duty first to hail and then tack'. My only comment is that, technically speaking, I believe L, having failed to comply with rule 43, and therefore not being eligible for its protection, by tacking infringes basic rule 41.1 – tacking too close.

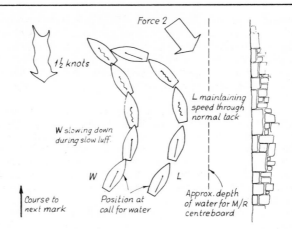

Force 2

1½ knots

L maintaining
speed through
normal tack

W slowing down
during slow luff

W   L

Course to
next mark

Position at
call for water

Approx. depth
of water for M/R
centreboard

Fig. 91

43.2

So far we have only reached the hail. The hailed yacht now has two choices she can either tack at the earliest possible moment after the hail or hail in return 'you tack' or words to that effect.

Taking W's first choice first, and it is the most usual case, she starts to get out of the way, and not only must she start as soon as she possibly can, but she must carry out the manoeuvre smartly. In RYA 82/6 (Fig. 91) we see a case where the hailed yacht began as soon as she could, but carried out such a delayed, slow tack that there was a collision. 'A yacht', said the RYA, 'that responds to a hail and begins to tack but luffs so slowly that she delays completion of the tack beyond a reasonable time is not responding "at the earliest possible moment after the hail".' Reading the cases it appears that W would be wisest not to hail in her turn, even a cry of 'right' has been mistaken by the leeward yacht for 'you tack' – she has and there has been a collision.

Now the hailing yacht must also tack. Virtually she must do so as soon as she can without colliding, when possible even before the windward boat has completed her tack. She too must not delay. RYA 73/5 (Fig. 92) shows W tacking, and then L continuing for three or four lengths before she also tacked. 'One of the objects of this rule is to ensure that both hailed and hailing yachts tack as nearly as possible at the same time.' L infringed rule 43 and obviously hailed before she needed to – which could have possibly led her trouble under rule 75.

The hailed yacht's other alternative is to hail 'you tack' when L must tack and W must keep clear. The onus is then on the yacht hailing 'you tack', ie W, to prove that she kept clear as promised. The object is to get the whole manoeuvre over as quickly and safely as possible.

Let us finally just see what normally happens, *Daisy*, L, sees she is nearing the shore and realises that when she has to tack she will not be able to tack clear of W on her starboard quarter. Some distance off (depending on weather and type of shore, speed, and draft of boat) *Daisy* will loudly hail 'water' (in the UK, perhaps 'shore room' in US), and her helmsman will make sure that he turns so that his voice carries. Almost immediately, W who has been expecting the hail, tacks (as soon as she can

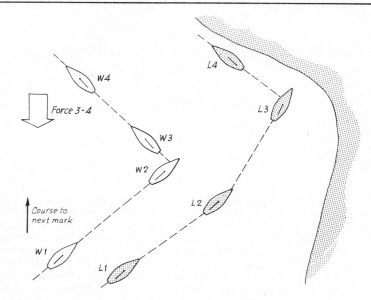

Fig. 92

let fly her genoa) and within a second or so *Daisy* tacks too, sure that she can now avoid contact. It is one of the most commonly used of all rules and over the years has been extremely successful.

43.3(a)(b)(c)

43.3(a) applies at a starting mark surrounded by navigable water from when the boats in question are approaching the line to start until they are clear of it (presumably this is what 'and after starting' means). The obstruction is stated to be the mark and its ground tackle. In such circumstances the yacht clear ahead or the leeward yacht is totally deprived of her rights under rule 43. If she tacks she will infringe rule 41, if she hails for room to tack she will not get it, or if she does will be subject to a protest under rule 41 for tacking too close. The windward (or clear astern) yacht is under no obligation to give room and can, in theory drive L into the committee boat so BEWARE. This rule was only adopted after long discussions in which it was considered more dangerous for L to hail for water and tack into a long line of boats than to take the other options open to her – go the other side of the committee boat or let her sheets go and stop. However rule 32 is, of course, still in effect which might make the right-of-way yacht think twice before causing an accident.

Rule 43.3(b). US 8 (Fig. 93) illustrates this rule well. 'Yachts A and B were ... approaching the finishing line near its leeward end which consisted of an angle in a breakwater. A could cross the finishing line and clear the breakwater and B could not. B, without hailing, tacked to starboard and collided with A. The PC disqualified B who appealed.'

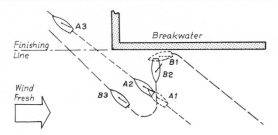

Fig. 93

In its decision the Appeals Committee said: 'B did not take advantage of the alternatives to sailing herself into an impossible situation such as: bearing away, or luffing, or easing her sheets before reaching the breakwater so as to obtain room to tack without fouling A and thereafter either establishing starboard tack rights on A or passing astern of her. Since the breakwater constituted a mark that A could fetch as well as an obstruction, B did not have the right to hail A about as provided in rules 43.1 and 43.2. In such a situation rules 43.3(b) was applicable and A, after being hailed twice, would have been obligated to give B room to tack and clear the other yacht and B, upon receiving it, would have been required to retire immediately.'

Finally 43.3(c), if W (or A in the above case) has made a mistake and refused room to tack to L (B) when in fact, as it turned out, she could not fetch the obstruction herself she at once becomes an infringing yacht and must either retire or exonerate herself as required by the SIs.

44   Returning to Start

44.1   (a) After the starting signal is made, a premature starter returning to *start*, or a yacht working into position from the course side of the starting line or its extensions, shall keep clear of all yachts that are *starting* or have *started* correctly, until she is wholly on the pre-start side of the starting line or its extensions.

(b) Thereafter, she shall be accorded the rights under the rules of Part IV of a yacht that is *starting* correctly; but when she thereby acquires right of way over another yacht that is *starting* correctly, she shall allow that yacht ample room and opportunity to keep clear.

44.2   A premature starter, while continuing to sail the course and until it is obvious that she is returning to *start*, shall be accorded the rights under the rules of Part IV of a yacht that has *started*.

Beginning back to front with rule 44.2 we see that rule 44.1 does not apply as long as a premature starter continues to sail the course and, further, until it is *obvious* that she is returning. So, when starting, even if you know that the boat ahead of you was a premature starter, and even if you have seen the recall signal, and perhaps heard her sail number given on the radio, she still retains all her rights under the rules of Part IV of a yacht that has started correctly until the moment that she clearly begins to

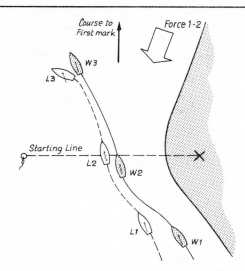

Fig. 94

go back. This is an obvious safety precaution.

IYRU 81 illustrates this. (Fig. 94) both L and W were premature starters, but only L knows that she was early. There was some delay in displaying the recall signal and L bore away sharply to return to the line while W was still unaware that either of them had started prematurely. In doing so L touched W. L admitted that she had been over the line, agreed she should have kept clear and stated that she had not been aware that W had also started early.

The protest committee disqualified both yachts, W under rule 37.1 and L under rule 44.1(a). Since L did not know that W was a premature starter, she was obliged to treat W as a yacht starting correctly and therefore keep clear of her. The decision was referred to the RYA. The decision read as follows: 'Under rule 44.2 both yachts, as premature starters continuing to sail the course, had all their rights under Part IV. At the moment when L bore away to return to the line, W acquired full rights of way in respect of L under rule 44.1(a). In bearing away, L was required by rule 44.1(a) to keep clear of W. As L failed to comply with her obligation, the decision to disqualify her was correct. The decision to disqualify W is reversed and she is to be reinstated.'

Having taken the rule out of order and looked first at a premature starter that does not return, now let us look at 44.1 and see what happens to one that does. As we saw above in IRYU 81, as soon as she turns, the premature starter loses all rights and with her, after the starting signal, a yacht working into position from the course side of the line. 'Both must keep clear of all yachts that have started correctly.' This loss of rights continues until the yacht is 'wholly' on the pre-start side of the line. Wholly, not just her bow; only when she is wholly back is she in a position to be able to start according to the definition. Even when she recovers her rights there is an intermediate stage – short though it may be – which constitutes one of the exceptions to rule 35 (rule 35, (b) (i)). Although she is assuming a proper course to start and is right-of-way yacht she must still give ample room and opportunity to

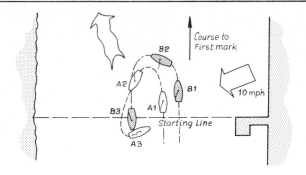

Fig. 95

keep clear to anyone starting correctly, this may mean the starboard tack yacht giving time and opportunity to a port-tack one.

US 98 is an interesting case where two yachts start prematurely on starboard tack, gybe round and return towards the line, A ahead of B, as shown in Fig. 95. As A reached the pre-start side of the line B, foreseeing that A would tack, hailed her not to do so, proclaiming rights under rule 41. As soon as A was wholly on the pre-start side of the line and was so advised by the race committee, she luffed and tacked. At this moment B was clear astern of A, but close aboard and straddling the starting line. The two collided. A protested B for infringement of rule 44.1, and B protested A for infringement of rule 41. B was disqualified and appealed.

Upholding the decision, the appeals committee said: 'A having returned wholly to the pre-start side of the line was a yacht starting correctly while B, not having done so, continued to be a premature starter and was obligated to keep clear of A.' The case was before rule 35(b) (i) existed; that rule, after exempting a right-of-way yacht from the constraints of rule 35 when assuming a proper course to start, then reimposes them by stating that the manoeuvre is subject to the second part of rule 44.1(b). However 44.1(b) says that she must give ample room and opportunity to keep clear only to a yacht that is starting correctly. B was not starting at all, let alone correctly and was therefore not protected by rule 35.

45 Re-rounding after Touching a Mark

45.1 A yacht that has touched a *mark*, and is exonerating herself in accordance with rule 52.2, (Touching a Mark), shall keep clear of all other yachts that are about to round or pass it or have rounded or passed it correctly, until she has rounded it completely and has cleared it and is on a *proper course* to the next *mark*.

45.2 A yacht that has touched a *mark*, while continuing to sail the course and until it is obvious that she is returning to round it completely in accordance with rule 52.2, (Touching a Mark), shall be accorded rights under the rules of Part IV.

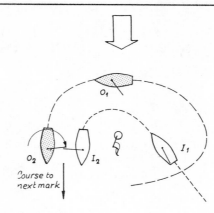

Fig. 96

How a yacht re-rounds a mark correctly in order to exonerate herself after touching it, is discussed in rule 52. Rule 45 deals only with her rights, or rather the lack of them, while she is re-rounding. As in rule 44.2 in the previous rule 45.2 gives the yacht that has touched the mark full rights under Part IV until the moment she does turn to go back.

IYRU 126 (Fig. 96) illustrates the rule. O and I rounded the windward mark together O outside. O had hit the mark on her first rounding and was re-rounding it in exoneration. Towards the end of the manoeuvre and before O had cleared the mark, I had an unexpected but controlled gybe, causing her sail to touch that of O. I protested, alleging that O had infringed rules 42.1(a) and 45.1. The protest committee disqualified O and she appealed, on the grounds that rule 42.1(a) had been incorrectly applied since gybing was not 'an integral part of the rounding manoeuvre'. Accordingly 41.1 applied and I had infringed it.

The decision dismissing the appeal reads as follows: 'The obligations of O were governed almost entirely by rule 45.1, and rules 42 and 41 had no application. To apply the rules otherwise could be substantially to nullify rule 45.1. This does not mean that I would sail anywhere she chose. She was still subject to rule 35 (Right-of-Way Yacht Altering Course), and O, in fulfilling her obligation to keep clear, was entitled to rely on I sailing a logical course that could reasonably be anticipated. Since the next leg was straight downwind, running on either tack was a proper course. Accordingly, I was at all times, during her rounding, on a proper course, and it was immaterial whether her gybe was intentional or accidental. By not allowing for it, O infringed rule 45.1.

Two additional points are worth noting. First, had O completed the rounding and cleared the mark, rule 41 would have applied, and I would have been the infringer. Secondly, had a re-rounding in exoneration of touching a mark not been involved in this incident, both yachts would have been subject to rule 42.

'In that event, I would have been entitled to room to gybe if gybing was "an integral part of the rounding manoeuvre". The meaning of "integral" in that phrase in rule 42.1(a) is "essential to completeness". Clearly, it was not necessary for I to gybe to complete her rounding and assume a proper

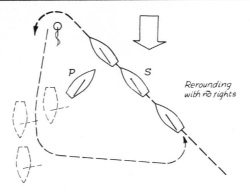

Fig. 97

course to the next mark. Therefore, had not rule 45.1 controlled, I would have infringed rule 41.1.

'It may seem to be drawing a fine line to distinguish among these three situations, but O in this case was a yacht that had touched a mark and was permitted to exonerate herself. Thus, her obligations were appropriately greater'.

Note that rule 35 permits I to alter course suddenly to assume a proper course at a mark, but it would not permit her to make unexpected changes.

Fig. 97 shows an interesting case – which happened but never came to protest. *Daisy* hit the mark and owing to the number of boats was unable to get clear to turn back for some time. To get back to the mark she resumed a beat and while on starboard encountered a yacht on port tack *that did not know* that *Daisy* was coming back. Thus both boats believed themselves, *Daisy* correctly and the other understandably, to be the burdened yacht. A dangerous situation, though in this case a collision was avoided and after the race an explanation led to neither boat lodging a protest. My view was asked, and for what it is worth, I believe that *Daisy* was *in fact* the burdened yacht. She should have realised that the other might not be able to tell and allowed for it. Meeting P she should either tack in good time or bear away sufficiently early for P not to have to consider keeping clear. It was dangerous because *Daisy* was not subject to rule 35 and could alter course as she pleased, while P also believed herself not to be subject to rule 35. Both believed they should keep clear and it would have been easy for them to turn into each other.

46   Person Overboard; Yacht Anchored, Aground or Capsized

46.1   A yacht under way shall keep clear of another yacht *racing* that:

(a) is manoeuvring or hailing for the purpose of rescuing a person overboard, or

(b) is anchored, aground or capsized.

46.2   A yacht shall not be penalised for fouling a yacht that she is attempting to assist or that goes aground or capsizes immediately in front of her.

46.3   A yacht anchored or aground shall indicate the fact to any yacht that may be in danger of fouling her. Under normal conditions, a hail is sufficient indication. Of two yachts anchored, the one that anchored later shall keep clear, except that a yacht dragging shall keep clear of one that is not.

When *Daisy* is on starboard tack, or leeward yacht with rights of way there are still some situations in which she must keep clear. First she must not get mixed up with anything that looks like a rescue job (46.1(a)), secondly she must keep clear of a boat that is anchored, aground or capsized, ie one that is absolutely beyond any hope of control. Some have taken these three words to be absolute allowing of no other condition, others believe the words not to be definitive but merely examples. FIV 71/7 stated: 'It is clear that the intention is to lay an obligation on a yacht underway to avoid a yacht which cannot move.' Well, perhaps up to a point, but not immovable because of lack of wind, but perhaps drifting with no sails set.

Rule 46.2 allows the protest committee to avoid penalising *Daisy* when she either goes to the assistance of another yacht and fouls her, or if she fouls a yacht that goes aground or capsizes just in front of her.

Rule 46.3 requires the yacht anchored or aground to hail or show in some way or other that she is out of control. The first half of the last sentence will serve to keep boats from kedging too close to each other, the second half is not something that one would think the yacht dragging her anchor can do anything about. Surely if there was enough wind to manoeuvre, the boat would not need to be kedged. However it would serve to resolve an otherwise insoluble problem! This is one of those rules where one feels each word reflects a single case which has given rise to hardship.

In RYA 77/4 the rule is applied rigidly. 'S heeled almost to the point of capsize, screwed round head to wind, her mast drawing an arc like a scythe and hitting P's mast well below the hounds.' However S did not capsize and P was unable to protect herself by citing rule 46.3 (she failed under rule 35 too).

(Numbers 47, 48 and 49 are spare numbers)

Part V—Other Sailing Rules

Obligations of Helmsman and Crew in Handling a Yacht

*A yacht is subject to the rules of Part V only while she is **racing**.*

50   Ranking as a Starter

A yacht whose entry has been accepted and that sails about in the vicinity of the starting line between her preparatory and starting signals shall rank as a starter whether she *starts* or not.

Whether a boat that has entered for a race or series and then does not start in any particular race, is to be ranked as a starter or not, is only important from the point of view of points systems that depend on the number of starters. In IRYU 34, the race was postponed 30 seconds before the starting signal. Some boats failed to see it, 'started' and sailed the course, being more than a mile beyond the starting area when the new preparatory signal was made. An attempt was made to have them disqualified as premature starters, but it failed. On appeal it was held that a yacht that neither started nor sailed about in the vicinity of the line between her preparatory and starting signals did not rank as a starter.

In IYRU 111, a boat coming out from harbour had nearly reached the starting line but was still on the course side when the starting signal went. No recall signal was made and she believed herself to have reached the pre-start side of the line when she set off on the race. She was held to have ranked as a starter (and a premature starter at that) even although she had never reached the pre-start side of the line. She was granted redress because she had been excluded from the results.

51   Sailing the Course

51.1   (a) A yacht shall *start* and *finish* only as prescribed in the starting and finishing definitions.

(b) Unless otherwise prescribed in the sailing instructions, a yacht that either crosses prematurely or is on the course side of the starting line or its extensions at the starting signal, shall return and *start* in accordance with the definition.

(c) Unless otherwise prescribed in the sailing instructions, when Code flag "I" has been displayed, and when any part of a yacht's hull, crew or equipment is on the course side of the starting line or its extensions during the minute before her starting signal, she shall return to the pre-start side of the line across one of its extensions and *start*.

(d) Failure of a yacht to see or hear her recall notification shall not relieve her of her obligation to *start* correctly.

51.2   A yacht shall sail the course so as to round or pass each *mark* on the required side in correct sequence, and so that a string representing her wake, from the time she *starts* until she *finishes*, would, when drawn taut, lie on the required side of each *mark*, touching each rounding *mark*.

51.3   A *mark* has a required side for a yacht as long as she is on a leg that it begins, bounds or ends. A starting line *mark* begins to have a required side for a yacht when she *starts*. A starting limit *mark* has a required side for a yacht from the time she is approaching the starting line to *start* until she has left the *mark* astern on the first leg. A finishing line *mark* and a finishing limit *mark* cease to have a required side for a yacht as soon as she *finishes*.

51.4   A yacht that rounds or passes a *mark* on the wrong side may exonerate herself by making her course conform to the requirements of rule 51.2.

51.5   It is not necessary for a yacht to cross the finishing line completely; after *finishing*, she may clear it in either direction.

All rules are equal, but if some rules are more equal than others, then rule 51 is one of the most important in the book since it is the rule that compels the competitors to sail the same course in the same way. Much of it is descriptive rather than mandatory, to make sure that there are no loopholes through which an unscrupulous competitor could get an unfair advantage.

51.1(a)

Not only may a race committee not set a course that starts or finishes other than in accordance with the two definitions but *Daisy* may not sail such a course. Fig. 98 shows a course set as follows 'start, 1, 2, 3, finish – all marks to starboard.' The course is then shortened at mark 2 and the committee boat anchored as shown. This means that *Daisy*, to finish correctly, must leave mark 2 to port – in spite of sailing instructions. The mark has changed its nature from a rounding mark to a finishing mark and the required sides for starting and finishing marks are fixed by *facts* on the water, unlike rounding marks fixed by sailing instructions. Usually there is no contradiction. IYRU 102 also illustrates a hook finish (Fig. 37).

The IYRU frowns on such a way of finishing because the race then finishes at a point rather than along a line, causing possibly serious bunching and crowding. When a race committee needs to overcome the

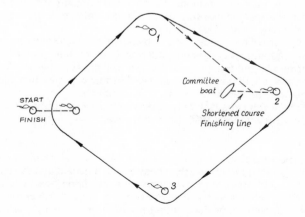

Fig. 98

problem an extra turning mark will allow the fleet to finish in the desired direction. It does not matter, remember, which side the committee boat is stationed, it is the *direction* that counts.

51.1(b) Premature starters

Rules 8.1 and 8.2 instruct the RC what to do, what signals to make etc. when a yacht starts prematurely. Rule 44 governs the premature starter as she struggles back to start correctly; now rule 51.1(b) contains the essential obligation – that of the yacht which is over the line at the start to return and *start* correctly if she is not to be disqualified. The common phrase 'over the line' is used deliberately because it covers both situations envisaged by the rule, that of the premature starter, approaching the line from the pre-start side pushing two inches of her bow across the line before the gun goes, and the yacht still on the course side of the starting line having arrived late and never reached the pre-start side, (see IYRU 111 p. 148) (Note that the word 'return' is used for her too, even though it is not quite accurate.)

51.1(c)

The Round-the-Ends rule. When there is a very large number of starters making race control difficult, there are several special starting systems that a race committee can employ of various grades of severity. The Round-the-Ends rule is the only one to be printed in the IYRR, and it can be used without any prescriptions in sailing instructions by means of the signals described in rule 4.1 'I'.

The rule can only be used when there is a committee-boat start with navigable water at both ends of the line, because when *Daisy* is over the line, not only at the starting signal but for period of a whole minute before that signal, she may not, as is usual, dip back across it but must go round one of the ends of the line (the committee boat or the ODM), across one of its extensions, before she can start correctly. In contrast the most punitive starting system disqualifies *Daisy* from that race and any resail of it if she sails into the forbidden area at any time after her preparatory signal.

The rule begins only one minute before the starting signal, but it is subject to a number of variations. Competitors should check carefully in sailing instructions to make sure that there are none, or if there are that they are absolutely clear. They should:

1 be sure of the shape of the forbidden area: the rule gives the course side of the line and its extensions, but some committees prefer to use a triangle formed by the two ends of the line and the weather mark.

2 check the time: the rule comes into effect one minute before the start, but this may be varied from one to five minutes.

3 check the penalty. It may be only to have to go round the one of the ends, but it may be total DSQ from that race.

51.1(d)

The responsibility of seeing and hearing the recall signals is here put fairly and squarely onto the competitors. Provided that the committee make the recall signals correctly 'didn't see' or 'didn't hear' will be no excuse.

Remember also that if a competitor *knows* he is over the line at the start he is cheating if he does not return and start correctly, even when no recall signal has been made. RYA 84/5 illustrates this. The RC failed to make a sound signal with the recall signal and a premature starter, that had been disqualified, was given redress on the understanding that she had believed herself to have started correctly. There is no onus on a yacht to respond when a sound signal is not made, unless she realises that she is a premature starter, when she is bound by rule 33.1 to retire or start correctly.'

51.2

Rule 3.2(a) (iii) requires sailing instructions to describe the courses, stating the order in which and on which side each mark is to be rounded or passed. Rule 51.2 obliges the competitors to follow this course and supplies a method for checking that they have done so. The Piece-of-String rule is frequently an aid to setting courses as well as deciding whether they have been sailed correctly. Looking at Fig. 99, we see that *Daisy* sailed the course that was posted, but not the one the course setter intended. If she was really meant to round mark 2 there were three ways of achieving it: require yachts to pass to the north of the beacon (rarely used), require it to be looped by sailing a 270° turn round it (undesirable), or more easily put S instead of P. If the race committee did none of these things then *Daisy* could not be disqualified for failing to sail the course. Naturally we can all guess that the race officer had mistakenly put P when he meant S, but courses cannot be set by telepathy. In the latest rules, the words 'touching each rounding mark' have been added. This will certainly stop clever corner-cutting when there is no doubt that the mark is a rounding (or turning) mark, as in Olympic courses. In the example in Fig. 99 if mark 2 is a rounding mark, *Daisy* will have to round it to port, looping it through 270° if she is to comply with the course instructions and rule 51.2. When she sails straight from mark 1 to mark 3 the string will not go near mark 2. But how is she to know that mark 2 is a rounding and not a passing mark?

RYA 85/4 (Fig. 100) shows that the problem may not be totally solved. The committee set 'all marks to port' and either intended Gaff to be looped or should have made it a starboard hand mark, *unless* they meant it to be a mark that merely bounded the leg from Prince Consort buoy to the finish. *Deva's* course, and her piece of string, went nowhere near Gaff buoy, so if

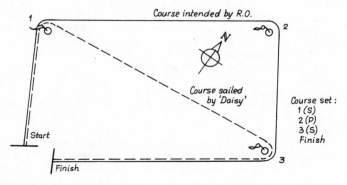

Course intended by R.O.

Course sailed by 'Daisy'

Course set :
1 (S)
2 (P)
3 (S)
Finish

Start

Finish

Fig. 99

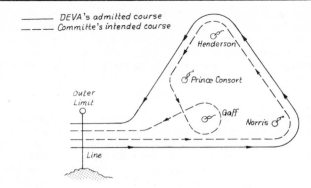

Fig. 100

Gaff was a rounding mark she did not comply with rule 51.2, but if it was not then she sailed the course. The RYA decision, in view of the ambiguity of the sailing instructions gave her the benefit of the doubt.

Note that the piece of string begins only when *Daisy* starts. It is for this reason that a buoy laid more than one length from the line cannot be a starting limit mark (see Mark and rule 51.3)

51.3

We have seen in the definition that a mark is 'any object that a yacht . . . must round or pass on a required side', in rule 3.2(a) (iii) that sailing instructions must describe the marks and state on which side each is to be rounded or passed, and in rule 51.2 that yachts must sail the course so as to round or pass each mark on the required side. Now we are told when those marks have a required side. There are three main categories of marks: starting marks (divided into starting line and starting limit marks), finishing marks (finishing line and finishing limit marks) and other marks (rounding and bounding marks).

1 Other marks. 'A mark has a required side for a yacht as long as she is on a leg which it begins, bounds or ends'. Looking at Fig. 101, course 1: Green is a mark for *Buttercup*, because Green ends the leg from Red to Green; Green is a mark for *Flame* because it begins the leg from Green to Blue; Green is not a mark for *Daisy* while she is on the leg from Blue to Red, she may pass either side of it (which she might want to do if she were on a beat) and would not infringe rule 52 by hitting it. Had course 2 been set, Green would be a bounding mark for *Daisy* on her leg from Blue to Red.

It is important to remember that the same buoy can, and often does, serve as starting mark, rounding mark and finishing mark. It must be considered according to its status at any given moment.

2 Starting marks. *Daisy* may not hit a starting mark after the preparatory signal (rule 52.1(a)(i)), but she may pass any side of it until she comes up to the start when the required side may be deduced from the definition of starting (it will also probably be stated in sailing instructions but if the two contradict each other the definition direction will prevail). A starting line

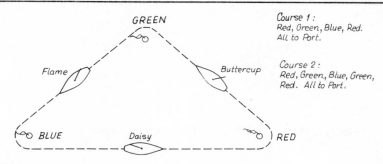

Fig. 101

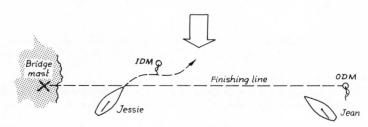

Fig. 102

mark is automatically on the line (see rule 6(a) and (b)) but a starting limit mark (see rule 6(c)) frequently is not. When a limit mark is on the course side of the starting line it acquires a required side as the yachts approach the line to start and no difficulties arise, but when it is laid on or has drifted to the pre-start of the line its object may be defeated. Over the last 50 years a number of cases have held that when the mark is more than one boat length from the line, on the pre-start side of it, it has no required side, and from that point of view can be ignored. This has been discussed under 'Mark' and rule 51.2, the situation is unsatisfactory, but not for want of efforts to right it, it is an intractable problem. (RYA 65/18 and RYA 68/12 refer.)

3 Finishing marks. A finishing mark holds its required side only until *Daisy* finishes, finishes correctly that is of course. If she touches the mark and 'unfinishes' she must re-round (see rule 52) and finish again, and during that period the mark retains its required side. In the rare situation of finishing on a transit line, if the limit mark is laid on the post-finish side of the line it may be useless. Fig. 102 (IYRU 124) shows just such a case. *Jessie* finished well beyond the intended mark and then sailed round it. *Jean* protested her, but in vain, for it was held that a limit mark that lay on the post-finish side of a finishing line did not rank as a mark. 'A yacht that has already finished cannot then be expected to continue her course to pass

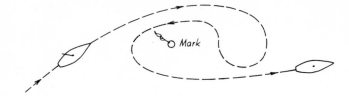

Fig. 103 *Mark to be left to port:* Daisy *unwinds correctly.*

yet another mark on a required side.'

I imagine that while *Daisy* would have to re-round a starting limit mark on the pre-start side of the starting line if she hit it, she would not infringe rule 51.2 by hitting a finishing limit mark laid as in Fig. 102.

51.4

This rule could well be tacked on to rule 51.2. It expresses in different words what the piece of string rule already says. It is illustrated in Fig. 103.

51.5

An explanatory rule, *Daisy* must clear the line before she ceases to race, but backwards or forwards will do unless SIs specifically state otherwise.

52   Touching a Mark

52.1   A yacht that either:

(a) touches:

> (i)   a starting *mark* before *starting*; or
>
> (ii)   a *mark* that begins, bounds or ends the leg of the course on which she is sailing; or
>
> (iii) a finishing *mark* while *racing*;

or
(b) causes a *mark* or *mark* vessel to shift to avoid being touched,

shall either exonerate herself in accordance with rule 52.2, or act in accordance with rule 68, (Protests by Yachts), when she alleges that she was wrongfully compelled by another yacht to touch it or cause it to shift, unless the other yacht retires or exonerates herself by accepting an alternative penalty when so prescribed in the sailing instructions.

52.2   (a) When a yacht touches a *mark* surrounded by navigable water, she may exonerate herself by completing the rounding of the *mark*, leaving it on the required side and thereafter re-rounding it or re-passing it without touching it, as required to sail the course in accordance with rule 51.2, (Sailing the Course), and the sailing instructions.

(b) When a yacht touches:

    (i)   a starting *mark*, she shall carry out the rounding after she has *started*;

    (ii)   a finishing *mark*, she shall carry out the rounding, and she shall not rank as having *finished* until she has completed the rounding and again crosses the finishing line in accordance with the definition of *finishing*.

(c) When a yacht touches a *mark* not surrounded by navigable water, she may exonerate herself by completing one 360° turn at the first reasonable opportunity.

52.1

This rule is to be read in the light of what has already been said in the definition of *mark* and under rule 51.3. Let us look at it from *Daisy's* point of view.

Daisy may not:

a) touch a starting mark before starting. The rule does not say for how long before starting, but since *Daisy* cannot be penalised for race infringements before the preparatory signal (see rule 31.1 and the definition of *racing*), she need not worry if she hits it before the five-minute gun. This phrase is not to be taken as meaning that she can hit it after starting. The starting mark then begins the leg she is sailing on – the first leg of the course – and is therefore covered by the next clause.

b) she may not touch a mark that begins, bounds or ends the leg she is on. Rule 51.3 described and defined the terms, rule 52 merely forbids *Daisy* to touch the marks at certain times. This rule, as we have said, includes a starting mark after starting, when it forms the beginning of the first leg, it also includes a finishing mark before finishing, when that mark ends the leg – the last – of the course.

c) she must not touch a finishing mark while racing. I believe this to mean 'a finishing mark after finishing while still racing'. It does not mean that when there is a finishing mark different from but near the starting line she would infringe rule 52 by touching it between the five-minute and starting signals. In US 188 a yacht's boom touched the committee boat after *finishing*. She infringed rule 52.1 and, since she failed to exonerate herself (in accordance with rule 52.2) she was disqualified.

Daisy may not cause a mark or a vessel to shift to avoid being touched. This comes from an 1895 case, *Britannia* v *Ailsa*. One can easily picture the small rowing boat, acting as mark, desperately trying to get out of the way of a thundering cutter under full sail. A Mirror dinghy would not be so intimidating.

If *Daisy* has touched one of the marks what can she do? She has two choices, she can re-round the mark or do a 360° turn when the mark is not in navigable water (rule 52.2), or she can protest another yacht which she believes has illegally pushed her onto the mark. Of course she can always retire. Occasionally re-rounding is forbidden in SIs (at night for example) and then she must retire if there is no other yacht to blame. The words 'she must protest' do not mean just putting up a flag and leaving it at that. They mean correctly carrying through the appropriate requirement of rule 68 so that the protest is valid and can go to a hearing and decision.

If *Daisy's* protest is found to be invalid she will be disqualified for not complying with rule 52.1. She cannot otherwise escape penalty, even if the other yacht later acknowledges her fault and retires (IYRU 41). Nor will it be sufficient for the other yacht to protest *Daisy*; *Daisy* will still be penalised if she has not herself protested according to the rule (IYRU 120). Finally remember that 'touch' means just that – a finger tip, a sheet end suffices to bring the rule into effect.

52.2

How then can *Daisy* exonerate herself under rule 52? IYRU 64 (Fig. 104) illustrates four possibilities. Pos. 1, *Daisy* touches the mark on the near side before rounding it, she rounds it to sail the course and then makes a penalty rounding without touching it. Pos. 2, she touches the mark on the far side while rounding it, she completes the rounding to sail the course and then completes a penalty rounding without touching it. Pos. 3, she touches it twice, on the near side and on the far side, she completes the rounding and makes her penalty rounding without touching it. Pos. 4, she touches the mark a second time while doing her penalty rounding, she must make a second penalty rounding without touching it. Of course she can only do these turns when the mark is surrounded with navigable water. When it is not, 52.2(c) allows her to do one 360° turn at the first reasonable opportunity.

Daisy cannot always exonerate herself when she likes. She must re-round a starting mark that she has touched, after she has started, and a

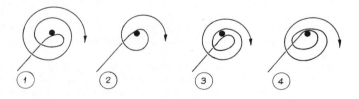

Fig. 104

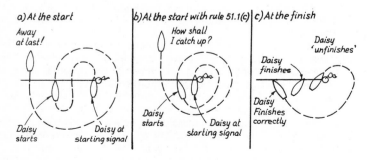

Fig. 105

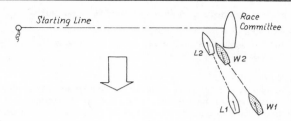

Fig. 106

finishing mark before she finishes (see definition of *finishing*). Otherwise the rounding would not be much of a penalty. Fig. 105(a) and (b) shows *Daisy's* obligations at a starting mark, described in US 236: 'A yacht is a premature starter and touches a mark. How does she exonerate herself? By returning to the pre-start side of the starting line or its extensions, starting (in accordance with the definition) and then executing the penalty rounding before recrossing the starting line.' Fig. 105(c) shows *Daisy* hitting a finishing mark.

Sometimes there are problems when the line has an inner limit mark, a small buoy laid just off the committee boat (usually to protect it). Must *Daisy*, having touched it, re-round only this small mark or must she re-round the committee boat? There is no 'correct' answer to this question; race committees laying such a troublesome mark, would do well to clarify in sailing instructions what they want *Daisy* and others to do if they touch it.

Rule 52.2(b)(ii) apparently presumes that *Daisy* has finished before she hits the finishing mark. As we say in the definition of 'finishing' she will then 'unfinish' (or become a premature finisher!) and must do a penalty round before she gets her gun. When she hits it before she has finished, then she will follow Fig. 104 (Pos. 1) as for a rounding mark.

In US 185 (Fig. 106) W tried unsuccessfully to slip through a gap between the committee boat and W. She hit both. She immediately did her 720° turns but did not re-round the committee boat. She was protested on the grounds that she had infringed two rules (37.1 and 52.2) and should have carried out two exonerations. However it was ruled that the dual violations '... occurred in such close proximity as to constitute a single foul even though more than one rule has been infringed ... Inasmuch as it was W's barging and her consequent infringement of rule 37.1, failure to keep clear of a leeward yacht, which brought about the accompanying infringement of rule 52, the appropriate penalty was the one for the infringement of rule 37.1 ...'

US 217 deals with another familiar problem. The start-finish line, set in the middle of the course, is made a prohibited area in SIs thus forbidding the crossing of the line except when starting or finishing. What, asked the question, was a yacht to do if she touched the committee boat at one end or the OLM at the other? If she were to re-round she would infringe SIs. The US Appeals Committee stated that this would be suitable occasion to use 52.2(c) and do a 360° turn. A good way out, when the committee boat is not surrounded by 'navigable' water from the point of view of the competitors.

53 Casting Off, Anchoring, Making Fast and Hauling Out

53.1 AT THE PREPARATORY SIGNAL

A yacht shall be afloat and off moorings at her preparatory signal, but may be anchored.

53.2 WHEN RACING

A yacht may anchor, but shall not make fast or be made fast by means other than anchoring, nor be hauled out, except for the purpose of rule 55, (Aground or Foul of an Obstruction), or to effect repairs, reef sails or bail out.

53.3 MEANS OF ANCHORING

Means of anchoring may include the crew standing on the bottom or any weight lowered to the bottom. A yacht shall recover any anchor or weight used, and any chain or rope attached to it, before continuing in the race, unless, after making every effort, she fails to do so. In this case she shall report the circumstances to the race committee, which may penalise her when it considers the loss due either to inadequate gear or to insufficient effort to recover it.

IYRU 94 which deals with an island used as a *mark* allows *Daisy* to haul out on such a mark without infringing rule 52 because she has touched it. 'Rules 53 and 55 then over-ride rule 52 because they serve a practical purpose and those permissible actions of the yacht in no way interfere with the proper sailing of the course.'

This is one of the rare occasions when the rules allow a protest committee discretion (in this part of the rules, 'race committee' still has the old meaning of 'race and protest committees'). I remember clearly a big American yacht anchored off Plymouth breakwater, struggling in the early morning breeze to get her anchor up so that she could finish the Fastnet race, with the minutes of her time allowance slipping by!

54 Means of Propulsion

54.1 BASIC RULE

(a) Unless otherwise permitted by this rule, a yacht shall be propelled only by the natural action of the wind on the sails and spars, and the water on the hull and underwater surfaces. A yacht shall not check way by abnormal means.

(b) Sails may be adjusted, and a competitor may move his body in order to maintain or change the angle of heel or fore and aft trim, or to facilitate steering. However, except as provided in rules 54.1(c) and 54.3, no actions, including *tacking* and *gybing*, shall be performed that propel the yacht faster than if the sails, hull and underwater surfaces had been trimmed to best advantage at the time.

(c) A yacht may promote or check way by means other than those permitted by this rule for the purpose of Fundamental Rule A, (Rendering Assistance).

(d) A yacht may anchor as permitted by rules 53, (Casting Off, Anchoring, Making Fast and Hauling Out) and 55, (Aground or Foul or an Obstruction). A yacht shall not recover an anchor in a manner that causes her to pass the point at which the anchor is lifted off the ground.

54.2   ACTIONS THAT ARE PROHIBITED
Examples of actions that are prohibited, except as permitted under rules 54.1(b) or 54.3:

(a) Repeated forceful movement of the helm (sculling).

(b) Persistent or rapidly-repeated trimming and releasing of any sail (pumping).

(c) Sudden movement of the body forward or aft (ooching).

(d) Persistent or rapidly-repeated vertical or athwartships body movement.

(e) Movement of the body or adjustment of the sails or centreboard that leads to persistent rolling of the yacht (rocking).

54.3   ACTIONS THAT ARE PERMITTED
The following actions are permitted for the sole purpose of accelerating a yacht down the face of a wave (surfing) or, when planing conditions exist, responding to an increase in the velocity of the wind.

(a) Not more than three rapidly-repeated trims and releases of any sail (pumping).

(b) Sudden movement of the body forward or aft (ooching).

There shall be no further pumping or ooching with respect to that wave or increase of wind.

A rule that forbids the use of engines, rowing and kinetics! Rule 54(a) contains a blanket prohibition of any form of propulsion except the 'natural action of the wind on the sails and spars and the water on the hull and underwater surfaces' – no towing, no paddling with plates. Nor may way be checked; a bailer may not be dragged in the water to slow the dinghy down. However there are some exceptions. First, Appendix 2 allows a board sailor to drag his foot in the water to check way. Secondly rule 54.1(c) allows *Daisy* when she is going to the assistance of someone in peril, obeying Fundamental Rule A, to use what means she can. Thirdly rule 54.1(d) allows *Daisy* to anchor according to rules 53 and 55 but she may not recover the anchor in such a way as to be carried beyond the point at which she let the anchor go.

So far so good, it is rules 54.1(b), 54.2 and 54.3 where the trouble arises, for it is these that prohibit kinetics; they aim to stop advantageous roll-tacking (or gybing), sculling, pumping, ooching, rocking. All these are given as examples of ways in which body movement can be used to drive the hull through the water. A little rocking in a flat calm to get you round the mark before the tide changes, a sharp spurt out of an awkward spot with a couple of roll tacks – it is hard for competitors to accept that such acts are just as reprehensible as motoring. It is also a runaway rule. If John pumps and gets away with it, *Daisy* must do so too or lose all chance of doing any good. Nor is it an easy rule to police. At one extreme it is clear that *Daisy* is rocking, at the other it is clear that she is not, what is not clear is the exact moment at which she passes the limit. It depends on the type of boat, the weather conditions and the views of the jury. World-wide consistency is greatly to be desired but most difficult to achieve.

There are few cases on the subject. US 132 held that, in a boat with a trim tab, the use of rudder and trim tab in opposite directions, although slowing her, did not infringe the rule. It was held to be comparable to backing sails which does not infringe it either.

US 56 absolved a helmsman who was trying to round a mark in light weather and had to move his tiller several times from centre to hard over before the boat would turn. It was held that it was not sculling because the object was to alter course (the reason for having a tiller), not go ahead.

In IYRU 14 two small dinghies, reaching at about hull speed were passed by a large power cruiser on a parallel course, creating several large waves. As each wave reached the quarter the helmsman moved his tiller across the centre-line in a series of alterations of course rhythmically timed to the passage of the waves under his yacht. No infringement was held to have taken place. 'While sculling in a very light wind or a calm can produce propulsion, it would be counter-productive for a yacht sailing at about hull speed. It would slow the yacht down. Taking advantage of wave action is well accepted as part of yacht racing . . . In taking advantage of the waves a helmsman may move his tiller as he thinks best to accomplish that purpose.'

In IYRU 92, a dinghy that roll-tacked nine times in less than three minutes was disqualified. She was propelled faster than if the sails, hull and underwater surfaces had been trimmed best advantage at the time, and her actions could not be justified changes in wind direction.

55   Aground or Foul of an Obstruction

A yacht, after grounding or fouling another vessel or other object, is subject to rule 57, (Manual and Stored Power), and may, in getting clear, use her own anchors, boats, ropes, spars and other gear; may send out an anchor in a boat; may be refloated by her crew going overboard either to stand on the bottom or to go ashore to push off; but may receive outside assistance only from the crew of the vessel fouled. A yacht shall recover all her own gear used in getting clear before continuing in the race.

Most of the rule permits yachts to infringe other rules in order to get clear. At the very end there is a mandatory phrase requiring any yacht concerned to recover all her own gear. Case law is naturally rather generalised each case being a one-off covering one particular set of circumstances.

IYRU 94 deals (as we have seen) with an island mark and states that rule 55 over-rides rule 52. I take this to mean that if *Daisy* ran aground on the island and if her crew went ashore to push off she would not have infringed rule 52.

56   Sounding

Any means of sounding may be used, provided that rule 54, (Means of Propulsion), is not infringed.

No comment is needed. It would be difficult to propel a boat with lead and line, but when sounding with a stick care must be taken not to turn it into a punt pole!

57   Manual and Stored Power

A yacht shall use manual power only and shall not use any device that derives assistance from stored energy for doing work; except that, when so prescribed in the sailing instructions, a power winch or windlass may be used in weighing anchor or in getting clear after running aground or fouling any object, and a power pump may be used in an auxiliary yacht.

Class rules will generally cover difficult points arising under this rule. In these days of robots it may not be easy to decide what is permitted and what is not. Remember that the IYRR do not forbid an automatic steering mechanism so in some cruiser classes it may be necessary to ban such devices in sailing instructions.

58   Boarding

Unless otherwise prescribed in the sailing instructions, no person shall board a yacht, except for the purposes of Fundamental Rule A, (Rendering Assistance), or to attend an injured or ill member of the crew or temporarily as one of the crew of a vessel fouled.

59   Leaving, Crew Overboard

Unless otherwise prescribed in the sailing instructions, no person on board a yacht when her preparatory signal was made shall leave, unless injured or ill, or for the purposes of Fundamental Rule A, (Rendering Assistance), except that any member of the crew may fall overboard or leave her to swim, stand on the bottom as a means of anchoring, haul her out ashore to effect repairs, reef sails or bail out, or to help her to get clear after grounding or fouling another vessel or object, provided that this person is back on board before the yacht continues in the race.

As in rule 55, case law concerns bizarre circumstances unlikely to happen again and from which it is therefore difficult to draw any interpretations of general application. IYRU 1 describes how a dinghy capsized 20 yards from the finishing line and the tide carried her and her crew across it. In answer to a question the RYA replied 'Provided that the complete crew remains with a capsized yacht they are considered to be "on board" for the purposes of rules 21 and 59. No rule was infringed. In another case the crew were separated from the hull and was not considered to be "aboard".'

In IYRU 66, the crew of a yacht fell overboard. During the time it took the helm to lower the spinnaker and turn back, a spectator craft picked the crew up and returned him to the yacht. After dealing with the question of Outside Assistance (see rule 60) the US Appeals Committee stated: 'Since the yacht made little or no progress until her crew was back on board, she did not infringe rule 59'.

US 237 also illustrates the last sentence 'provided that this person is back on board before the yacht continues in the race'. On a beat P lost both crew members and as a result bore off, forcing S to tack. P tacked, gybed and retrieved one crew, tacked and gybed again and retrieved the other crew, thus in the process performing 720° turns. Its decision, disqualifying P for failing to execute valid turns, states: '... making forward progress on the course is continuing in the race. It brings the yacht nearer to the time of finishing. A yacht is also nearer to the time of finishing after completing

720° turns than before doing so. The turns therefore can count for exoneration only when all conditions are present that allow a yacht to continue in the race. Accordingly, P was required to pick up both crew members before . . . [doing her turns].

'The last clause of rule 59, as applied to crews overboard, is an important safety rule. Until a crew member overboard has been retrieved, a yacht must have no incentive or opportunity and indeed must not be able to improve her finishing position or time – and that is what the rule provides.' This conforms to an old RYA case, 67/14, where the helmsman fell overboard and the crew managed to cross the finishing line single-handed. On appeal she was held to have infringed rule 59.

60 Outside Assistance

Except as permitted by Fundamental Rule A, (Rendering Assistance), rule 55, (Aground or Foul of an Obstruction), and rule 58, (Boarding), a yacht shall neither receive outside assistance nor use any gear other than that on board when her preparatory signal was made.

No outside assistance, not a screwdriver, not a spare sheet, not a sandwich after the preparatory signal, unless someone is overboard or ill or under rule 55, assistance from the crew of a vessel fouled. It would presumably be impossible to unravel who did what when pushing off. US 75 is about a spectator swimming over to help right a capsized catamaran. This was held to be outside assistance as no one was in any danger. In IYRU 66 (US 161) in a very similar case, outside assistance was permitted when a spectator boat picked up a crew member in the water; 'since any person in the water should be considered in some degree of peril; outside assistance in recovery does not infringe rule 60.' So each case must be considered individually.

The more difficult problems with this rule arise when the outside assistance is given orally. In US 182 the question was asked: 'Should we notify a skipper of an improper finish, as we do an improper start? Can a hail in these circumstances be construed as outside assistance . . .?' The answer was given: 'Notification to a yacht that she has not finished properly is appropriate as soon as it is apparent that she thinks she has finished, provided the action is the same in all such cases. There is no rule against such notification by the RC. It should not be construed as outside assistance prohibited by rule 60 but simply as prompt notification of a fact of which a yacht will be notified sooner or later.' The US Appeals Committee goes on to say that it would be unwise for the RC to offer advice as to how to correct the fault, there was no rule against it but it made the committee vulnerable to claims for redress. The second question went as follows: 'Should infringers of rule 51.1(c), the Round-the-Ends rule, be advised immediately or should they not be hailed until after the start?' The answer: 'Notification . . . is entirely permissible under the rules provided the procedure is covered by SIs . . .' The message is clear, hails by the race officer will not be considered outside assistance when all boats receive the same treatment, otherwise they may be.

In RYA 78/1 dinghies were racing in bad visibility and had difficulties in finding one of the marks. In the race an unknown number of competitors received advice from motor yachts cruising around near the mark in the fog, as to the direction of the mark. As this advice was given to some and not to others the PC did not see how any equitable arrangement could be made to retain the race as valid. For various reasons the appeal was sent back for a re-hearing on the question of redress, the decision stating: 'the RC should concern itself solely with the question whether, and to what extent, the finishing position of each yacht was prejudiced by an action or omission of the RC' – obviously visibility diminishing during a race and oral advice and conversation are excluded from such actions or omissions. The RYA went on to say: 'It is well established that oral advice volunteered by a third party is not within the intention of rule 60'. This had been established in RYA 63/27 and 63/28. 'There is no other rule', it continued, 'which can be infringed by the giving or receiving of oral advice, so it is irrelevant which non-racing yacht spoke to which racing yacht'. I cannot say that I think this decision would be binding in some circumstances. Imagine a Ruritanian team in the Admiral's Cup, being given information at a mark, in Ruritanian by a team coach. I believe that an international jury would hold that to be outside assistance.

In an Italian case (FIV 67/5) where, during a cadet race, a coach gave individual advice at a mark the decision said: 'It is intuitive that competition between individuals must be based on the ... skill of the competitor, the cases covered by rule 60 must not be limited to purely material help but must also include any suggestion or information furnished during the race to the competitor by a third person who can be considered to have some connection with the competitor himself and which places those that receive it in a position of unfair advantage with respect to the others.'

So we see that there are different points of view. When organisers wish to be sure they should either exclude support boats from the race area (as in the Olympics), and ban radios, or lay down rules about the use of private frequencies for weather forecasts etc. In the Mediterranean wind on the water can be seen from the air and yachts directed to it. There is no ruling as to the acceptability of this, I imagine that if such information were given on a private frequency it would be considered outside assistance, but if it were on a frequency carried by all but given in Ruritanian what then. Would it be assisting the Ruritanian crew or would each boat be expected to carry a Ruritanian speaking crew-member?

61 Clothing and Equipment

61.1 (a) Except as permitted by rule 61.2, a competitor shall not wear or carry clothing or equipment for the purpose of increasing his weight.

(b) Furthermore, the total weight of clothing and equipment worn or carried by a competitor shall not be capable of exceeding 15 kilograms, when soaked with water and weighed as provided in Appendix 10, (Weighing of Wet Clothing), unless class rules or the sailing instructions prescribe a lesser or greater weight, in which case such weight shall apply, except that it shall not exceed 20 kilograms.

61.2 When so prescribed by the class rules, weight jackets of non-metallic material (excepting normal fasteners), with or without pockets, compartments or containers, shall be permitted, provided that the jacket:

(a) is permanently buoyant,

(b) does not extend more than 30 mm above the competitor's shoulders, and

(c) can be removed by the competitor in less than ten seconds,

and that ballast carried in the pockets, compartments and containers shall only be water. For the purpose of rule 61.1(b), the pockets, compartments and containers shall be filled completely with water and included in the total weight.

61.3 When a competitor is protested or selected for inspection, he shall produce all containers referred to in rule 61.2 that were carried while *racing*.

61.4 The organising authority of an offshore event or events for cruiser-racer type yachts may prescribe that rule 61.1(b) shall not apply to the event or events.

Like rule 26 this is an IYRU policy rule and is included to for reasons of health and safety to stop light people weighting themselves down dangerously with extra weight. No cases have reached the case books, possibly because its main use is at championship meetings where there is often an international jury from whose decisions there is no appeal. The rule applies to all classes and all crews but may be altered by an organising authority (rule 61.4) for 'cruiser-racer type yachts'. A large man in the Southern Ocean might well need more than the permitted clothing weight if he were to keep warm. (It is an interesting thought as to who would weigh him too!) Appendix 10 – Weighing of Wet Clothing recommends the method to be used.

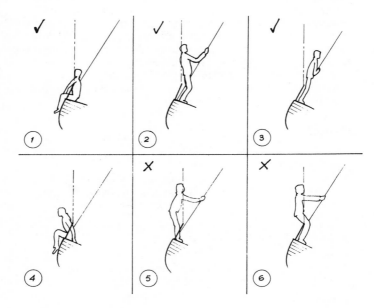

Fig. 107 *N.B. 4 is allowed only with two wire lifelines.*

62   Increasing Stability

Unless otherwise prescribed by her class rules or in the sailing instructions, a yacht shall not use any device, such as a trapeze or plank, to project outboard the weight of any of the crew, nor, when lifelines are required by the conditions for the race, shall any member of the crew station any part of his torso outside them, other than temporarily. On yachts equipped with upper and lower lifelines of wire, a crew member sitting on the deck facing outboard with his waist inside the lower lifeline may have the upper part of his body outside the upper lifeline.

Even the crews of off-shore boats now sit huddled on the weather rail like little birds on a branch showing that lifeline rules need to be strictly controlled both for reasons of safety and so that misuse does not lead to increased and unfairly gained stability. IYRU 83 (Fig. 107) shows what is allowed and what not.

63   Skin Friction

A yacht shall not eject or release from a container any substance (such as polymer) the purpose of which is, or could be, to reduce the frictional resistance of the hull by altering the character of the flow of water inside the boundary layer.

64   Setting and Sheeting Sails

64.1   CHANGING SAILS

While changing headsails and spinnakers, a replacing sail may be fully set and trimmed before the sail it replaces is taken in, but only one mainsail and, except when changing, only one spinnaker shall be carried set.

64.2   SHEETING SAILS TO SPARS

(a) Unless otherwise prescribed by the class rules, any sail may be sheeted to or led above a boom regularly used for a working sail and permanently attached to the mast to which the head of the working sail is set, but no sails shall be sheeted over or through outriggers.

(b) An outrigger is any fitting so placed, except as permitted in rule 64.2(a), that it could exert outward pressure on a sheet at a point from which, with the yacht upright, a vertical line would fall outside the hull or deck planking at that point, or outside such other positions as class rules prescribe. For the purpose of this rule: bulwarks, rails and rubbing strakes are not part of the hull or deck planking. A boom of a boomed headsail that requires no adjustment when *tacking* is not an outrigger.

64.3   SPINNAKER: SPINNAKER BOOM

A spinnaker shall not be set without a boom. The tack of a spinnaker when set and drawing shall be in close proximity to the outboard end of a spinnaker boom. Any headsail may be attached to a spinnaker boom, provided that a spinnaker is not set. Only one spinnaker boom shall be used at a time and, when in use, shall be carried only on the side of the foremost mast opposite to the main boom and shall be fixed to the mast. Rule 64.3 shall not apply when shifting a spinnaker boom or sail attached thereto.

64.4   HEADSAIL
Unless otherwise prescribed by the class rules, the following distinction shall apply between spinnakers and headsails. A headsail is a sail in which its mid-girth, measured between the mid-points of the luff and leech, does not exceed 50% of the length of the foot, and in which any other intermediate girth does not exceed a value similarly proportional to its distance from the head of the sail. A sail tacked down abaft the foremost mast is not a headsail.

Although class rules vary these four rules to a certain extent, they still form the basis of what is or is not permitted. IYRU 7 states that it is permissible for the crew to hold the sheet of a headsail or spinnaker outboard, since a human is not a fitting. US 125 agrees, but in this case the sheet was held out by a crew member's foot. No part of a human body can be an outrigger.

US 148 saw the mid section of a spinnaker being supported, in very light weather, with a paddle. The yacht was protested on the grounds that the paddle was either an outrigger or a spinnaker pole unattached to the mast. The protest and the appeal failed. 'Rules 64.2 and 64.3 deal with sheeting and setting headsails at points outside a vertical line from the hull ... of a yacht when upright. Since the paddle neither extended beyond the verticals, nor exerted outward pressure on a sheet, the manner in which it was used did not contravene [these rules]'.

65   Flags

A national authority may prescribe the flag usage that shall be observed by yachts under its jurisdiction.

66   Fog Signals and Lights

Every yacht shall observe the International Regulations for Preventing Collisions at Sea or Government Rules for fog signals and, as a minimum, the exhibition of lights at night.

(Number 67 is a spare number)

Part VI—**Protests, Penalties and Appeals**

Definitions

When a term defined below is used in its defined sense in Part VI and associated appendices, it is printed in **bold type**. *The definitions rank as rules.*

Rules—

(a) These racing rules, and

(b) the prescriptions of the national authority concerned, when they apply, and

(c) the sailing instructions, and

(d) the appropriate class rules, and

(e) any other conditions governing the event.

Protest—A written allegation by a yacht under rule 68, (Protests by Yachts), that another yacht has infringed a **rule** or **rules**.

The term **protest** includes when appropriate:

(a) a request for redress under rule 69, (Requests for Redress); or

(b) a request for a hearing under rule 70.1, (Action by Race or Protest Committee), or Appendix 3, rule 2.6, (Alternative Penalties); or

(c) a notification of a hearing under rule 70.2, (Action by Race or Protest Committee); or

(d) an investigation of redress under rule 70.3, (Yacht Materially Prejudiced); or

(e) a report by a measurer under rule 70.4, (Measurer's Responsibility).

Party to a Protest—The protesting yacht, the protested yacht, the race committee or any yacht involved in the incident that might be penalised as a result of the **protest**.

Protest Committee—The body appointed to hear and decide **protests** in accordance with rule 1.5, (Authority for Organising, Conducting and Judging Races), namely:

(a) the race committee or a sub-committee thereof; or

(b) a separate and independent protest committee or jury; or

(c) an international jury.

Interested Party—Anyone who stands to gain or lose as a result of a decision of a **protest committee** or who has a close personal interest in the result.

There are five definitions in this section. When the word, or phrase, appears in the rules in bold, the defined sense is intended. This defined sense will be seen to embrace alternatives or explanations; by this means tedious repetition in the rules is made unnecessary. Little comment is required.

1 Rules

(a) These racing rules: that is the current IYRR without appendices. When an appendix is to apply to a race it must be cited specifically in the sailing instructions.

(b) the prescriptions of the national authority: these are directed mainly at organising authorities and race committees, only a very few are addressed to competitors. When they apply those few can usefully be reprinted in sailing instructions so that foreign competitors do not require new rule books.

(c) the sailing instructions

(d) the appropriate class rules: one class is likely to have two sets of rules which must be adhered to, measurement rules and championship rules. The latter will cover such matters as crew members, special safety regulations, number and types of sails to be used etc such as is found in the Green Book (Rules for the World Championships of the Level Rating Classes).

(e) any other conditions: such as safety regulations, or local authority bye laws. It is important to ensure adequate information on these for the competitor, and, where pre-race preparation is necessary, only fair to give advance warning by printing the requirements in the notice of race.

2 Protest. The word, defined in its original meaning of an action brought by one yacht against another, embraces all the actions that a yacht, a race committee or a protest committee may bring with one exception. The action taken by a race committee, independent protest committee or international jury under rule 75.1 for gross infringement of the rules or misconduct is not included. Rule 75.1 gives powers to deal with difficult and special cases where all the procedures used for other actions may not be suitable.

3 Party to a Protest: Part VI refers to 'parties to the protest' in several places; note that only parties to the protest have the right to appeal under rule 77.1(a). Note too that a yacht dissatisfied with a redress decision is not a party to the protest unless she has been involved in the hearing. She must seek redress on her own behalf and only after she has extracted a decision from the protest committee may she then appeal if she sees fit. This is made clear in IYRU 119.

4 Protest Committee: notice that the race committee itself can be the protest committee.

5 Interested Party: of necessity, given the wide variation in circumstances, this definition is vague. It does not specifically state that competitors are interested persons although most competitors would stand to gain or lose by the decision. It will always be wiser to choose the protest committee from non-competitors but it is not always possible to do so. Rule 73 makes it clear that when someone *is* an interested party, he *cannot* sit on the protest committee although he can testify. In RYA 84/2 it was stated: 'An interested party does not cease to be such because a party to the protest is willing to accept him as a member of the protest committee'.

Members of the race committee are not interested parties but they are advised not to serve on a protest committee dealing with a request for redress under rule 69(a) when they have been personally involved. Appendix 6 (Protest Committee Procedure) para 2.1(d) reads: 'When a hearing concerns a request for redress ... involving a member of the race committee it is desirable that he is not a member of the protest committee and would therefore appear only as a witness'.

As far as 'close personal interest' is concerned, no rule can draw the line between husband and wife at one extreme and cousins three times removed at the other. The good judgement of those concerned will decide.

SECTION A—Initiation of Action

Three actions are possible:
1 Yacht(s) v Yacht(s) – rule 68.
2 Requests for redress by one or more yachts – rule 69 (often incorrectly called 'protesting the race committee').
3 Race Committee v Yacht(s) – rule 70. However it would be fair to say that 70.3 is rather RC *for* a yacht, as it allows the committee to initiate redress.

68   Protests by Yachts

68.1   RIGHT TO PROTEST
A yacht can protest any other yacht, except that a **protest** for an alleged infringement of the rules of Part IV can be made only by a yacht directly involved in, or witnessing an incident.

The basic right to protest is formulated in this rule, namely that a yacht may protest any other yacht. That rule 68.1 continues with only a single exception ... serves to emphasize the broad scope of the right to protest. The right should be liberally interpreted to permit any yacht, which is eligible to race in a series and whose entry has not been rejected or rescinded, to protest or seek redress from the race committee whether or not she actually ranked as a starter in the particular race.' This wide interpretation from US 205 is confirmed by IYRU 2. Here yacht A infringes a rule in an incident with B, continues to race and is then involved in another incident with C. Although A is disqualified as a result of the incident with B, her protest against C is still valid. Again, a yacht may protest another in a different race, and she may protest after she has retired, even when the infringement is seen when the protestor is already ashore (RYA 67/15). The single exception is that a protest for an alleged infringement of the rules of Part IV may only be made by a yacht directly involved in or witnessing an incident. That is, Part IV protests cannot be lodged by protestors who have only heard of an incident. Look at the difference between Part IV and Part V protests. A spectator sees two incidents. In the first A and B collide, neither fly a protest flag; in the second, A touches a mark and fails to re-round. The spectator reports what he has seen to a third yacht, C, which had not seen either incident. C can now protest A under rule 52 for touching the mark, and call the spectator as a witness; she cannot however protest A or B for the collision because she did not see it and was not involved. (When the spectator is not an interested party he can get his oar in by making a report to the race committee which, however, may or may not take action – see rule 70.2(d).)

When two yachts touch, one or both of them must (if neither retires or takes a penalty) protest (see rule 33.2), but with that exception there is no need for a yacht to protest if she does not wish to. However there is a moral obligation. We all know protesting is unpopular; it stops the poor protest committee from going to the cocktail party, it takes the prize away from a deserving (?) boat, it prevents your crew from getting away home – in other words its a bore. Nevertheless the health of the sport depends on regular steady policing which can usually only be done by the competitors. Forebearance leads to indiscipline and disregard for the rules which, in its turn, leads to cheating and the disintegration of competitive sport.

68.2 DURING A RACE—PROTEST FLAG

(a) An intention to protest an infringement of the **rules** occurring during a race shall be signified by the protesting yacht conspicuously displaying a flag. Code flag 'B' is always acceptable, irrespective of any other provisions in the sailing instructions.

(b) The flag shall be displayed at the first reasonable opportunity after the incident.

(c) (i) Except as provided in rule 68.2(c)(ii), the flag shall be displayed until the yacht *finishes* or, when the first opportunity occurs after *finishing*, until acknowledged by the race committee.

(ii) In the case of a yacht sailed single-handed, it will be sufficient to display the flag at the first reasonable opportunity after the incident and to bring it to the notice of the race committee when the protesting yacht *finishes*.

(d) When the yacht retires, the flag shall be displayed until she has informed the race committee or has left the vicinity of the course.

A protest flag must be flown when a rule is infringed 'during a race', not, you will notice, 'while *racing*'. It is necessary from before the preparatory signal when the yachts begin to sail about in the vicinity of the starting line (or starting area if there is one) until they have left the vicinity of the course. That is to say the rule covers all the time a yacht is racing and, in addition, the time envisaged by rule 31.2. It applies whether the protesting yacht was actually involved in the incident or merely noticed its occurrence (US 67). As we shall see in greater detail under rule 68.3, there are very few acceptable excuses for not displaying a flag: a dismasted yacht was allowed to get away with it (US 153), and US 190 relieves a protesting yacht of the necessity for a flag in a measurement protest, but IYRU 88 limits this, so, when in doubt – up with the flag!

No particular flag is specified, but flag 'B' is frequently prescribed by sailing instructions and its exclusion is specifically prohibited (see rule 3.1). It is unwise to argue about what is or is not a flag; what is important is that it is a conspicuous, eye-catching signal which is not normally flown, and that its meaning as an intention to protest is obvious to competitor and race committee alike. 'When SIs do not specify a particular flag the term "flag" should be broadly interpreted and may include such makeshifts as a handkerchief . . . or a red cellophane tell-tale' (US 88). The exception is a flag that means something else. In US 187 one boat hoisted a yellow flag (being used instead of 'I' with Appendix 3.2) and later changed it for a red protest flag. However, said the Appeals Committee 'a' flag is not the same as 'any' flag. 'It would thwart the very purpose of the requirement for displaying a protest flag to say that another flag, which under the rules signals a clearly contrary intention, could be used as a protest flag. Here the yellow flag signalled an admission that the yacht displaying it had committed a foul; the red protest flag signalled her belief that another yacht has committed a foul against her. To say that either flag could be used for either purpose would destroy the value of both as signals.'

The flag must be displayed at the first reasonable opportunity. As long ago as 1935, US 3 stated: 'While the phrase "at the first reasonable opportunity" is not synonymous with "immediately" it implies that a protest flag must be flown within a reasonably short time after a contestant has infringed a rule ... In fairness to such a competitor he should be notified promptly of this alleged infringement in all ordinary circumstances when a flag could be flown, if it was not flown, the race committee should refuse to hear the case. The spirit of the rule is that the protesting party must signal his intention at the time prescribed.'

More recently RYA 83/4 concerns an occasion in the Fireball Worlds when an incident occurred at the gybe mark. The boats were planing on and off to the leeward mark where the protest flag was at last hoisted. The protest was held to be invalid and on appeal this was confirmed. 'The wind was moderate on the leg from the gybe to the leeward mark and the crews were not continuously using the trapezes. The flag had been flown ... at the first convenient opportunity, not at the first reasonable opportunity'. Whether or not the flag is flown in time is, within limits, a question of fact, to be decided by the protest committee before a hearing. Committees will be most sympathetic when a protesting yacht would manifestly lose places in a race if she were to struggle with a flag. A Dutch appeal (KNVW 70/4) for instance, permitted a delay from the gybe to the leeward mark because of a strong gusty wind which kept the crew fully occupied sitting the boat out and continually trimming sheets. But such leniency is rare, and although excuses (or reasons) for not displaying a flag within a moment or two of an incident are many and varied, few succeed.

The flag must be displayed until the yacht finishes, as is shown by US 60. A protest was refused when the protestor finished without a flag. It had been hoisted after the incident but had blown overboard. It might seem unreasonable to expect a boat to carry more than one protest flag, but she did not hoist any other signal and the refusal of the protest was held to be correct. Although the rule permits the flag to be removed as soon as the yacht has finished she would be unwise to do so unless she is fairly sure that it has been seen by the race committee. The requirement is there for just that purpose, and it is the race officer's evidence which will count in any eventual hearing. Indeed if the incident has happened at the finishing line and the flag is flown after finishing it is obligatory to get his acknowledgement.

A yacht that retires but wishes to protest must also fly a flag and keep it up until acknowledged by the race committee or until she leaves the area of the race. That is, a boat retiring to Cherbourg when the race ends in Cowes may lower her flag in harbour, but one that retires on, say, the last leg of an Olympic course will be expected to make sure her flag is seen by a race officer. Whatever the rule, it is always courteous to tell the race committee that a protest is pending so that a hearing can be arranged.

Rule 68.2(c)(ii) mitigates the stringent rules for single-handers. It allows the flag to be displayed only twice, instead of continuously, at the first reasonable opportunity and again at the finish. For sailboards, Appendix 2.5 waives this rule so that a man on a sailboard is not required to display any flag, although he is required to hail.

68.3 AFTER A RACE

A yacht may protest without having displayed a protest flag:

(a) when she has no knowledge of the facts justifying a **protest** until she has *finished* or retired, or

(b) when a yacht, having displayed a protest flag, fails to lodge a valid **protest** as required by rule 33.2, (Contact between Yachts Racing) or rule 52, (Touching a Mark).

When the facts of an infringement are not known until a race is over, no protest flag is necessary. But this general statement is not as comprehensive as it might at first glance appear. To begin with the rule is limited by the fact that Part IV protests have to be witnessed by the protesting yacht (see rule 68.1); secondly appeal committees have continually narrowed its scope. In US 210, *Tior* believed that *Minuteman* had retired as a result of a collision between them and flew no flag. The protest committee disqualified both boats under rule 33.2 because neither had displayed a protest flag. Confirming this decision the Appeals Committee said: 'Retirement by itself does not necessarily indicate acknowledgement of an infringement, especially when serious damage has occurred. Without evidence of such acknowledgement the other yacht is obligated to protest by rule 33.2 and may not claim lack of knowledge of the facts ... as grounds for being exonerated for failure to display a flag'. A similar situation arose in RYA 81/1 where one yacht also did not display a protest flag because she believed the other to have retired. But she had been aware of the facts of the incident and the protest was invalid.

In IYRU 47, *Hocus Pocus* protested three yachts for starting outside a limit mark, but, because she was not sure of her facts until she got ashore and looked at the course instructions, she did not fly her flag. The protest committee refused to hear the protest and its decision was confirmed on appeal: 'All competitors are presumed to be aware of the SIs. A yacht that has reason to believe that another has infringed a rule and wishes to protest must show a protest flag ... If after finishing she is satisfied that no infringement occurred, she need take no further action.'

RYA 81/7 deals with the same subject. After an incident between A and B, A accepted responsibility and agreed to do her 720° turns. C, which had seen the incident, did not see a protest flag on either of the others. C did not fly a flag herself, but on coming ashore she protested A for failing to complete her turns. The race committee correctly held that the protest was not valid since the protestor had not displayed a protest flag.

Look at an example where the rule did apply. In RYA 83/4, A witnessed a collision between B and C, she then saw a protest flag on B. Only when the results were posted the morning after the race did A learn that B's protest had been refused as invalid. A then lodged a protest against B and C and the protest committee correctly disqualified them both under rule 33.2.

Finally there seems to be a slight variance on the two sides of the Atlantic in the interpretation of rule 68.3(b). In US 229 (1980) A saw a collision between B and C. Neither B nor C displayed a protest flag, nor did A. When no protest was lodged by B or C at the end of the race A protested both yachts, her protest was held to be valid and B and C were disqualified. The US Appeals Committee confirmed the protest committee's decision. This is not in line with the trend of RYA decisions which hold that A's failure to display a flag after seeing an incident between B and C with no subsequent flags, invalidates her protest. So again, when in doubt – up with the protest flag! The rule now supports the RYA view.

Note that rule 69 specifically states that a yacht about to request redress need not display a protest flag. IYRU 88 states that a protest flag is necessary for protesting a class rule, US 190 that it is not needed for a measurement protest. Certainly a flag would be required if the infringement were noticed during the race (wrong sail, main hoisted above black band etc), may be it would not be necessary for a scantling protest already notified to the race committee. But if in doubt hoist it.

68.4   INFORMING THE PROTESTED YACHT
A protesting yacht shall try to inform the yacht she intends to protest that a **protest** will be lodged. When an alternative penalty is prescribed in the sailing instructions, she shall hail the other yacht immediately.

In spite of the fact that this rule comes after the rule requiring a flag until the finish etc it does not follow that the protested yacht cannot be informed until after the race is over. On the contrary, ideally, the intention to protest will be made clear by a loud hail immediately after the incident, even before the protest flag is flown. When Appendix 3 (720° Turns and Percentage Penalties) is in force or any other system of alternative penalties, such a hail is obligatory. It is not however always possible to inform the protested yacht immediately and in recognition of this the protestee may be told at any time until the protest is lodged. Indeed, because it would be easy for the protestee to avoid being informed, by hiding or going away, the rule uses the words 'shall try to inform'. It is enough to try, it may not be possible to succeed. However a protest committee will naturally expect the attempt to be genuine. If nothing can be done on the water, then the protestee should be informed on coming ashore, and if he has disappeared then an effort to reach him, by phone or a message on the notice board will probably be accepted as 'trying'.

Usually it is perfectly possible to get the message across, but if not, as IYRU 92 points out, the failure to succeed does not invalidate the protest. The mere claim by the protested yacht that she did not know that she was being protested, is not a ground for not hearing the protest, but a little more time may be needed for preparation of the defence (see rule 72.3).

68.5   PARTICULARS TO BE INCLUDED

A **protest** shall be in writing and be signed by the owner or his representative, and include the following particulars:

(a) the date, time and whereabouts of the incident;

(b) the particular **rule** or **rules** alleged to have been infringed;

(c) a description of the incident;

(d) unless irrelevant, a diagram of the incident.

There are two essential conditions for the validity of a protest. It must be in writing, signed by the owner or his representative, and it must identify the incident (see rule 68.8). There is no necessity for an official form unless sailing instructions so require. The rule lists the simple particulars to be supplied and rule 68.8 allows these to be altered later when they are not correct. Often there is not much time to write out the protest, but protestors will find it worth their while to spend a little time on the diagram and, however brief, the description of the incident. If for example everything depends on there having been no overlap at the mark and the original sketch shows the boats overlapped then the case is inevitably weakened despite later correction. It is important for protests not to be refused for mere technicalities but likewise protestee and committee alike must be aware of what the protestor is alleging.

In RYA 85/2 the protestor gave an approximate time and place for the incident, then added 'rule 36' and nothing more: no diagram, no description of the incident. Arriving at the hearing the committee invited him to complete the form, but he waved it aside saying that it was so simple as to be unnecessary. The committee, instead of insisting, went ahead and disqualified the protestee, who appealed on the grounds that the protest did not comply with the requirements of the rule.

68.6   TIME LIMIT

Unless otherwise prescribed in the sailing instructions, a protesting yacht shall deliver or, when that is not possible, mail her **protest** to the race committee:

(a) within two hours of the time she *finishes* the race or within such time as may have been prescribed in the sailing instructions, unless the **protest committee** has reason to extend this time limit, or

(b) when she does not *finish* the race, within such time as the **protest committee** considers reasonable in the circumstances.

The period from when a yacht finishes to the latest time for her to lodge a protest is often called 'protest time'. Rule 68.6 gives protest time as being two hours, but this can be altered by sailing instructions. When she does not finish (retires or fails to finish within the time limit etc) then the protest committee will decide what is reasonable; perhaps for instance two hours from when she entered harbour. The protest may be mailed, necessary perhaps when the protesting yacht goes to another harbour from that of the race office. In such a case, a phone call to the race office or to the protestee would be a courteous act, and a wise one too.

The protest committee has the right to extend protest time when it is reasonable to do so, but the committee does not have unqualified authority to extend the time limit for lodging. 'Reason to' must not be capricious or arbitrary. (USYRU 88). There is no absolute limit, but since everything must come to an end, it would only exceptionally be later than the prize giving.

A race committee is entitled to make protest time very brief, 15 minutes for example, and a yacht, by entering, is taken to have accepted the terms of the sailing instructions, but when the time is so short, the protest committee is under a duty to take particular care in considering whether it should extend the time limit or not (RYA 82/15).

The principle is, that while not hurrying him unfairly, the protestor should be forced to 'accuse' the protestee as soon as possible after the facts become known to him. In an unpublished case, decided by an International Jury, A brought a measurement protest against B for certain bumps and hollows in the hull. These had last been seen a day or two before the series began when B was out of the water. The protest was lodged after the fourth race of a five-race series. This meant that the facts had been known for a fortnight with no action taken, and the jury threw the case out as being out of time.

VI

68.7 FEE
Unless otherwise prescribed in the sailing instructions, a **protest** shall not be accompanied by a fee.

No fee is required. However a race committee may ask for one by prescribing it in sailing instructions. I like the suggestion that any fees should go to a good cause named in the sailing instructions (Olympic fund, clubhouse roof etc.).

68.8 REMEDYING DEFECTS IN THE PROTEST
The **protest committee** shall allow the protesting yacht to remedy during the hearing:

(a) any defects in the details required by rule 68.5, provided that the **protest** identifies the nature of the incident, and

(b) a failure to deposit such fee as may be required under rule 68.7.

Rule 68.8 allows the protesting yacht to remedy any defects in the details required by rule 68.5 provided that *the protest identifies the nature of the incident*. These are not the same words as those used in rule 68.5(c) which speaks of *a description of the incident*. This is deliberate. The description of the incident may be scanty, or indeed missing, but yet the incident can be perfectly identified by the diagram together with the time, place and rules alleged infringed. To quote USYRU 88 again, discussing a protest that was said to be deficient in some points: 'The written protest adequately met the minimum requirements. It identified the incident by date, approximate time and whereabouts. It clearly designated the rule believed infringed as the Opposite Tack rule. It gave a brief but clear statement of the facts ... It did not contain a diagram of the incident and while a diagram was certainly relevent, its omission in this case did not warrant invalidation of the protest since the essential facts were clear without it. The protest committee was correct in asking for and accepting the diagram at a later date'.

However a limit can be reached. As we saw in RYA 85/2 there was no diagram and no description of the incident, the rule cited was 36, but there was no indication as to whether the yachts were beating or running or as to what action either of them had taken. When invited at the preliminary examination to complete the form the protestor declined, saying that it was not necessary, and nevertheless the protest committee proceeded to hear the case without requiring him to do so. On appeal the protest was held to be invalid. It is not, after all as if much were needed, 'we were running on opposite tacks and as s-tack I had to luff to avoid a collision' would be adequate (see also rule 68.5).

The clauses of rule 68 that relate to yacht to yacht relationships are interpreted strictly, but those that govern procedure ashore are more liberally interpreted and a protest committee has considerable freedom of manoeuvre provided that it always tries to be fair towards all the parties.

We have seen in rule 68.5 the particulars that must be included in a protest form for the protest to be valid. This rule makes sure that the protestor, tired and cross after a long race, is not held to some slip of the pen made while writing out the protest. It is surprising how often S can be written for P or L for W. Additionally any fee required under rule 68.7 may be paid in late. However one thing cannot be remedied. When the protest fails to identify the nature of the incident, then it is invalid, the defect cannot be remedied and the protest cannot be heard.

68.9 WITHDRAWING A PROTEST
When a written **protest** has been lodged, it shall not be withdrawn, but shall be decided by the **protest committee**, unless prior to the hearing one or more of the yachts acknowledges the infringement, except that, when the **protest committee** finds that contact between two yachts was minor and unavoidable, a protesting yacht may withdraw her **protest**.

You can hoist a protest flag and then decide to let it be, you can write out a protest form and decide not to hand it in at the office, but once lodged (filed – US) then a protest cannot be withdrawn and the committee will have to deal with it. The exceptions are when, before the hearing, another yacht takes the blame for the incident (although when you think about it its not so much that the protest is withdrawn but rather that it becomes irrelevant), and when a protest is brought only because of rule 33.2 and contact is found by the PC to have been minor and unavoidable, then the protestor may withdraw it.

69 **Requests for Redress**

Rule 69 should be read in conjunction with rule 70.3 (Yacht Materially Prejudiced) and rule 74.2 (Consideration of Redress). Note that no protest flag need be displayed when it is intended to claim redress.

A yacht that alleges that her finishing position has been materially prejudiced through no fault of her own by:

(a) an action or omission of the race committee, or

(b) rendering assistance in accordance with Fundamental Rule A, (Rendering Assistance), or

(c) being disabled by another vessel that was required to keep clear, (a yacht is "disabled" when, in the absence of other yachts, she is significantly impaired in her ability to proceed at normal speed or to manoeuvre or to proceed in safety), or

(d) a yacht infringing Fundamental Rule C, (Fair Sailing), or against which a penalty has been imposed under rule 75.1, (Penalties by the Race Committee or Protest Committee),

may request redress from the **protest committee** in accordance with the requirements for a **protest** provided in rules 68.5, 68.6, 68.7 and 68.8, (Protests by Yachts). A protest flag need not be displayed. The **protest committee** shall then proceed in accordance with rule 74.2, (Consideration of Redress).

Rule 69 is designed to help *Daisy* when her placing in the results has been adversely affected by one of four things: a mistake by the race committee; the time she has spent assisting others; being disabled in certain circumstances; and being done down by the bad behaviour of another competitor. There are two prerequisites common to all four categories: first *Daisy's* finishing position must have been materially prejudiced and, secondly, the worsening of her position must have happened through no fault of her own.

IYRU 95 states: 'A yacht is entitled to redress from a race committee's alleged failure to fulfil requirements of the sailing instructions only when she can demonstrate that her finishing position was thereby materially prejudiced'. In this case SIs provided for the first leg to be sailed to windward. After one class had started the wind backed some 55°. The first mark could not be moved for the start of the second class as the first had not yet rounded it. When the Finns started, none could fetch the first mark on a single tack, but further backing of the wind permitted some to do so. "A" requested redress, holding that the race committee had contravened the sailing instruction.

The protest committee was satisfied that the first leg of the course was not a 'windward' leg. On the other hand it found no evidence to suggest that, within the terms of rule 69, the race was unfair, or that any yacht was materially prejudiced. The request was refused and, on appeal, the decision of the protest committee was upheld.

A winning yacht will not get redress when other yachts have suffered but she has not. Suppose that *Daisy* has won a race in a series but because "B" came second it would pay *Daisy*, points-wise, to have the race abandoned. Suppose also that the RC has made an error, nevertheless *Daisy* is not eligible for redress for her finishing position in that race has not been materially prejudiced by the mistake.

In one curious case (US 230) yacht no. 388 chose not to start in the fifth race of the series. In that race one of the marks was missing, however most competitors turned in more-or-less the right place and the race was scored as if the mark had been present. This arrangement was accepted by all the yachts that started. 388 requested redress, claiming that her position in the

VI

series had been materially prejudiced. Refusing redress, the US Appeals Committee stated that rule 69 related to the finishing position of a yacht in a particular race. Having, with some difficulty, accepted that the race committee had acted within its powers to let such a bizarre race stand, it added: 'A yacht is not entitled to redress for proper action by the RC simply because alternative action which is also available to the committee would give her a better standing in the series'.

US 223 is one of the rare cases that deals with the phrase 'through no fault of her own'. A right-of-way yacht avoided a collision by taking violent avoiding action, but in so doing she ripped her headsail on the spreader. However she was held not to be eligible for redress under 69(c) because 'proper anticipation and sail-handling ... would have avoided any damage to her headsail'.

69(a)

It is only too easy for a RC to make mistakes. Think of the number of times starting and finishing lines and course marks are laid wrongly, how often there are errors in starting procedures or in recalls, how often sailing instructions are ambiguous. The scope for mistakes is large and varied. Now while a yacht can get redress for such mistakes (subject always to the prerequisites we saw above) she cannot protest the RC. RYA 82/3 illustrates this. The race officer made a mistake in the timing sequence (the starting signal was one minute early). At a redress hearing the PC held that no yachts had been materially prejudiced and let the results stand, two yachts appealed. The appeal was dismissed, the PC's decision was not at fault since it had been held that no yachts had been materially prejudiced and therefore no redress was required. It is a fairly common mistake to believe that when the RC have done something wrong the race is automatically 'null and void'. But this is not so and indeed rule 5.1(d) specifically forbids the abandonment or cancellation of a race already completed without considering whether it is the fairest thing to do. See also rule 74.2.

It is not the mistake itself that is actionable, but the fact that the mistake has prejudiced one or more yachts. In US 198, a case where two marks were laid instead of one, it was stated: 'A's request for redress under rule 69(a), claiming prejudicial procedure by the RC, is resolved in three steps. The first step is to determine whether the RC took some action it should not have taken, or failed to take some action it should have taken. In this case, it clearly took improper action by unnecessarily establishing a replacement mark two miles from the location of a turning mark which was in fact in place. Having found that the RC erred, the second step is to determine whether the improper action was prejudicial to any yacht or yachts ... the third step is to determine what equitable arrangement is to be made ...'

It is clear from this decision that the action or omission of the RC must be contrary to the rules. IYRU 123 corroborates this, stating 'redress can be granted under rule 69(a) only when the RC acts incorrectly', and RYA 82/3 which we have looked at earlier, confirms this again. I would make one proviso: that the RC acts reasonably. Were a RC to act unfairly and unreasonably although technically within their powers I do not believe that any appeals authority would hesitate to reverse this.

IYRU 110 illustrates a situation where the RC got it wrong and gave redress where none was due. Competitors asked for the race to be abandoned because of windshifts and redress was granted, the race being abandoned. However, on appeal, it was held that no redress should have been given. Windshifts are a common occurrence in yacht racing. Anticipating predictable windshifts is part of the art of sailing and cannot be said to affect the fairness of the competition within the meaning of rule 5.1(b). Note rule 69(a) speaks of 'the race committee', not protest committee. There is virtually no redress from the decision of a protest committee, only appeal is available. The exception is where a protest committee in granting redress to some yachts harms the positions of others that have not been parties to the protest. The yachts may seek redress against the decision, indeed must do so, no appeal until hearing. Of course what this is *in fact* saying is that the PC have not heard all the relevant evidence at the first hearing and that it has therefore reached a mistaken result and should take another look at it. IYRU 119 which lays this down is discussed under rule 77 (Appeals).

VI

Let us look finally at two other cases from the States. In US 209 the committee started a race in winds which one of the competing Sunfish considered too strong. She chose not to start and then claimed that her finishing position had been materially prejudiced by 'starting the race under the existing wind and sea conditions and jeopardising their safety'. Her request for redress was refused and confirmed on appeal. 'The decision whether to start, postpone or abandon a race is a matter solely within the jurisdiction of the RC. Rule 69(a) should not be interpreted to materially restrict or interfere with the authority and responsibility of the RC in matters of race management.'

US 243 shows to what lengths competitors will go. In the second race of the series the RC scored a yacht in second place which had started prematurely and failed to return and start correctly. The posted results were not corrected until two days later when the yacht's score was changed to DNS. She claimed redress and the protest committee gave it!! The appeal committee stated: 'If a yacht is scored incorrectly, she is not prejudiced within the meaning of rule 69(a) by having the score corrected at a later date. It follows that there is no justification for reinstating her incorrect score ... Not to disqualify a premature starter would be prejudicial to others in the fleet, and conversely, the posting of an incorrect score is not an error which prejudiced her performance in that race.'

69(b)

Fundamental Rule A (FRA) orders *Daisy* to go to the assistance of any 'vessel or person in peril' – when possible of course. It is therefore only fair that *Daisy* should have redress for the time she spends. The decision in IYRU 38 shows how unrestrictedly race and protest committees are to interpret FRA – 'A yacht in a position to assist another that may be in peril is bound to do so. That she offers assistance not requested is irrelevant'. It will also be irrelevant when adjudicating on redress.

In offshore races there are numerous occasions each year when one boat stands by another, perhaps rudderless, or without a mast, until the rescuer is satisfied that all is well. On finishing she requests redress. Her elapsed time is then usually shortened as appropriate. Sometimes such rescues become very complicated. In a One Ton Cup at night, a blazing vessel (it turned out to be a chartered motor boat) was seen. A number of competitors went to the scene and *Gumboots*, then leading on points picked up the ship-wrecked family from the liferaft. *Gumboots* intended to finish the race, but in the early hours of the morning a rescued child was ill and had to be taken ashore. After three days of discussion, *Gumboots* was awarded her position at the mark before the incident, and this was good enough for her to win the series.

69(c)

This rule says another 'vessel', not another yacht, thus redress can be granted for disablement by a spectator craft, or a committee vessel as well as another competitor. The yacht must be disabled. This is not the same as damaged, she may be damaged but yet able to sail on with no loss of speed. In US 253 it is envisaged that a yacht is wrongfully forced by an outside leeward yacht to pass between a distance mark and the mark boat at the finish, becoming entangled with, but not damaged by, this marker and losing 14 places before being able to finish properly . . .

'Question. Is physical damage required in order to entitle a yacht to redress under rule 69 as having been "disabled" due to a rule infringement by another yacht?

'Answer. Physical damage is not a requirement for disablement under rule 69. Disabled is defined as being incapable or incapacitated. This is further defined by US 223 which states, "A yacht is disabled if her speed has been reduced or her manoeuvrability be impaired."

'Question. If physical damage is not required and the definition of "disabled" quoted above applies, to what extent and for what duration must the yacht's speed be reduced or her manoeuvrability be impaired in order to determine that her finishing position was prejudiced?

'Answer. The determination of the extent and the duration that a yacht's progress has been hindered in order to establish that she has been "materially prejudiced" and that she is thus entitled to redress under rule 74.2, is a matter of fact which can only be decided by a protest committee'.

'When, in the absence of other yachts' is a phrase designed to prevent *Daisy* from maintaining, say, that she cannot proceed at normal speed because she has been forced into a group of yachts that are blanketing her. However if she was driven onto the shore and lost some minutes getting off she might be eligible for redress.

69(d)

When *Daisy* is the victim of foul play she may now request redress, but only when the offending yacht (or presumably person where appropriate) has been found to have infringed FRC or has been found guilty of some misdemeanour under rule 75. If we look at IYRU 78 we see a case in which A harrassed B throughout the race. A was thrown out of the series under rule 75 (see that rule) but there was no redress for B. This rule 69(d) has been adopted since that case, and now B could be given redress, provided that she could show that she had suffered material prejudice to her finishing position as a result of A's actions.

70   Action by Race or Protest Committee

We have seen how a yacht can get a protest on the road and how and when she may ask for redress, now let us see the powers given to the committee to discipline yachts. Just as there is no compulsion on a yacht to protest (except under rule 33.2) there is no compulsion on a race or protest committee to act either, except in so far as rule 13 may compel a committee to act when the yacht concerned is a prize-winner.

70.1   WITHOUT A HEARING

The race committee may act in accordance with rule 74.4, (Penalties), without a hearing against a yacht that:

(a) fails either to *start* or *finish*, except that she shall be entitled to a hearing when she satisfies the **protest committee** that an error may have been made, or

(b) when the Percentage Penalty as set out in Appendix 3 is in effect, displays Code flag "I" during a race but fails to report the infringement and is thus subject to Appendix 3, rule 2.6.

A yacht so penalised shall be informed of the action taken, either by letter or by notification in the race results.

Only the race committee is empowered to disqualify a boat without a protest or hearing and only in very limited circumstances: when a yacht fails to *start* or *finish*. The words 'start' and 'finish' are used in their defined sense, thus restricting wide use of this rule. A yacht can be penalised without a hearing for crossing the line the wrong way (not in the direction of the first mark when starting or from the last when finishing), for starting prematurely and failing to return, and for infringing a starting rule such as Round-the-Ends or Five-minute; there are few other examples. Seeing such infringements with their own eyes, race officers (as delegates of the race committee) have the right to mark the results DNS or DNF (did not start/finish). However since everyone can make mistakes the rule provides the yacht with the right to a hearing when she can satisfy the protest committee that an error has been made. This is a request for a hearing, not a request for redress (see definition of *protest* (b)), the action being by the protest committee against the yacht. This is an important difference because of the consequences that may flow from a redress hearing. Furthermore IYRU 118 places the responsibility for satisfying the protest committee that the race officer was wrong, firmly on the yacht.

The other occasion for summary justice arises from the percentage penalty system in Appendix 3.2.5 and is self-explanatory. An infringing yacht must, naturally, be informed of what has happened, but the results are considered adequate for this purpose. Unless deliberately and specifically altered by sailing instructions, the rule cannot be used for other infringements, such as touching a mark (IYRU 18). The race officer must turn to rule 70.2 to deal with those.

70.2   WITH A HEARING

The race committee or the **protest committee** may call a hearing when it:

(a) sees an apparent infringement by a yacht of any of the **rules** (except as provided in rule 70.1), or

VI

(b) learns directly from a written or oral statement by a yacht (including one contained in an invalid **protest**) that she may have infringed a **rule**, or

(c) has reasonable grounds for believing that an infringement resulted in serious damage, or

(d) receives a report not later than the same day from a witness who was neither competing in the race nor otherwise an **interested party**, alleging an infringement, or

(e) has reasonable grounds for supposing, from the evidence at the hearing of a valid **protest**, that any yacht involved in the incident may have committed an infringement.

For such hearings, the race committee or **protest committee** shall notify the yacht involved thereof in writing, delivered or mailed not later than 1800 on the day after:

    (i)   the finish of the race, or

    (ii)   the receipt of the report, or

    (iii)   the hearing of the **protest**.

When rule 70.2(e) applies, this notice may be given orally at the hearing. The notice shall identify the incident, the **rule** or **rules** alleged to have been infringed and the time and place of the hearing.

Both race and protest committees are entitled to protest a yacht for infringing any rule and bring her to a hearing. For the action to be valid the evidence may only come to the notice of the committee in a limited number of ways. There is no compulsion to protest a yacht (except in so far as concerns a prize-winner in rule 13) if the committee prefer not to and it may sometimes be better not to take notice of minor infringements that have no effect on the speed of the boat. The principle of a jury protesting a yacht for, say, infringing rule 54 by pumping and then itself hearing the protest is unpopular, but when a jury refrains from taking action it is roundly accused of being weak: 'Why can't they do something, it happened under their noses' is the cry. One easy answer is to say that the jury should not go out on the water, but then you might have no jury at all if its members were not allowed to go and watch.

The yacht must be notified in writing (although the way the sentence is written there is enough ambiguity about it for oral notice to be sometimes acceptable) and, however brief, ranks as a protest. Protest time is rather arbitrarily limited to 1800 on the day after the finish, or the receipt of the report (70.2(d)), or the hearing of the protest (70.2(c)). There are five clauses under which action may be taken when:

(a) the race committee sees apparent infringement (other than those summarily dealt with under rule 70.1) with its own eyes. For example, the race officer sees a boat hit a mark and fail to re-round it and he initiates a protest. This happened in USYRU 111 where it was said: 'The race committee in initiating action under rule 70.2 is not in the position of a prosecutor, but of an umpire, with one rather significant difference. An umpire who sees what he believes to be an infringement, rules forthwith, and his decision is usually final. A race committee or a member thereof in a similar situation, however, calls a hearing to give the "apparent infringer" an opportunity to provide evidence as to the facts or support his action by a rule in his favour. The race committee at the hearing is still in the position of an umpire.' But see rule 73.3.

(b) the committee learns directly from a written or oral statement that she may have infringed a rule. It is quite common in off-shore racing for a declaration to be qualified. The yacht admits that some rule was infringed – perhaps the nav lights failed or a life belt was lost overboard – then this technical infringement will be digested by the protest committee which often decides not to proceed with a protest. However the rule was included partly because of an incident similar to that recounted in IYRU 18. Within half an hour of finishing a race a winning helmsman admitted to two members of the race committee that he had touched a mark. The committee were entitled to disqualify him under this rule.

The rule now specifically includes an admission written on a protest form when the protest is found to be invalid. Some may not like this, but it is hard to ignore a piece of paper, bearing the owner's signature, that states that his yacht has hit a mark and not acted correctly according to rule 52. The fact that the signed piece of paper is *also* an invalid protest seems of no consequence. It would surely not be fair to the rest of the fleet to allow such yacht to retain a leading position.

(c) the committee has reasonable grounds for believing that an infringement resulted in serious damage, then these circumstances in themselves authorise an intervention.

(d) the committee receives (in writing or orally) a report of an alleged infringement. This report will only be acceptable when it comes from someone who has witnessed the incident (thus preventing the race or protest committee acting on bar gossip) who is not a competitor (a competitor has his own right of protest) and who is not an interested party. To be valid this report must be made not later than the same day. RYA 1968/13 held that this 'report time' may be prolonged by the protest committee just as protest time may be prolonged under rule 68.5.

(e) the grounds for action appear during the hearing of evidence at a valid hearing. There is a difference between this and (b). If in an A v B protest, it seems that C, which has not been present, is or may be the infringing yacht, the protest committee may take action against her and, after hearing her, penalise her without any admission on her part.

70.3   YACHT MATERIALLY PREJUDICED

The race committee or the **protest committee** may initiate consideration of redress when it is satisfied that any of the circumstances set out in rule 69, (Requests for Redress), may have occurred.

This rule gives the race, or protest committee, discretionary power to initiate a redress hearing when it believes that it is right to do so. This may arise from any one of the four grounds in rule 69. Once decided that some redress is due a hearing will be called in accordance with rule 73 and the action dealt with under rule 74.2. IYRU 88 points out that there is no compulsion on a race committee to avail itself of this rule.

This will be simple when redress is given to a yacht that has, say, stood by another with a broken mast or when she has been disabled by a vessel required to keep clear, but a committee will tread warily and make sure it has heard all the evidence before abandoning or cancelling a race because of its own mistake.

Appendix 6 (Protest Committee Procedure) recommends (in para 2.1(d)) that when a hearing concerns a request for redress involving a member of the race committee it is desirable that he is not a member of the protest committee and would therefore appear only as a witness. However with rule 70.3, the hearing will probably be called by the race officer who is trying to be fair and he will remember that before abandoning or cancelling a race after its completion, particular care must be taken.

70.4 MEASURER'S RESPONSIBILITY
When a measurer concludes that a yacht does not comply with her class rules or measurement or rating certificate:

(a) before a race or series; he shall request the owner or his representative to correct the defect. When the defect is not corrected, he shall report the matter in writing to the race committee, which shall reject or rescind the yacht's entry or approve the entry in accordance with rule 19, (Measurement or Rating Certificates). The yacht shall be entitled to a hearing upon her request.

(b) after a race; he shall make a report to the race committee or to the **protest committee**, which shall then notify the yacht concerned and call a hearing.

The measurer shall not have the authority either to rescind an entry or to disqualify a yacht.

Measurement is a difficult and sensitive area of race administration. When class rules are poorly written, or ambiguous, or when development in a class puts a strain on the rules, problems arise which need to be treated strictly by the book in order to be fair to all parties concerned. Rule 70.4 is addressed to administrators, to measurers and race committees, not to yachts. When a yacht wishes to protest another for not measuring she will allege an infringement of rule 19 or of class rules in that a measurement, scantling or flotation rule has been infringed while racing. A hearing will be called as usual and the committee will proceed under rule 74.3.

Note that rule 74.4 states: 'The measurer shall not have the authority either to rescind an entry or to disqualify a yacht.' No need for comment, but it needs to be remembered by measurers and committees alike.

A yacht may be under the control of a race committee or not. The committee governs her from the time she enters a race or series, and, for the purposes of this rule, her certificate is accepted, until the presentation of the prizes or the finalisation of all protests and appeals arising from the series, whichever is the later. The racing rules have no application to yachts not under the control of a race committee and we need not concern ourselves with them, they are provided for by the various class associations or rating authorities. The opening sentence speaks of a measurer not referring to any old measurer, but to one officially appointed for the race or series, when he is an agent of the race committee. IYRU 123 states: 'It is not open to an outside measurer to lodge a report within the meaning of rule 70.4. Before the racing starts the owner is given a chance to put things right on the spot, but when this may not happen because the defect is impossible to correct or because the owner maintains that there is no defect. Then the measurer will report in writing to the race committee, stating what he believes to be wrong. The committee shall then take action'. It is not open to it to sweep the matter under the carpet. The RC will call a hearing and let the yacht state her case. It will not rescind the entry except when all else has failed.

It is interesting to note that the ORC have strengthened this rule. Some defects, such as ballast moving are easily corrected but may be evidence of an attempt to cheat, and it is not permitted to correct them without reference to the race committee. When the measurer reports after a race, and entry cannot be rescinded, the committee will call a hearing and then proceed according to rules 73 and 74.3.

SECTION B—Protest Procedure

This section provides a framework for dealing with protests, from the moment a protestor hands in a protest form to the race office (or the race officer) until, after the hearing, a party to the protest (probably a would-be appellant) requests, and is supplied with, details of the decision in writing. However much the procedure varies with time and place, certain basic rights remain constant, such as the right to state one's case, to question witnesses, and not to be judged by a possibly biased committee member. Sailing instructions are permitted to alter this section, with very clear and specific reference to the alterations (see rule 3.1),and we will look at some of those, but such changes should only be made when it is essential to do so and without prejudicing the competitors.

Incorrect procedure may be appealed, but it is safe to say that, in general an appeals committee will not upset a decision when the appellant has neither raised an objection at the time nor been harmed by the mistake. Section B should be read in conjunction with Appendix 6 (Protest Committee Procedure). This Appendix is not mandatory but should not be disregarded without good reason, the two sections enable a committee to come to a fair conclusion.

71   Procedural Requirements

71.1   REQUIREMENT FOR A HEARING
A yacht shall not be penalised without a hearing, except as provided in rule 70.1, (Action by Race or Protest Committee).

'A yacht shall not be penalised without a hearing ...' – no taxation, no representation. A pillar of the system, this rule should appear in rule 74.4 as well as in rule 71.1. Note that the reverse side of this does not follow: there is no implication that the committee may dismiss the protest – once lodged it must be heard. The only exception to this rule is rule 70.1 which permits, as we have seen, very limited cases where penalisation can be summary.

US 130 illustrates rule 71.1. M and W were the parties in a complicated three-boat situation, the rights and wrongs of which depended on the luffing rights between them at various stages of the incident. L was not included in the hearing (we do not know why), her evidence was missing and although it seemed quite probable that she had caused the trouble she could not be penalised. US 110 shows us a committee trying its damnedest to get rid of *Windsock*, a boat which infringed rule 25. But in spite of

infringing a number of rules, she was re-instated because she never had a
hearing.

Occasionally the stringent requirements of this rule are deliberately
reduced by Sls. When all yachts come in to the same harbour after
finishing, it is easy for the PC to protest them in the normal way, but when
they scatter after finishing, each going to her own marina, it is sometimes
more satisfactory to penalise *Daisy* summarily for, say, lack of navigation
lights at the finish. When she does not accept the penalty she should
always be given a hearing as soon as she asks for one. It is possible to justify
such specified alterations in limited circumstances, but it is a facility that
should be used extremely sparingly.

In US 104 a protestee arrived at the hearing half an hour late, through no
fault of his own, to find that he had already been disqualified. He appealed
successfully and the case was sent back to the race committee for a re-
hearing (see also 73.1 and 73.4). 'Without a hearing' does on occasion have
to be interpreted as 'without a reasonable chance of appearing at a
hearing'. When a protest cannot be heard at once the (wretched) organiser,
who has to fix a hearing, will have to try to find a time and place possible,
even if not convenient, for the parties and their witnesses. When it is
apparent however that one of the parties is deliberately avoiding the
hearing, then the committee can go ahead without him.

71.2   INTERESTED PARTIES

(a) No member of a **protest committee** shall take part in the discussion or
    decision upon any disputed question in which he is an **interested party**,
    but this does not preclude him from giving evidence in such a case.

(b) A **party to a protest** who wishes to object to a member of the **protest
    committee** on the grounds that he is an **interested party** shall do so
    before evidence is taken at the hearing or as soon thereafter as he
    becomes aware of the conflict of interest.

We saw among the definitions at the beginning of Part VI those who are
interested parties, now we must consider the restraints on them. Rule
71.1(a) absolutely bars an interested party from sitting as a member of a
protest committee, and this is confirmed by RYA 1984/2 where it was held
that an interested party did not cease to be such because a party to the
protest was willing to accept him as a member of the protest committee. In
this case, at a redress hearing, the chairman of the protest committee had
taken part in the race. The decision reads: 'Council accepts that sometimes,
unavoidably, fellow competitors sit on a protest committee, but it is
nevertheless undesirable.'

Naturally an interested party may give evidence, indeed pertinent
evidence is mostly given by interested parties (the protestor, protestee and
their crews). Members of the RC are not interested parties, but should not
sit on protest committees when redress under 69(a) is at point. This is
discussed under Interested Party. See also US 111 under rule 70.2(a).

71.3   PROTESTS BETWEEN YACHTS IN SEPARATE RACES
        A **protest** occurring between yachts competing in separate races organised
        by different clubs shall be heard by a combined committee of the clubs
        concerned.

When more than one organising club organise races in the same area at the same time incidents may occur between yachts in different races. It is not laid down which of the two clubs shall receive the protest form, nor what time limit governs when they are different but the protestor would be well-advised to lodge his protest within the time limit set by his own club. However, at the same time he should inform the other club so as to put them in a position to comply with the requirement for a combined committee of the clubs concerned.

72   Acceptance or Refusal of a Protest

72.1   ACCEPTING A PROTEST

When the **protest committee** decides after examination that a **protest** conforms to all the requirements of rule 68, (Protests by Yachts) and is valid, it shall then call a hearing as soon as possible.

The protest committee is now chosen, accepted and ready to work, and the first thing it must do is to check the validity of the protest; ie that the various requirements of rule 68 have been complied with. When the protestor states on the form that the flag has been flown at the proper time and that he informed the protestee and when the latter makes no demur, the PC, if satisfied on the other counts, may declare the protest valid and go ahead with the hearing. An appeal on defects in the protest form usually fails when the appellant has raised no objection until after he has lost the case. When it is not clear that rule 68 has been complied with the PC will have to take evidence from the parties, and from outside parties if necessary before deciding whether the protest is valid.

Rule 68.5 allows forms to be made good, defects to be remedied, a process more honoured in the breach than the observance. However a permissive approach by the protest committee may rebound on the protestor.

The committee should not therefore proceed without a completed form, and it does not take much to fill in a few words. The PC shall then call a hearing as soon as possible. Usually this is immediately and the hearing follows straight on from the examination, but there may well be occasions when it is wiser to wait until, say, the next day, either because it is very late, or because some essential witness such as a measurer is not available, or for some other reason. Sometimes hearings are held, unavoidably, weeks after the event when memories have faded. This is always undesirable however necessary.

When two protests arise from the same incident, or from very closely connected incidents, it is advisable to hear them together in the presence of all the yachts concerned. This useful ruling from IYRU 112 will prevent having to hear all the evidence about one incident twice over.

72.2   REFUSING A PROTEST

When the **protest committee** decides that a **protest** does not conform to the requirements of rule 68, (Protests by Yachts), all **parties to the protest** concerned shall be notified that the **protest** will not be heard and of the reason for such decision. Such a decision shall not be reached without giving the protesting party an opportunity of bringing evidence that the requirements of rule 68 were met.

When there is doubt about the protest, the protestor may bring evidence if he so wishes to try to prove its validity. However, when nevertheless the protest committee still believe that the requirements of rule 68 have not been complied with, the protest must be refused. All parties to the protest must then be informed of the decision and the reason for it.

A protest committee's refusal of a protest cannot be justified by the fact that the rule alleged to have been infringed and cited in the protest was not the right one. (IYRU 44). Until facts are known it is not always possible to pick the right rule. In the law courts this problem is overcome by the police charging an accused with every possible misdemeanour, but this would not be useful on a protest form.

72.3   NOTIFICATION OF PARTIES
The **protest**, or a copy of it, shall be made available to all **parties to the protest**, and each shall be notified of the time and place of the hearing. A reasonable time shall be allowed for the preparation of a defence.

A paragraph which protects the protestee from being hurried or from not knowing what is alleged against him. The sooner he (and any other party to the protest) is in possession of a copy of the protest the better. The protest form is sometimes treated as if it were subject to the Official Secrets Act, but this is not so. A good photo-copier is of the greatest assistance for protests. However it is not essential for a copy to be *given* to the protestee, indeed it is often impossible and US 133 makes it clear that the protest need only be made available to the protestee. US 54 and US 82 are cases where the appeal was upheld, the latter reads (in full!): 'Since a copy of the protest was not made available to him, although requested both before the hearing and at it, the disqualification of the protestee is annulled.'

In IYRU 109 the appellant alleged that he was aware of the hearing only when he was told to attend it; he was refused permission to read the protest outside the room and had to read it during the hearing and that he was not given enough time to prepare a defence. The PC commented that the time of the hearing had been posted on the official notice board, that the protest had been available for over an hour before that time; the protestee had been informed that a protest had been lodged; that he had made no effort to prepare a defence; that he had had to be summoned from the club's dining room when the PC, the protestor and the witnesses were already assembled and ready to proceed. The appeal was dismissed: it is the duty of a protestee to protect himself by acting reasonably before a hearing.

73   **Hearings**

Rule 73 should be read in conjunction with Appendix 6 para 2.2 – para 2.6. which gives useful advice on procedure at the hearing. All is now ready: a suitable protest committee is assembled, the protest has been examined and found valid, the protestee has read the protest, prepared his defence and found his witnesses, other protests relating to the same incident have been conjoined and the show is ready to roll.

73.1   RIGHT TO BE PRESENT
The **parties to the protest**, or a representative of each, shall have the right to be present throughout the hearing of all the evidence and to question witnesses. Each witness, unless he is a member of the **protest committee**, shall be excluded, except when giving his evidence. Others may be admitted as observers at the discretion of the **protest committee**.

The parties to the protest or a representative of each have a right to be in the protest room from the beginning to the end, they also of course have a right to be present at any postponed hearing after an adjournment, at a re-opening in accordance with rule 73.5 or at a re-hearing required by the national authority after an appeal. Owners often try to include another member of the crew but such an attempt should be sternly resisted. One yacht one man, except for an interpreter when necessary. When an owner's representative has not sailed in the race and is neither a close relative nor known to be closely connected with the owner, it will be wise to ask for a letter of appointment. In US 144 the skippers were asked to leave the hearing and did so without objection at the time. On appeal the case was remanded for a re-hearing: 'The right of the parties to a protest to be present throughout the hearing is important and fundamental. The appellant was asked to leave the hearing before the taking of evidence from witnesses was completed and obeyed, but he should not have been asked to do so.'

When possible observers should be welcomed. There are two rules, that observers must not be potential witnesses and that they leave the room while the PC is reaching its decision. It is a good way to train protest committee members and sailors alike and I personally believe that the presence of others lessens the likelihood of lying.

In IYRU 122 the appeal was dismissed because although he had been excluded wrongly from the room during the hearing he was fully aware of the situation at the time and made no complaint about it. 'An adult yachtsman must take some share of the responsibility for protecting his rights including the obligation to make a timely objection when a PC fails to follow the procedural requirements of the rule. Additionally in this case the appellant did not allege any incorrect conclusions in his grounds for appeal.' When therefore you believe the PC is making a mistake say so, firmly and politely.

73.2   TAKING OF EVIDENCE
The **protest committee** shall take the evidence presented by the **parties to the protest** and such other evidence as it deems necessary.

The few words in this simple rule conceal the fact that the taking of evidence is a skilled art. If this were not so, lawyers would not command such high fees. It is difficult to grasp the fundamental situation clearly so that the correct questions can be asked. We all know how, in the discussion at the end of the hearing, someone says 'but we need to know whether she luffed or not,' or 'we never asked what the relative speeds of the two boats were.' With hindsight it appears almost impossible that one missed such obvious questions and one starts to appreciate counsels' skill. Never be afraid to recall witnesses or parties to ask another question, but remember that if a witness comes back the parties must come back too so that they can

VI

examine him. It surprised me when I first sat on the appeals committee to find how often at an incident near a mark the committee had failed to ask whether the inside yacht had established an overlap in proper time or not.

Theoretically a strict question-and-answer routine should happen between committee, protestor and protestee in turn, but in fact they too are usually inexperienced interrogators and, provided that the chairman keeps complete control of the hearing and does not let things run away, it is often possible to get the two parties discussing the incident freely. The more relaxed they become the more likely it is they will say something of use to the listening judges.

The question often heard is 'How many witnesses?' Since time is rarely unlimited, must all the witnesses be heard? US 212 tried to answer this question in a case where the protest committee had allowed the parties only one additional witness each, to which the protestee objected that he had four witnesses waiting to testify, two from his yacht and two independent competitors who had seen the incident. 'There may be circumstances where the protest committee would be fully justified in limiting the number of witnesses it will hear, particularly when the additional testimony would merely corroborate that of the prior witnesses. However ... when additional witnesses are offered from yachts other than those which are parties to the protest, a protest committee should be bound to investigate the nature of their testimony to a greater degree than in the case of additional witnesses from the crews of the yachts involved'. True if wordy! Of course there is the other point, that if you listen to all six crew members, instead of each telling the same tale, one or two often come out with a quite unexpected viewpoint which throws a new light on the whole incident.

'The protest committee shall take ... such other evidence as it deems necessary.' The committee is free to call whom it will. It need not advertise for witnesses – as do the police – but it should protect the interests of all the competitors by calling useful witnesses overlooked by the parties.

Hearsay evidence. The rules of hearsay evidence prevent what one person said being reported by another. It is not permitted in law courts hence the awkward policeman's phrase: 'I spoke to the inn keeper and as a result of what he told me, I went to the Marina ...' I do not suggest that the complicated laws of hearsay should be rigidly applied to protests, but remember that when the protestor says 'My crew said the distance was 6ft,' it is not evidence. And indeed when the crew is eventually called as a witness he may say something quite different, such as 'I couldn't see, I was behind the genoa'. Never take such reported evidence when it is possible to call the persons concerned and, when they are not available, largely discount its value. A protestor's statement such as 'The protestee did not hail for room, he shouted "your main is torn",' is not hearsay, it is direct evidence about the incident.

Leading questions. A leading question is not an important question as many people seem to think, it is a question which leads the questionee to give the required answer. 'Did you then alter the setting of the sails?' is not a leading question, 'You then pulled in your main, didn't you?' is. It expects the answer 'yes'. In the courts a lawyer may not lead his own client – for obvious reasons – he may only lead when cross-examining his opponent's witnesses. Again with untrained people (on both sides of the table) the rules cannot be rigidly applied, but a stern warning if a party begins to lead his witness can be enough. Otherwise the evidence is virtually worthless. 'Would you not say that the distance between the boats at that moment was about 6 feet?' asks the helmsman of his crew. The answer is unlikely to be reliable.

Normally when a statement is made by one party and not refuted or questioned by the other it may be accepted as fact. In RYA 68/32 it was held that the unsupported evidence of an interested party may be accepted by a PC as discharging an onus of proof, particularly if that evidence was not disputed by the other party or if it was considered by the PC to be consistent with other evidence.

Rule 9.2 introduces an interesting exception. It states that: 'when races are sailed in fog or at night, dead reckoning alone need not necessarily be accepted as evidence that a mark has been rounded or passed'. I take this to mean that if you refuse to believe a man when he says he saw and rounded a mark you are, to all intents and purposes accusing him of lying; with this rule you may disbelieve his DR without impugning his honour in any way.

Written evidence may be accepted at the discretion of the PC (RYA 63/35) but of course there will need to be a good reason why the witness cannot come in person to testify. The written evidence must be made available to the other side – or to both sides when the evidence comes from a third party. PCs will naturally be alert to the disadvantages of not having the witness available for questioning.

Anyone wishing to present photographic evidence (photograph or video) and anyone on a committee looking at it as evidence should read Appendix 11, Photographic Evidence.

73.3   EVIDENCE OF COMMITTEE MEMBER
Any member of the **protest committee** who speaks of his own observation of the incident shall give his evidence as a witness in the presence of the **parties to the protest**, and may be questioned.

When a member of the PC has seen the incident and wishes to give evidence he may do so, but only in the presence of the parties. The other members of the PC should be careful to ask him all the questions they want to at that time. The parties MUST feel secure that when they leave the room the witness's privileged position will not permit him to tell other aspects of the incident after they have left the room. It is the extension of this rule to permit juries to act as referees, in particular with regard to infringements of rule 54 such as rocking, ooching and pumping that is so unwelcome and criticised. Or at least it is unwelcome and criticised by those who get penalised. However it is not criticised by the class associations to such an extent that they are moved to alter the rule.

Appendix 8 now permits a member (or members) of an international jury who has instituted a protest under rule 70.2(a) to withdraw after giving his evidence without automatically down-grading the jury status and thereby voiding the waiver of right of appeal.

73.4   FAILURE TO ATTEND
Failure on the part of any **party to the protest**, or a representative, to make an effort to attend the hearing may justify the **protest committee** in deciding the **protest** as it thinks fit without a full hearing.

Note that when a party to the protest makes a genuine effort to attend a protest committee is not entitled to go ahead without him. In US 104 the skipper of no. 331 arrived at the meeting shortly before 8.30pm without dinner having had late business commitments and having encountered heavy traffic. On arrival he was informed that the protest of 438 v 331 had been heard at 8 o'clock and that 331 had been 'disqualified' – a rehearing was ordered. However he cannot deliberately make himself 'unavailable' and get away with it. As we have seen in IYRU 109, he must behave reasonably.

73.5 RE-OPENING A HEARING

A hearing may be re-opened when the **protest committee** decides it may have made a significant error or when material new evidence becomes available within a reasonable time. Requests from yachts for re-opening a hearing shall be lodged no later than 1800 of the day following the decision, unless the **protest committee** has reason to extend this time limit.

74 Decisions and Penalties

This rule is closely linked with rule 73.2 (Taking of Evidence), it is quite impossible to arrive at the facts without hearing the evidence first. The better the evidence the easier to arrive at the facts.

74.1 FINDING OF FACTS

The **protest committee** shall determine the facts and base its decision upon them. The finding of facts shall not be subject to appeal.

What is a fact or rather what is not a fact? – for PC's must keep facts and interpretations separate. The protestor makes a statement that she bore away and passed six feet astern of P. P states that S did not bear away, that P passed 6 feet ahead of S and S half a length astern of her. These are two contradictory statements. The jury now questions witnesses and comes to the following conclusions: that S did bear away, that S passed six feet astern of P and that there is doubt as to whether P could have passed ahead without a collision had S not borne away. These are 'the facts', Now the rules pertaining to these facts (Opposite Tacks – Basic Rule) rule 36, must be applied to them, together with the considerable amount of case law on such a much-used rule and the rule 'interpreted' for the case in question. It is this interpretation that an Appeals Authority can reverse, it cannot alter the facts. But the line is sometimes fine and difficult to draw.

IYRU 58 makes a very important point. Decisions must be made on facts, not on intent. A yacht that luffed with every intention of tacking was held not to have infringed rule 41.1 (Tacking) because she never went beyond head-to-wind (see definition of 'tacking'). In the fair-sailing rule and rule 75 intent will of course have to be considered. A man spills beer over the chairman of the jury: he did it in a temper – he infringed rule 75; he did it by mistake – he did nothing wrong; he put out a fire caused by a pipe in the chairman's pocket – he deserves a medal! Thus can circumstances alter cases.

IYRU 77 lays a heavy burden on a PC. When it is found that there has been a collision the PC may not dismiss the case. This is discussed under rule 74.4.

74.2   CONSIDERATION OF REDRESS

(a) When consideration of redress has been initiated as provided in rule 69, (Requests for Redress), or rule 70.3, (Yacht Materially Prejudiced), the **protest committee** shall decide whether the finishing position of a yacht or yachts has been materially prejudiced in any of the circumstances set out in rule 69.

(b) If so, the **protest committee** shall satisfy itself by taking appropriate evidence, especially before *abandoning* or *cancelling* the race, that it is aware of the relevant facts and of the probable consequences of any arrangement, to all yachts concerned for that particular race and for the series, if any, as a whole.

(c) The **protest committee** shall then make as equitable an arrangement as possible for all yachts concerned. This may be to let the results of the race stand, to adjust the points score or the finishing time of the prejudiced yacht, to *abandon* or *cancel* the race or to adopt some other means.

VI

We have already seen in rule 69 when redress may be granted; in many respects that rule cannot be separated from this one and the two should be studied together.

Rule 74.2(a) points out that it is the protest committee that must decide whether the yacht that is seeking redress is eligible for it or not. Sometimes it will be obvious; for example when a yacht has spent a long time rescuing another. At other times evidence will be needed. Sadly a lot of time is often wasted proving that the race committee has made a mistake because the amour propre of the race officer will not permit him to admit it.

Rule 74.2(b). Once decided that a yacht is, or as so often that several yachts are eligible for redress, the protest committee can proceed to considering what redress to give. The possibilities available to it and its duty are made clear in IYRU 38, a case in which one dinghy had gone to the assistance of another which had capsized. The decision went as follows: 'A yacht that, in rendering assistance, prejudices her chance of winning a prize, may seek redress, even when subsequent examination shows that no peril has arisen. From the evidence in this case there seems little doubt that the appellant prejudiced her finishing position. While a decision to take action under rule 69 lies within the discretion of the protest committee it ought to have agreed that rule 69 applied and have decided what action was to be taken.

'In regard to the committee's expressed fear of possible exploitation by an unscrupulous helmsman of such a situation, the rules are not based upon contemplation of misuse. Should instances of misuse occur rule 75.1 will suffice.

'A protest committee's options are not confined to abandoning or cancelling a race. Rule 74.2 states that a protest committee, after satisfying itself that redress is warranted, "shall make as equitable an arrangement as possible for all yachts concerned." To abandon or cancel a race merely because one yacht at the rear justifiably seeks redress might be most inequitable to all the other yachts. Depending upon circumstances, such an arrangement could include one of the following options:

1 to arrange a sail-off between the prejudiced yacht and those ahead of or close by her at the time, if they could be identified;

2 to award the prejudiced yacht breakdown points;

3 if the incident occurred close enough to the finishing line for her probable finishing position to be determined with some certainty, to consider her as having finished in that position;

4 to award the average points scored in the other races of a series, less the score of her worst race, when a discard is allowed.'

The object of the committee must be to be as fair as possible to all the competitors. While this is comparatively easy when the incident occurs at or near the finish, it is impossible when there is a mistake at the start. An error in the starting procedure which affects one or more yachts and which is let go ruins the race. Like Humpty Dumpty it cannot be put together again. When the race is abandoned, those which won will object; when places are given (or time) the prejudiced yachts will say they are given too few and the others will say too many; when average points are awarded to a good calm-weather yacht, others will maintain that she got average points on a day of high winds when she would have done badly. However there is no getting out of it, the jury is compelled by the rules to play at 'god' and must make as 'equitable arrangement as possible'. As much evidence as possible should be heard to get a good picture of the incident before redress is awarded.

One thing a jury may not do is to put yachts that have made a mistake ahead of those which have made no mistake. IYRU 102 states: 'It is not open to a race committee to override the definition of finishing, . . . when the race committee is satisfied that the course ordered was such that the other yachts were prejudiced so as to alter the result of the race, it is open to the race committee to award points to such yachts, but it would not be equitable for such yachts to rank higher than those yachts that finished correctly'.

74.3   MEASUREMENT PROTESTS

(a) A **protest** under rule 19, (Measurement or Rating Certificates), or class rules that a measurement, scantling or flotation rule has been infringed while *racing*, or that a classification or rating certificate is invalid, may be decided by the **protest committee** immediately after the hearing, provided that it is satisfied there is no reasonable doubt as to the interpretation or application of the rules. When the **protest committee** is not so satisfied, it shall refer the question, together with the facts found, to an authority qualified to resolve such questions. The **protest committee**, in making its decision, shall be governed by the report of the authority.

(b) In addition to the requirements of rule 74.7, the body that issued the certificate of the yacht concerned shall also be notified.

(c) When an appeal under rule 77, (Appeals), is lodged, the yacht may compete in further races, but subject to the results of that appeal.

Although the rule speaks of 'a protest under rule 19 *or* class rules,' an infringement of a class measurement rule must automatically be an infringement of rule 19. There are two sorts of protest;

1 that a rule has been infringed while racing – eg too big a genoa has been used, the main has been hoisted above the black band, the mast has been raked further aft than is permitted, etc;

2 that the certificate is invalid: eg out of date, hull scantlings not to class rules etc.

When the race or protest committee is faced with a measurement protest it will call a hearing, as for any other protest, and proceed to hear the parties and witnesses – expert witnesses such as measurers and class officials. There is a great possibility that the committee will be able to arrive at an answer without outside help, and when it can it must do so. However the occasion may arise when it cannot interpret the rule without help and must refer the question to a qualified authority. Class rules sometimes define the qualified authority, or there may be a chief measurer to whom ultimate reference can be made. It is wise, when possible, to know the whereabouts of this person or persons, before a series starts, so that problems can be dealt with as expeditiously as possible.

Case law varies on the question as to whether a protest flag is necessary for a measurement protest or not. When the infringement occurs while racing the protest flag should be hoisted as for any other protest, when the protest comes under **2** (above) and notice has been given to the yacht concerned and to the race committee probably not. The time limit for protests of this kind was discussed under rule 68.3. It is only fair to bring measurement protests as soon as the facts become known, not, as in US 190, where the protest alleged the carrying of incorrectly stamped and unmeasured sails for the whole series, the protest being lodged after the last of seven races. The IOR states that the rating authority in whose waters the yacht is lying is the 'authority qualified' and goes on to require that rating authority to help a protest committee when asked to do so. Appendices 5 and 6 lay down details of Administrative Protests, ie protests made when there is no racing and procedure when measurement errors are found during a series.

74.4 PENALTIES
When the **protest committee** after finding the facts, or the race committee acting under rule 70.1, (Action by Race or Protest Committee), decides that:

(a) a yacht has infringed any of the **rules**, or

(b) in consequence of her neglect of any of the **rules**, a yacht has compelled other yachts to infringe any of the **rules**,

she shall be disqualified, unless the sailing instructions applicable to that race provide some other penalty and, in the case of (b), the other yachts shall be exonerated. Such disqualification or other penalty shall be imposed irrespective of whether the **rule** that led to the disqualification or penalty was mentioned in the **protest**, or the yacht that was at fault was mentioned or protested, e.g., the protesting yacht or a third yacht may be disqualified and the protested yacht exonerated.

The authority of all protest committees to disqualify or otherwise penalise a yacht stems from this rule. It is therefore one of the most important in the book and we need to look at its words and implications very carefully.

Action under rule 74.4, to penalise, or indeed not to penalise, can only follow a decision that a yacht has infringed a rule – a decision reached either by the protest committee after finding the facts during the hearing of a valid protest or, summarily, by the race committee under its powers to disqualify without a hearing in accordance with rule 70.1.

The options open to the committee are as follows:
1 When there was no collision it may decide that no rule has been infringed

and dismiss the protest(s).

2 It may decide that a rule has been infringed and penalise the infringing yacht, or that both yachts have infringed rules and penalise both. Occasionally this means disqualifying the protestor herself, as occurred in US 176 when *Menehune* protested *Rambler* (for infringing what rule is not disclosed) but was disqualified herself under rule 52 for hitting the committee vessel and failing to protest.

3 It may decide that a third yacht was the cause of the trouble and penalise her instead (see 74.4(b)).

4 It may permit a protest to be withdrawn under 68.9 when the protest has been brought with the object of satisfying rule 33.2 and contact has been found, as a fact, to have been 'minor and unavoidable'.

5 It may not dismiss a protest where there has been a collision (IYRU 77) because when two yachts collide there must have been an infringement of a rule. (Competitors should remember this; when poor Muggins has infringed a rule he did not know existed, he will be disqualified because the protest committee *has no other choice*).

6 When there has been an infringement of rule 26, it may warn or otherwise act according to rule 26.5.

7 In spite of 5 above, protest committees are obliged to dismiss any protest under 46.2 'A yacht shall not be penalised for fouling a yacht that she is attempting to assist . . .'

8 It may at its discretion, decide not to penalise a yacht losing gear and thereby infringing rule 53.3 – Means of Anchoring.

9 It may not disqualify when flag 'Y' is displayed after the warning signal see rule 4.1 'Y'.

Rule 74.4(b) permits the exoneration of an infringing yacht when she was compelled to infringe a rule by another yacht. In IYRU 19 (Fig. 108) P tried and failed to cross ahead of M, M tacked to avoid her, hailing as she did so. S tried to respond but there was contact. P retired, S protested M under rule 36 and the protest committee, commenting that M had had sufficient time to take avoiding action to keep clear of both P and S, disqualified M under rule 32(!) M appealed, successfully. 'P, which properly retired', went the decision, 'infringed rule 36. She caused the problem and M, in the circumstances, took proper action to mitigate the effects of P's error of judgement. Both M and S were the innocent victims of P's failure to observe the rules. M is re-instated and S not to be penalised.'

US 138 (Fig. 6) is another good example where A was exonerated for hitting the mark because B had wrongly pushed her into it. This sort of situation most commonly arises at marks where A tries to barge, not having a timely overlap. To avoid a collision B bears away, as does C, but in so doing touches D outside her. Then, provided that the evidence shows that B was entitled to room from C and C from D, A will be penalised and take the blame for the collision down the line. In real life it often does not happen so neatly. There is often a missing link because of unsatisfactory evidence etc.

The protest committee must disqualify a yacht for infringing rule XX even when rule XX has never been mentioned in the protest or by the protestee at the hearing. In US 186 (a case looked at under rule 35) the two boats protested each other under rules 37, every clause of 41 and 42.2, but the decision was based on rule 35. This marks a very big departure from the law where, if you have not been charged under section 1234 you cannot be

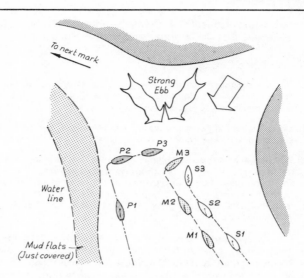

Fig. 108

found guilty of breaking section 1234. Although at first sight this provision may seem unreasonable, if it were not so every protest would cite every rule – just to make sure. When the committee's decision is correctly based on the facts found at the hearing the subject matter of the relevant rule must have been discussed.

The committee must impose a penalty on an infringing yacht irrespective of whether the yacht was at fault was mentioned or protested. That is to say the protesting yacht herself may be penalised (as we saw) or a third yacht. Naturally this is subject to this third yacht being proceeded against according to rules 70.2(e) and 73, with all her rights to a hearing and to call and question witnesses undiminished.

74.5   ALTERNATIVE PENALTIES
When so prescribed in the sailing instructions, the procedure and penalty for infringing a rule of Part IV shall be as provided in Appendix 3, Alternative Penalties for Infringement of a Rule of Part IV.

The IYRR only supplies systems of penalties for infringements of Part IV. These are the 760° Turns and the Percentage Place Penalty systems, both described in Appendix 3. Many clubs use other systems however, penalising rather than disqualifying for infringements of rules other than those of Part IV. Such systems need to be carefully explained in SIs so that competitors know what to expect. It is desirable for protest committees to have some idea before they start judging what they are going to impose for each kind of infringement. They are by name and nature juries, not judges, and should have only to decide 'guilty' or 'not guilty', not the amount of the fine – a very subjective business. This problem never arose with the old system when disqualification was the only penalty, but now it is important to make sure that like infringements receive like punishments.

74.6   POINTS AND PLACES

(a) For the purpose of awarding points in a series, a retirement after an infringement of the **rules** shall not rank as a disqualification. This penalty can be imposed only in accordance with rule 74.4.

(b) When a yacht either is disqualified or has retired, the following yachts shall each be moved up one place.

(c) When a yacht is penalised by being removed from a series or a part of a series, no races are to be rescored and no changes are to be made in the scores of other yachts, except that, when the incident from which the penalty resulted occurred in a particular race, she shall be disqualified from that race and yachts *finishing* behind her in that race shall each be moved up one place.

Rule 74.6(a) is an encouragement to retire rather than go to a hearing and be disqualified, rule 74.6(b) is simple with respect to one race but its problems are shown in US 214 where a boat was disqualified after the sixth race of a series from the whole series because of the misbehaviour of the crew. The alteration to the points system caused by moving boats up various places made a difference to who won the series and on appeal it was held that, when penalising in retrospect, places should not change. Most points systems try, in vain, to be totally fair. But the sting is taken out of what may appear arbitrary results when they can be foreseen.

74.7   THE DECISION

(a) After making its decision, the **protest committee** shall promptly communicate the following to the **parties to the protest**:

     (i)   the facts found,

     (ii)   the **rule** or **rules** judged applicable,

     (iii)   the decision and grounds on which it is based,

     (iv)   the yacht or yachts penalised, if any, and

     (v)   the penalty imposed, if any, or the redress granted, if any.

(b) A **party to the protest** shall on request be supplied with:

     (i)   the above details in writing, and

     (ii)   unless irrelevant, a diagram of the incident endorsed by the **protest committee**.

This is an administrative rule usually dealt with by reading out the PC's decision to the parties and then sticking it up on the board for all to see. The detail will depend on the time available. When there is a long queue of protests to be heard, one can read a brief decision and then post a fuller written version on the notice board. When all the facts are found it is surprising how easily the correct rule to apply follows. When there is time it is always advisable for the PC to make a diagram. It may be possible to endorse the protestor's or even the protestee's, but early action takes much of the labour out of the preparation of an appeal if such becomes necessary.

SECTION C—Special Rules

75 Gross Infringement of Rules or Misconduct

75.1 PENALTIES BY THE RACE COMMITTEE OR PROTEST COMMITTEE
After a finding of gross infringement of the **rules** or of a gross breach of good manners or sportsmanship, the race committee or **protest committee** may exclude a competitor, and a yacht when appropriate, either from further participation in a series or from the whole series, or take other disciplinary action, proceeding in accordance with rules 73, (Hearings), and 74.1, (Finding of Facts). The committee shall report any penalty imposed to the national authority and to the national authority of the competitor and of the yacht.

VI

Action under rule 75.1 is not a protest within the defined sense of the word. It is not a rule that can be infringed by a yacht but an action brought by the race or protest committee against someone for 'gross infringement of the rules or of a gross breach of good manners or sportsmanship'. It is a rule to be used with the greatest care because, in my opinion, it reflects on the person's character because he or she has acted with intent. It is this 'intent' that differentiates the action under this rule. Naturally a committee will limit the scope of its action. It will not act under rule 75.1 when a man beats his wife or defrauds his company, that is, when the action is not linked to the sport in any way. But the rule is properly invoked when a competitor *during* the regatta or series, *at* the site of the event (host club, marina, race area) conducts himself improperly towards someone connected with the event (organisers, fellow competitors, marina staff, press). Apart from anything else some protection needs to be given to the good name of the sport. The enormous quantity of volunteer assistance on which every race rests would not be forthcoming so willingly if some stand were not taken. No rules can be laid down, each sad case is unique, fortunately a heartfelt apology and a dressing down is often all that is necessary.

Case law is rare; In US 249 a crew beat up the skipper of another, competing, yacht. The committee recommended to clubs in the area that both the owner and the crew (an owner being responsible for the behaviour of his crew) be prohibited from racing for five years. On appeal this was reduced to two.

IRYU 78 shows the power of rule 75.1 in comparison with FRC – The Fair Sailing Rule. As the sixth and final race of a championship series began A's accumulated score was such that the only way she could lose the prize was for B to finish ahead of her and among the first three of the 48 competitors. A started prematurely and was recalled by loud hailer. About 70 to 100 metres beyond the starting line she turned back but she had sailed only some 20 to 30 metres toward the line when she met B which had started correctly. Instead of continuing toward the pre-start side of the line A turned and sailed on top of B.

The race committee hailed A again that she was still a premature starter and received a wave of acknowledgement in return but A continued to sail the course harrassing B throughout the windward leg. When A and B reached the windward mark they were last but one and last respectively, whereupon A retired. B ultimately finished in 22nd place.

Since it was obvious to the race committee that A continued to race solely for the purpose of harrassing B it called a hearing on its own initiative under rule 70.2(a). A was disqualified under rule 51.1(b) (Sailing the Course) and the Fundamental Rule – Fair Sailing. She then discarded the race and won the championship. She also appealed her disqualification under the Fair Sailing rule, asserting that she believed she had returned and started correctly.

Dismissing the appeal the Norwegian Yachting Association said: 'The facts established by the race committee show gross infringements of the rules and of sportsmanship. Such deliberate attempts to win by unfair means should be dealt with severely. To disqualify A in the sixth race only is not enough, since she would then achieve the purpose of her unfair action and become the winner of the championship. Rule 75.1 can be applied to exclude A from the entire series and such action would be well within the spirit of the racing rules. A, therefore, is excluded from the whole series and all her results shall be struck from the records as if she had not started in any of the races.'

In a rather similar case (RYA 84/7) it was stated that when a competitor infringed a rule he was obliged to retire promptly. A competitor who did not do so and then deliberately hindered a yacht that was racing, committed a gross breach of good sportsmanship. Occasionally a case arising from an incident not on the water comes to appeal. In RYA 77/12, it seems that a competitor made defamatory remarks about the integrity and capability of the flag officer and race committee of the club in front of a lot of people. The committee demanded an apology before the next race in the series, and when it was not forthcoming disqualified the offender under rule 75.1. On appeal the RYA stated: 'An allegation of gross misbehaviour has to be proved, this necessarily involves a hearing and the taking of evidence ... Thereafter, the race committee having decided that such an infringement occurred, rule 75.1 does not place any restrictions on the freedom of a race committee to take disclipinary action.'

75.2 PENALTIES BY THE NATIONAL AUTHORITY

Upon receipt of a report of gross infringement of the **rules** or a gross breach of good manners or sportsmanship or a report of a penalty imposed under rule 75.1, a national authority may conduct an investigation and, when appropriate, a hearing and take such action as it deems appropriate against the person or persons or the yacht involved. Such action may include disqualification from participating in any race held in its jurisdiction for any period or other disciplinary action. The national authority shall report any penalty imposed to the national authority of the competitor and of the yacht and to the International Yacht Racing Union. The IYRU shall inform all national authorities, which may also apply a penalty.

It is not within the scope of this book to discuss the powers of national authorities. Provided they do not conflict with a man's rights under the law of the land, they are presumably limitless (though if they do not find approbation from organising authorities and class associations they may be ineffective). Each national authority will prescribe the procedure to be adopted.

76 Liability

76.1 DAMAGES

The question of damages arising from an infringement of any of the **rules** shall be governed by the prescriptions, if any, of the national authority.

76.2 MEASUREMENT EXPENSES

Unless otherwise prescribed by the **protest committee**, the fees and expenses entailed by a **protest** on measurement or classification shall be paid by the unsuccessful party.

The only point worth noting is that where measurement expenses are concerned the protest committee may decide about the fees. It may decide that the unsuccessful party pays the costs, as is written in the rule, but it may consider that the other side has also been negligent or careless and caused some of the expense unnecessarily, in which case it may apportion the costs between the parties.

SECTION D—Appeal Procedure

77 Appeals

77.1 RIGHT OF APPEAL

Except when governed by rule 1.7 (Authority for Organising, Conducting and Judging Races), the following appeals and references may be made to the national authority concerned:

(a) a yacht that is a **party to a protest** may appeal against a decision of a **protest committee**;

(b) a race committee may appeal only against a decision of an independent protest committee constituted as provided in rule 1.5(c), (Authority for Organising, Conducting and Judging Races);

(c) a race committee or protest committee may refer its own decision for confirmation or correction of its interpretation of the **rules**;

(d) a person or a yacht penalised under rule 75.1, (Penalties by the Race Committee or Protest Committee), may appeal against the decision.

77.2 TIME LIMIT AND DEPOSIT

An appeal or reference shall be made within such period after receipt of the **protest committee's** decision and be accompanied by such deposit as the national authority may prescribe.

77.3 INTERPRETATION OF RULES

An appeal or reference shall be made solely on a question of interpretation of the **rules**. A national authority shall accept the **protest committee's** finding of facts, except that, when it is not satisfied with the facts presented, it may, when practicable, request further information or return the case to the **protest committee** for a re-hearing.

77.4   WITHDRAWAL OF APPEAL

An appeal lodged with the national authority may be withdrawn when the appellant accepts the original decision.

77.5   INTERESTED PARTIES

No **interested party** nor any member of the **protest committee** concerned shall take part in the discussion or the decision upon an appeal or reference.

77.6   POWER TO UPHOLD OR REVERSE A DECISION

The national authority shall have the power to uphold or reverse a decision, and when it is of the opinion, from the facts found by the **protest committee**, that any yacht that is a **party to the protest** has infringed an applicable **rule**, it shall disqualify or penalise her, irrespective of whether the **rule** that led to the disqualification was mentioned in the decision.

77.7   DECISIONS

The decision of the national authority shall be final and shall be communicated in writing to all the **parties to the protest**, who shall be bound by the decision.

The most useful long-term work of an appeals committee is probably to ensure that there is consistency in the decisions and judgements of protest committees throughout the area it governs. If there were no appeals authority it would be easy to conceive of a protest committee in Cowes interpreting the rules in a different way from that at Grafham Water; or perhaps the Dragon class would sail to a slightly different understanding of rule 37 from that of the Lasers. This would make it almost impossible for helmsmen to change area or, alternatively, classes. The IYRU, by its November meetings and its case book strives continually to arrive at international consistency, so that at international meetings such as World Championships or the Olympic Games, helmsmen from all over the world will be sailing to the same interpretations of the rules.

It follows from this that appeals on new or difficult interpretations are always welcome, while appeals on facts are not acceptable. Provided that the protest committee has followed the requirements of Part VI for a fair and valid hearing, an appeal committee will not reverse its findings of fact. After hearing all the evidence, when the protest committee states that L was six feet from W, an appeals committee will not change that figure to 10, for it has no reliable knowledge on which to base such a change. However, the interpretation of that number, whether six feet was or was not 'ample room', may well belong in the province of an appeals committee.

By means of prescriptions, national authorities arrange their appeal systems in different ways. In the UK, the RYA is the only appeal authority, cases being heard by the Racing Rules Committee at approximately monthly meetings. In the USA there is a two-tiered system of, first, district appeals and then the USYRU Appeals Committee. Most of the work of the latter is carried out by correspondence.

Appeals and references can only be made after a decision. No decision, no appeal. It would be most unsatisfactory if the appeals committee had to do the protest committee's work for it. Even when there has been a decision the yacht appealing, the appellant, must have been a party to the protest. For instance, when there has been a redress hearing, a yacht that was not at the hearing, and whose point of view has not been taken into account, cannot turn directly to the appeals committee for help. She must seek redress in her turn from the protest committee and, if she does not like the new decision, *then* she may appeal (IYRU 119).

While any protest committee may refer its decision for confirmation or otherwise by the national authority, a race committee may only appeal against the decision of an independent protest committee. When the protest committee is a sub-committee of the race committee itself – as is normal in all club racing – the race committee is expressly forbidden by rule 77.1(a) to appeal. This occurred in IYRU 111, where an appeal was refused, but the problem was solved by accepting the case as a reference.

No further comment is needed about appeals as the procedure is clearly laid down. However as one who has struggled with appeals for years, I must make a personal appeal to all readers who have anything to do with the preparation of appeals. Remember that the appeals committee knows *nothing*. The names of the people, the class of boat, the weather, tides, geography, timing, the incident, the outcome – nothing, so make sure you supply it. If possible ask a total outsider to read the papers before sending them in to see if you have covered all the points.

VI

78   Particulars to be Supplied in Appeals

78.1   The appeal or reference to the national authority shall be in writing and shall contain the following particulars, so far as they are applicable:

(a) a copy of the notice of race or regatta, the sailing instructions and amendments thereto, and any other conditions governing the event;

(b) a copy of the **protest** or **protests** prepared in accordance with rule 68.5, (Protests by Yachts), and of all other written statements that may have been submitted by the **parties to the protest**;

(c) the observations of the **protest committee** thereon, a full statement of the facts found, the decision and the grounds thereof;

(d) a diagram, prepared or endorsed by the **protest committee** in accordance with the facts found by it, showing:

    (i)   the course to the next *mark*, or, when close by, the *mark* itself with the required side;

    (ii)   the direction and force of the wind;

    (iii) the set and rate of the tidal stream or current, if any;

    (iv)   the depth of the water, if relevant, and

    (v)   the positions and tracks of all yachts involved. It is preferable to show yachts sailing from the bottom of the diagram towards the top;

(e) the grounds of the appeal to be supplied by the appellant in accordance with rule 77.3, (Appeals);

(f) the observations, if any, upon the appeal by the **protest committee**, the race committee or any of the **parties to the protest**.

78.2   The race committee shall notify all **parties to the protest** that an appeal will be lodged and shall invite them to make observations upon it. Any such observations shall be forwarded with the appeal.

The Particulars to be supplied in Appeals. This is really a list of instructions to club secretaries or whichever flag officer has been volunteered for the job. I would add to the list in the rules the following points: date each document, avoiding the situation where the poor appeals committee do not know which was written first. Check that sail numbers, boat names and helmsmens' names are cross referenced. It is possible to spend hours discovering that K666, helmed by J Smith is the same boat as *Daisy* owned by R Green! Mark supporting letters with the relevance of the writer: the signature 'John' (or illegible) may be the appellant, the protestor, a witness, the commodore or whoever.

Appendices

In the rules of the International Yacht Racing Union 1985–88, there are no less than thirteen appendices. Only the first four appendices and commentary are given here. National authorities may be found to have added or substituted different appendices.

APPENDIX 1—Definition of an Amateur and Eligibility Regulations

1   Amateur

1.1   For the purpose of international yacht races in which yachts are required to have one or more amateurs on board and in other races with similar requirements, an amateur is a yachtsman who engages in yacht racing as a pastime as distinguished from a means of obtaining a livelihood or part-time compensation. No yachtsman shall lose amateur status by reason of his livelihood being derived from designing or constructing yachts, yacht parts, sails or accessories; or from similar professions associated with the sport; or solely from the maintenance (but not the *racing*) of yachts.

1.2   Competing in a race or series in which a monetary prize is offered, or a prize having a value greater than US$300, other than a prize awarded only for temporary possession, is ground for loss of amateur status unless prior to the event:

(i)   the competitor assigns to the IYRU, his national authority or his national Olympic committee all his rights to such prize, or

(ii)   the organising authority obtains its national authority's consent to a prize (not being money) having a value greater than US$300.

1.3 Any yachtsman whose amateur status is questioned or is in doubt may apply to his national authority for recognition of his amateur status. Any such applicant may be required to provide such particulars and evidence and to pay such fees as the national authority may prescribe. Recognition may be suspended or cancelled by the national authority granting it, and, upon application by the competitor affected, the authority may reinstate recognition of amateur status following a period of at least two years absence from the sport.

1.4 The Permanent Committee of the IYRU or any tribunal nominated by the chairman of that committee may review the decision of any national authority affecting the amateur status of a yachtsman for the purpose of competing in international races.

1.5 For the purpose of participation in the Olympic Regatta an amateur is required to conform to the eligibility rules of the International Olympic Committee. Information on these eligibility requirements is available from all national authorities.

2 I.O.C. Rule 26—Eligibility Code

To be eligible for participation in the Olympic Games, a competitor must:

— observe and abide by the Rules of the International Olympic Committee (IOC) and in addition the rules of his or her International Federation (IF), as approved by the IOC, even if the Federation's rules are more strict than those of the IOC;

— not have received any financial rewards or material benefit in connection with his or her sports participation, except as permitted in the bye-laws to this rule.

BYE-LAWS TO RULE 26

A. Each IF is responsible for the wording of the eligibility code relating to its sport, which must be approved by the Executive Board in the name of the IOC.

B. The observation of Rule 26 and of the eligibility codes of IFs are under the responsibility of IFs and National Olympic Committee (NOC) involved. The Eligibility Commission of the IOC will ensure the application of these provisions.

C. All cases of infringement of Rule 26 of the IOC and of the eligibility codes of IFs shall be communicated by the respective IF or NOC to the IOC to be taken in consideration by its eligibility commission. In accordance with Rule 23 and its bye-law, the accused competitor may request to be heard by the Executive Board whose decision will be final.

GUIDELINES TO ELIGIBILITY CODE FOR THE IFs

A. The following regulations are based on the principle that an athlete's health must not suffer nor must he or she be placed at a social or material disadvantage as a result of his or her preparation for and participation in the Olympic Games and international sports competitions. In accordance with Rule 26, the IOC, the IFs, the NOCs, and the National Authorities will assume responsibility for the protection and support of athletes.

B. All competitors, men or women, who conform to the criteria set out in Rule 26, may participate in the Olympic Games, except those who have:

1. been registered as professional athletes or professional coaches in any sport. Each National Authority shall provide a means for registering professional yachtsmen and women, and professional coaches. In this connection:

   (a) Professional yachtsmen or women shall be persons who do not comply with the definition of an amateur as defined in Appendix 1 of the current Yacht Racing Rules.

   (b) Professional coaches shall be persons who obtain their principal means of livelihood from teaching the skills of yacht racing.

2. signed a contract as a professional athlete or professional coach in any sport before the official closing of the Olympic Games.

3. accepted without the knowledge of their IF, National Authority or NOC a material advantage for their preparation or participation in yachting competition except:

   (a) either from, or with the permission of their National Authority; or

   (b) from funds held by the National Authority however obtained which are being held by that Authority or Trust for or on behalf of either an individual or class of yachtsmen.

   (c) National Authorities may issue guidelines for the receipt of such material advantages which shall cover:

   (i) Reimbursement of expenses properly incurred in preparation for, and competing in an international or Olympic event.

   (ii) The provision of equipment for such events.

   (iii) Living and accommodation allowances and including allowances in lieu of normal salary, etc., if the same is lost due to the yachtsman engaging in such preparation or competition.

   (d) The receipt of money as a prize, or otherwise, not exceeding US$300 shall not be a breach of this clause.

4. allowed their person, name, picture, or sports performances to be used for advertising, except when their IF, NOC or National Authority has entered into a contract for sponsorship or equipment. All payment must be made to the IF, NOC or National Authority concerned, and not to the athlete.

5. carried advertising material on their person or clothing in the Olympic Games and Games under the patronage of the IOC, other than trademarks on technical equipment or clothing as agreed by the IOC with the IFs.

   In the absence of any special agreement by the IOC with the IF's, advertising material on clothing shall not exceed that on clothing commercially available to the public *provided however* that only one maker's mark may be displayed on clothing worn by yachtsmen and provided that such a mark shall fit within a square not exceeding 100mm by 100mm.

6. in the practice of sport and in the opinion of the IOC, manifestly contravened the spirit of fair play in the exercise of sport, particularly by the use of doping or violence.

APPENDIX 2—Sailboard Racing Rules

A sailboard is a yacht using a free sail system. A free sail system means a swivel-mounted mast not supported in a permanent position while sailing. Sailboard races shall be sailed under the International Yacht Racing Rules modified as follows:

1 Part I—Definitions

1.1 *Leeward* and *Windward*—The *windward* side of a sailboard is the side that is, or, when head to wind or with the wind astern, was, towards the wind, regardless of the direction in which the sailboard is sailing, except when the wind is coming over her stern from the same side as her sail and boom are on, in which case the *windward* side is the other side. The opposite side is the *leeward* side.

When neither of two sailboards on the same *tack* is *clear astern*, the one on the *windward* side of the other is the *windward sailboard*. The other is the *leeward sailboard*.

1.2 *Capsized* and *Recovering*

(a) *Capsized*—A sailboard shall rank as being *capsized* from the moment her masthead touches the water until her masthead is lifted from the water.

(b) *Recovering*—A sailboard shall rank as *recovering* from a *capsize* from the moment her masthead is lifted from the water until her sail is out of the water and has filled.

2 Part III—General Requirements

2.1 Rule 19—Measurement or Rating Certificates

Rule 19.1—When so prescribed by the national authority, a numbered and dated device on the board, daggerboard and sail shall rank as a measurement certificate.

2.2 Rule 23—Anchor

An anchor and chain or rope need not be carried.

2.3 Rule 24—Life Saving Equipment

A safety line shall prevent the mast separating from the hull.

2.4 Rule 25—Class Insignia, National Letters and Sail Numbers

Rule 25.1(a)—The class insignia shall be displayed once on each side of the sail. It shall fit within a rectangle of 0.5 m², the longer dimension of which shall not exceed one metre. It shall not refer to anything other than the manufacturer or class and shall not consist of more than two letters and three numbers. When approved by the IYRU or a national authority within its jurisdiction, this insignia shall not be considered to be advertising.

Rule 25.1(c)—A sailboard shall carry on her sail a sail number allotted either to the board or to its owner. This number shall be issued by a national authority or its duly authorised body.

3   **Part IV—Right of Way Rules**

3.1   Rule 33.2—Contact between Yachts Racing

As between each other, rule 33.2 shall not apply to sailboards.

3.2   Rule 38.2—Same Tack—Luffing and Sailing above a Proper Course after Starting

Rule 40—Same Tack—Luffing before Starting

For "mainmast" read "foot of mast".

3.3   Recovering from a Capsize

A sailboard *recovering* from a *capsize* shall not obstruct a sailboard or yacht under way.

3.4   Sail out of the Water when Starting

When approaching the starting line to *start*, a sailboard shall have her sail out of the water and in a normal position, except when *capsized* unintentionally.

3.5   Sailing Backward when Starting

When approaching the starting line to *start* or when on the course side of the starting line, a sailboard sailing or drifting backward shall keep clear of other sailboards or yachts that are *starting* or have *started* correctly.

4   **Part V—Other Sailing Rules**

Rule 54.1—Means of Propulsion

Dragging a foot in the water to check way is permissible.

5   **Part VI—Protests, Penalties and Appeals**

Rule 68—Protests by Yachts

A sailboard need not display a flag in order to signify her intention to protest as required by rule 68.2, but, except when rule 68.3 applies, she shall notify the other sailboard or yacht by hail at the first reasonable opportunity and the race committee as soon as possible after *finishing* or retiring.

6   **APPENDIX 3—Alternative Penalties for Infringement of a Rule of Part IV**

6.1   720° Turns

Two full 360° turns of the board shall satisfy the provision of the 720° turns penalty. The sailing instructions may prescribe a greater penalty by increasing the number of turns required.

6.2   Percentage

A sailboard need not display Code flag "I" to acknowledge an infringement. She shall notify the other sailboard or yacht by hail immediately and the race committee as soon as possible after *finishing* or retiring.

7   Rules for Multi-Mast Sailboards

7.1   Part IV—Rule 38.2 and Rule 40

The normal station of the helmsman is the normal station of the crew member controlling the mainsail. The mainsail is the foremost sail and the mainmast is the foremost mast.

7.2   Appendix 2—Rule 1.2(a) *Capsized*

A multi-mast sailboard shall rank as being *capsized* from the moment all her mastheads touch the water until one masthead is lifted from the water.

7.3   Appendix 2 —Rule 1.2(b) *Recovering*

A multi-mast sailboard shall rank as a sailboard *recovering* from a *capsize* from the moment one masthead is lifted from the water until all her sails are out of the water and they have filled.

7.4   Appendix 2—Rule 3.4—Sail out of the Water when Starting

For "sail" read "sails".

Board sailors should be aware that this Appendix is not fixed for four years as is the rest of the rules, it is subject to change each November, although naturally change will only be made when considered essential. The appendix consists of a number of adjustments to the rules themselves, defining capsized and recovering, redefining leeward and windward (because sailboards can sail in either direction), coping with such situations as waiting for the start capsized (not allowed except by mistake), sailing backwards when starting (must keep clear), dragging a foot in the water (allowed) 720° turns (board only – but more turns suggested) and finally rules for multimast sail boards. There is nothing difficult about the appendix, (and no case law) it just needs to be read.

APPENDIX 3—Alternative Penalties for Infringement of a Rule of Part IV

Experience indicates that the 720° turns penalty is most satisfactory for small boats in relatively short races, but that it can be dangerous for large yachts and in restricted waters and not sufficiently severe in long races. The 20% penalty is relatively mild and is designed to encourage acknowledgement of infringements and willingness to protest when not acknowledged. Both systems keep yachts racing.

Either of the following alternatives to disqualification may be used by including in the sailing instructions a provision such as the following (or if preferred the selected penalty may be quoted in full):

"The 720° turns penalty (or the percentage penalty) as provided in rule 74.5, (Alternative Penalties), and Appendix 3, Alternative Penalties for Infringement of a Rule of Part IV, of the yacht racing rules shall apply for infringement of a rule of Part IV."

1	**720° Turns**

A yacht that acknowledges infringing a rule of Part IV may exonerate herself by making two full 360° turns (720°), subject to the following provisions:

1.1   When the yacht infringed against intends to protest, she shall act in accordance with rule 68, (Protests by Yachts), and hail the infringing yacht immediately.

1.2   With or without such notification, a yacht that realises that she has infringed a rule of Part IV shall acknowledge her infringement by immediately starting to get clear of other yachts and, when well clear, shall forthwith make her turns. While doing so, she shall keep clear of all other yachts until she has completed her turns and is on a *proper course* for the next *mark*.

1.3   The turns may be made in either direction but both in the same direction, with the second full 360° turn following immediately on the first.

1.4   When the infringement occurs before the starting signal, the infringing yacht shall make her turns after the starting signal.

1.5   When an infringement occurs at the finishing line, the infringing yacht shall make her turns on the last leg of the course before being officially *finished*.

1.6   When a yacht acknowledges fault but claims that the other yacht involved in the incident has infringed a rule of Part IV, she shall act in accordance with rule 68, (Protests by Yachts), hail the other yacht immediately and exonerate herself by making her turns. She shall not be further penalised for the infringement she has acknowledged by making her turns, except as set out in paragraphs 1.9 and 1.10.

1.7   When neither yacht acknowledges fault, a **protest** may be lodged in accordance with rule 68, (Protests by Yachts), and the sailing instructions.

1.8 Failure to observe the above requirements will render a yacht that has infringed a rule of part IV liable to disqualification or other penalty, but when an infringing yacht's turns do not conform to the above requirements, the yacht infringed against is relieved of further obligations under rule 33.2, (Contact between Yachts Racing).

1.9 An infringing yacht involved in a collision that results in serious damage to either yacht shall be liable to disqualification.

1.10 The **protest committee** may disqualify a yacht for an infringement of the rules that results in an advantage to the infringing yacht after completing the 720° turns, whether or not serious damage results. The **protest committee's** action shall be governed by rule 70.2, (Action by Race or Protest Committee).

Rule 68.4 (Informing the Protested Yacht) has already told us that when *Daisy* intends to protest another yacht when this appendix is in force, she must hail 'immediately'. It may not be possible to put up a protest flag immediately, but a hail is always possible. Not only must she hail but she must try to inform *the* yacht that she wishes to protest, not yachts in general. In IYRU 100, three yachts were overlapped while rounding the leeward mark, with three others directly astern. One or more rule infringements occurred whereupon A protested B which did her turns. A then shouted 'I'm going to protest the whole bunch.' About five minutes later, A displayed her protest flag, intending that to signify her protest against C. She made no specific hail to C, then or previously. The protest committee declined to hear A's protest, owing to her failure to follow the requirements of paragraph 1.1 of Appendix 3. A appealed.

The district appeals committee reversed the decision and C appealed. Upholding C's appeal the US Appeals Committee said: 'Whichever of the two systems of alternative penalty, under Appendix 3, is in effect, it is essential that a yacht alleged to have infringed a rule be notified immediately ... It is especially necessary when the alternative penalty is the 720° turn, for that penalty must be carried out by "immediately starting to get clear ... and forthwith make her turns." The quickest means of notification is by hail and it must be made immediately to satisfy paragraph 1.1.

'In addition, it is equally important, in equity, for such a hail positively to identify the yacht to which it is directed. When two yachts are alone on the course this poses no problem but when there are several yachts in close proximity to an incident specific identification becomes essential. Such identification might be a yacht's sail number, her name, her helmsman's name or even her hull colour.

'In the case at hand, there were six yachts in close proximity but A's general hail, "I'm going to protest the whole bunch," was more in the nature of a threat than a notice of protest. While her display of a protest flag may or may not have been made at the first reasonable opportunity, there was nothing to prevent her from hailing C, immediately and specifically, as soon as the alleged infringement occurred.'

Little else needs to be said. Note that paragraph 1.6 allows *Daisy* to do her turns *and* protest. She may genuinely not know whose fault the incident was, she exonerates herself 'without prejudice', as it were, to her action against the other. Paragraphs 1.9 and 1.10 extend the committee's powers to disqualification in certain circumstances even when turns have been executed.

2   Percentage

2.1   A yacht that acknowledges infringing a rule of Part IV shall receive a score for the place worse than her actual finishing position by 20% of the number of starters but not less than three places, subject to the limitation in paragraph 2.8. A yacht infringing a rule in more than one incident shall receive a penalty for each infringement.

2.2   The **protest committee** may disqualify a yacht for serious infringement of the rules, whether or not serious damage resulted.

2.3   When a yacht infringed against intends to **protest**, she shall hail the infringing yacht immediately and act in accordance with rule 68, (Protests by Yachts).

2.4   A yacht that acknowledges infringing a rule of Part IV shall, at the first reasonable opportunity, display Code flag "I" and keep it displayed until she has *finished*. She shall report ackowledging her infringement and identify the yacht infringed against to the race committee within the time limit for lodging protests.

2.5   A yacht that fails to acknowledge an infringement fully as provided in paragraph 2.4 and that, after a **protest** and hearing, is found to have infringed a rule of Part IV, shall be disqualified. However, a yacht that *finishes* and subsequently acknowledges an infringement of a rule of Part IV prior to a hearing shall be penalised 50% or at least six places.

2.6   A yacht that has displayed Code flag "I" during a race and has not reported the infringement to the race committee shall be liable to the 50% penalty of paragraph 2.5 without a hearing except that she may request a hearing on the two points of having displayed the flag and having reported the infringement to the race committee.

2.7   When a yacht has failed to fully acknowledge infringing a rule of Part IV, but the yacht infringed against has not met the requirements of paragraph 2.3, the penalty shall be 20%.

2.8   The penalty shall be computed as 20% (or 50%) of the number of starters in the event to the nearest whole number (round .5 upward), such number to be not less than three (or six), except that a yacht shall not receive a score worse than for one position more than the number of starters. (Examples: an infringing yacht finishing 8th in a start for 19 yachts would receive a score for 12th place: $8 + (19 \times 20\% = 3.8$ or $4) = 12$. Another infringing yacht, finishing 18th, would receive the score for 20th place.) The imposition of a percentage penalty shall not affect the scores of other yachts. Thus, two yachts may receive the same score.

Close inspection of the appendix itself reveals the answers. It is worth noting that, again, the hail by a yacht intending to protest must be immediate. The 'I' flag once hoisted cannot be withdrawn. Even late acknowledgement is worth something. An analysis of what the infringing yacht will be penalised is as follows:

A yacht that infringes a rule of Part IV will receive:

(a) a 20% penalty when

1 she acknowledges an infringement correctly,

2 she acknowledges the infringement incorrectly because she has learnt of the facts late, or

3 she acknowledges the infringement incorrectly but the other yacht also acts incorrectly: or

(b) a 50% penalty when: she acknowledges an infringement after finishing but before the hearing, or

(c) a disqualification when she acknowledges an infringement incorrectly, or not at all, and, after a hearing, is found to have infringed a rule.

'Correctly' means in accordance with para 2.4 which requires:

1 that the 'I' flag be hoisted at the first reasonable opportunity after the incident,

2 that it is kept flying until the yacht finishes and

3 that she reports the matter to the race committee identifying the boat infringed against within protest time.

APPENDIX 4—Team Racing Rules

Team racing shall be sailed under the International Yacht Racing Rules supplemented as follows:

1   Sailing Rules

1.1   A yacht may manoeuvre against a yacht sailing on another leg of the course only when she can do so while sailing a *proper course* relative to the leg on which she herself is sailing. For the purpose of this rule, each time a leg is sailed, it shall be regarded as "another leg of the course".

1.2   Except to protect her own or a team mate's finishing position, a yacht in one team that is completing the last leg of the course shall not manoeuvre against a yacht in another team that has no opponent astern of her.

1.3   Right of way may be waived by team mates, provided that in so doing, rule 35, (Limitations on Altering Course), is not infringed with respect to an opponent; but when contact occurs between team mates and neither retires immediately, the lower-scoring team mate shall automatically be disqualified or otherwise penalised. This rule overrides rule 33.2, (Contact between Yachts Racing). The benefits of rule 69, (Requests for Redress), shall not be available to a yacht disabled by contact between team mates.

1.4   When two *overlapping* yachts on the same *tack* are in the act of rounding or passing on the required side of a *mark* at which their *proper course* changes:

(a) When the *leeward yacht* is inside, and has *luffing* rights, she may hold her course or *luff*. When she does not have *luffing* rights, she shall promptly assume her *proper course* to the next *mark*, whether or not she has to *gybe*:

(b) When the *windward yacht* is inside, she shall promptly *luff* up to her *proper course* to the next *mark*, or when she cannot assume such *proper course* without *tacking* and does not choose to *tack*, she shall promptly *luff* up to *close-hauled*. This clause does not restrict a *leeward yacht's* right to *luff* under rule 38, (Same Tack—Luffing and Sailing above a Proper Course after Starting).

Para 1.1 limits one yacht manoeuvring against another to when both are on the same leg of the course, or when the manoeuvrer can do so while sailing what is a proper course for herself, on her leg of the course. It is an enigmatic sentence. It implies that in ordinary racing a yacht may manoeuvre against another while on a different leg of the course, or perhaps it means that maneouvring is allowed in team racing but not otherwise.

Para 1.2 again limits the right to maneouvre against another boat. In teams A, B, C v X, Y, Z, B cannot, on the last leg of the course, maneouvre against Z when neither A or C are astern of her.

Para 1.3 permits waiving of right of way between team mates with some limitation. When there is contact between team mates one must retire or be disqualified. The benefits of rule 69(c) in respect of such a collision are withdrawn.

Para 1.4 lays down the right and obligations of the inside of two overlapped yachts at a mark, using different words from rule 42, but amounting to the same. The rest of this appendix deals with scoring and administration of team racing.

2 Scoring Each Race

2.1 Yachts shall score three-quarters of a point for first place, two points for second place, three points for third place, and so on.

2.2 A yacht that does not *start*, (including a premature starter that does not respond to a recall), shall score points equal to the number of yachts entitled to *start* in the race.

2.3 A yacht that infringes any rule and retires with reasonable promptness shall score one point more than the number of yachts entitled to *start* in the race, but when her retirement is tardy, or when she fails to retire and is subsequently disqualified, she shall score four points more than the number of yachts entitled to *start* in the race.

2.4 A yacht that infringes a rule shortly before or when *finishing* shall be considered to have retired with reasonable promptness when she notifies the race committee of her retirement as soon as is reasonably practicable.

2.5 A yacht that does not *finish* for a reason other than an infringement shall score points equal to the number of yachts entitled to *start* in the race, except as provided in rule 2.6.

2.6 After all the yachts of one team have *finished* or retired, the race committee may stop the race and award to each yacht of the other team that is still *racing* and under way, the points she would have received had she *finished*.

2.7 The team with the lowest total point score shall be the winner of the race.

3 Reports

3.1 A yacht that retires shall promptly report that fact and the reason therefore to the race committee. When it resulted from a rule infringement, she shall state:

(a) when the infringement occurred;

(b) which yacht(s), if any, was involved in the infringement; and

(c) when she retired.

The sailing instructions may require her to submit within a prescribed time a signed statement covering a, b and c.

3.2 A yacht that fails to report her retirement in accordance with rule 3.1 shall be awarded points on the assumption that she retired tardily owing to a rule infringement.

4   Determining the Winner

4.1   THE WINNER

(a) When two teams only are competing:
The winner shall be the team winning the greater number of races.

(b) When more than two teams are competing in a series consisting of races, each of which is between two teams, the winner shall be the team winning the greatest number of races.

(c) When more than two teams are all competing in each race, the winner shall be the team with lowest total point score in all races.

4.2   BREAKING TIES

(a) A tie shall, when practicable, be broken by a sail-off. The time of the sail-off, if any, shall be set out in the notice of the race or regatta and the sailing instructions.
When a sail-off is impracticable, the tie shall stand, unless progress into a further round requires it to be broken.

(b) When progress into a further round is necessary, the breaking of ties shall be:

    (i)   When two teams only are competing:

        1 The winner shall be the team with the lower total point score.

        2 When the tie remains, it shall be broken in favour of the winner of the last race.

    (ii)   When more than two teams are competing in a series consisting of races, each of which is between two teams:

        1 When there is a tie between two teams:
The winner shall be the team that won when the two tied teams met.

        2 When there is a tie between more than two teams:
          (a) The winner shall be the team with the lowest total point score for the races in which the tied teams met each other.
          (b) When a tie remains between two of the teams it shall be broken in accordance with subsection 4.2(b)(ii) *1* of this rule.

    (iii) When more than two teams are all competing in each race:

        The winner shall be the team that has beaten the other tied team or teams in most races, or when still tied, the team that beat the other tied team or teams in the last race.

Addendum to Team Racing Rules

Rules recommended to apply when the Home Team provides all racing yachts

5   Allotment of Yachts

The home team shall provide the visiting team with a list of the yachts to be used and of the sail numbers allotted to each yacht for the match. The home team shall divide these yachts into as many equal groups as there are competing teams and these groups shall be drawn for by lot for the first race. The yachts shall then be allotted to the crews by each team, except that a helmsman shall not at any time steer the yacht of which he is normally the helmsman. The groups of yachts shall be exchanged between races so that, as far as possible, each group will be sailed in turn by each team. In a two team match after an even number of races, if either team requests that the yachts be regrouped, the home team shall re-divide them into new groups that shall be drawn for by lot; except that for the final odd race of a two-team match, the visiting team may select the group it wishes to sail.

6   Allotment of Sails

When sails as well as yachts are provided by the home team, the sails used by each yacht in the first race shall be used by her throughout the series. The substitution of a spare or extra sail shall not be permitted, unless, because of damage or for some other valid reason, a change is approved by the race committee after notification to all teams.

7   Group Identification

One group shall carry no markings. The second group shall carry dark coloured strips or pennants, and additional groups shall carry light or differently coloured strips or pennants. Strips or pennants should usually be provided by the home team and should be attached to the same conspicuous place on each yacht of a group, such as the after end of the main boom or the permanent backstay.

8   Breakdowns

8.1   When a breakdown results in material prejudice, the race committee shall decide whether or not it was the fault of the crew. In general, a breakdown caused by defective equipment, or the result of an infringement by an opponent, shall not be deemed the fault of the crew, and a breakdown caused by careless handling or capsizing shall be. In case of doubt, the doubt shall be resolved in favour of the crew.

8.2   When the race committee decides that the breakdown was not the fault of the crew and that a reasonably competent crew could not have remedied the defect in time to prevent material prejudice, it shall award the broken-down yacht the number of points she would have received had she finished in the same position in the race she held when she broke down, or order the race to be resailed, or *cancel* the race. In case of doubt as to her position when she broke down, the doubt shall be resolved against her.

9   **Spares**

The home team shall be prepared to provide one or more extra yachts and sails to replace any that, in the opinion of the race committee, are unfit for use in the remaining races.

Notes on rule 26

At the time of writing, this IYRU policy rule is new and untested. The following points are worth noting:

1 While racing all advertising is forbidden unless national authority permission is granted within the limits imposed by rules 26.2 – 26.4, except for the sailmakers', builders' and other marks that have always been allowed;

2 The opening sentence also forbids advertising in any series of races for the duration of that series, giving the time the prescription begins and ends. But this can be altered by the notice of race – *not* the sailing instructions, *not* the national authority, but the notice of race. It is therefore possible for the organisers to plan for, say, team advertising between races when visiting teams from far away are in need of sponsorship money. Presumably a series includes a series that runs from April to September, there is no indication to the contrary.

3 The dispensation in rule 26.4 is not intended to condone old advertising yacht names. If *Daisy* (whose owner is chairman of '*Daisy* & *Buttercup* plc') has got away with it since before November 1983 she is not therefore entitled to a whitewash and cannot use the name any more than she theoretically could before. The rule is meant to cover such races as the Whitbread Round the World Race, in which advertising names have been allowed for more than a decade.

A universal index of the yacht racing rules

This index is of words and subjects used in the yacht racing rules and tells you where to find them. It applies to the rules found in this book, though as rule numbers are used (not pages) you can use this index with any official manual or reproduction of the rules.

How to use this index. Headwords (or phrases) are in alphabetical order and printed in bold type; references to the definitions in Parts I and VI are printed in italics. A hyphen represents the headword when required by the sense. References for each headword are in rule order. Each complete reference ends with a semi-colon. Brackets mean that the word is understood in the rule in question but does not actually appear.

Each headword embraces the derivations from the root, ie **anchor** includes anchors, anchored, anchoring etc; the context will determine which.

For example look at:

mainsail: *gybing*; *tacking*; *leeward and windward*; numbers and letters 25.1; (25.2); (54); only one to be set 64.1

This means that the word 'mainsail' appears in the three definitions quoted, it does not appear in rule 25.2 which deals with numbers and letters on the sails of 'other' yachts. Neither does it appear in rule 54 where the rule deals with 'any sail', which may of course be a mainsail. It appears in rule 64.1 in the instructions for setting sails and nowhere else in the rules.

Do not try to use this index instead of the rules. It guides you to the rule you seek but is deliberately ambiguous as to what the rule says.

The following abbreviations are used: NA national authority; N of R notice of race; FR fundamental rule; OA organising authority; PC protest committee; RC race committee; SI sailing instructions; IJ international jury.

ABANDONMENT: racing 3.2(b) (xvii); – signal, and resail signal 4.1 "N" "N" over "X"; – after timing error 4.2(d); RC's powers to – 5.4; RC to check rule 74.2 before – 5.5; – and resail 5.6; (when mark missing 9.1(b)); RC considering – to act equitably 74.2(b) (c)

abnormal means of checking way 54.1(a)

accident 24

action *(or omission)* of RC 69, (70.3)

advertising 26

afloat 53.1

aground: keeping clear of yacht – 46.1; yacht – fouled by another 46.2; yacht – to indicate fact 46.3; permitted ways to get clear 55;use of winch after running – 57

altering course (by a yacht): *luffing; bearing away; obstruction;* hailing before – 34.1; limitations on – 35; before starting 40; changing tacks, other yacht – 41.2; substantial – before hailing for room to tack 43.1

amateur Appendix 1

anchor: 23; keeping clear of yacht – 46; yacht – fouled by another 46.2; yacht to indicate fact 46.3; when racing 53.2; – standing on bottom 53.3, 59; methods of – and recovery 53.3; recovering 54.1; using – when aground, – sent out in boat 55; weighing – 57

anti-barging rule 42.4

appeal: denying right of 1.7; N of R and SI to state when no right of – 1.7(c), 2(m), 3.2(b) (xxx); procedure 77; particulars with – 78; App. 8

area *obstruction;* 7.1

ashore 55

assistance: rendering – obligatory FR A; fouling yacht after – her 46.2; exception to propulsion rule 54.1(c); limitations on receiving outside – 55; exception to boarding rule 58; outside – forbidden 60; redress after rendering – 69(b)

award of prizes 13; – of points 74.6

bailing 53.2, 59

ball (or shape) 4.1 "AP"(b)

ballast: movement restricted 22.1; shipping and unshipping, water as – 22.2 (61.3, 62)

BEARING AWAY: *tacking, proper course;* (39)

beat: *tacking;* 42(a)

blue flag (or shape) 4.1, 4.4

board sailing see **sailboard**

boarding 58; to give outside assistance 60

boat (see also **committee boat**): *mark;* (9.1), 55

body movement 54.1(b); 54.2(c)(d)(e); 54.3(b)

boom: *mark;* advertising on – 26.3 – headsail 64.2; spinnaker – 64.3; main – 64.3

builder's mark 26.1(b)

buoy: *obstruction;* as mark 4.1 "M"; bounding or starting area 7.1;

replacing missing mark 9.1

buoyancy: 3.2(b)(xix); – signal, individual's responsibility, wet suit inadequate 4.1 "Y"; replacing life-saving equipment 24

bulkheads 22.1

bulwarks 64.2(b)

CANCELLATION: *racing*; – signal 4.1 "N over 1st sub"; RC's powers to – 5.3(d), 5.4(c); RC to check rule 74.2 before – 5.5; (when mark missing 9.1(b)); RC considering – to act equitably 74.2(b)(c)

capsized 46.1, 46.2; on sailboard – Appendix 2.1.2

casting off 53

centre line: *gybing.* 27

certificates: 19, 70.4 (see also **measurement**)

chain: 23, 53.3

championships: limitations on refusing entry 1.3; – and national letters 25.1(e)

changes (in SI): 3.2(b)(iv), 3.4 (3.5)

change of course (by RC): 3.2(b)(xv); before start 5.3(b); after start 5.4(b)

charter: 20, 25.3

checking way 54.1(a)

class association: as OA 1.1(d); permits refusal of entry 1.3; appoints IJ 1.6(b); allots sail number 25.1(c)

class flags: 3.2(b)(vii); under other visual signals 4.1; as warning signal 4.2(a) System 1; not later than preparatory signal 4.2(a) system 2; at dip 8.1(a)(i)

class insignia: 25; when required 25.1(a); placing 25.1(d); for "other" yachts 25.2

class rules: govern RC, conflict with IYRR, modified 1.4; 2(b); 3.2(a)(i) (b)(i); observance of – checked before awards 13; entry form requires compliance with 18; require measurement certificate 19.1; deviation in excess of tolerances in –, owner to maintain yacht in accordance with – 19.2; on anchors 23; on life-saving equipment 24; sail insignia etc. 25.1(d); size of sail numbers 25.1(f); control sail numbers etc for "other" yachts 25.2; sail numbers in contravention of – 25.3; permit or ban advertising 26.2 prescribe on forestays and jib-tacks 27; prescribe on clothing 61.1(b), 61.2, on trapezes 62, on sheeting sails to spars 64.2; differentiate spinnaker and headsail 64.4; *rules*; not complied with 70.4

classification certificate 74.3

CLEAR ASTERN and CLEAR AHEAD (see also **overlap**): *leeward and windward*; same tack not overlapped 37.2; same tack transitional 37.3; luffing after starting 38.1; on free leg of course 39; onus on c-ahead yacht 42.1(c); obligations of c-astern yacht 42.2 (a)(b) obligations on c-ahead yacht 42.2(c)(d); establishing overlaps from c-astern 42.3(a), at a continuing obstruction 42.3(b); c-ahead yacht hails for room to tack 43.1

clearing – the finishing line: *racing*, 51.5
– the starting line: 38.1, 40
– after grounding etc.: 55, 57, 59

CLOSE-HAULED: *tacking*; central tack-point when not – 27; luffing above – course 40; luffing above – at mark 42.2(b); (42(a)); above – at starting mark 42.4; hailing for room to tack when – 43; two – yachts on same tack at obstruction 43.1

clothing: and advertising 26.1(d), 26.2, 26.3; and equipment 61; Appendix 10

club: organises races 1.1(c); enters yacht, member of – enters yacht 20.1; member on board 21; two combine to hear protest 71.3

collision: immaterial to disqualification 31; reasonable attempt to avoid 32, (33.2 – see *contact*); lack of hail causes – 34.1; altering course to avoid – before starting 40; unavoidable at obstruction 43.1; hailing yacht tacks when – unavoidable 43.2

committee boat: (3.2(b)(xiv)); and finishing line 4.1 "S" (c); displaying signals 4.1 "red" "green" "blue"; at starting and finishing lines 6

compass bearing 42.4

consent for advertising 26.2

contact (see also *collision*): – between yachts 33.2; protest withdrawn after – 68.9

contents (of SIs) 3.2

course: (see also *proper course*) 3.2(a)(iii); change – 4.1 "C"; shorten – 4.1 "S"; – signal before or with warning signal 5.1(a); when – can be changed 5.1(b); when – can be changed after preparatory signal 5.3(a)(b); sailing the – 51; – to or from last mark: *starting, finishing*, 42.4; – on which mainsail fills *tacking*

crew: *starting; finishing*; personal buoyancy and – 4.1 "Y"; over line at start 8.1, 51.1(c); and advertising 26.1, 26.2, 26.3; make contact 33.2; obligations of – Part V Title; standing on bottom 53.3,55; refloating yacht 55; – of vessel fouled 55; boarding to tend sick – 58; fall overboard, swim 59; not to be stationed outboard 62

crossing (the finishing line) 51.5

curtailing a luff 38.5 (see also *luffing*)

damage: affects measurement certificate 19.2; caused by right-of-way yacht 32; caused by right-of-way yacht failing to hail 34.1; caused by infringement 70.2(c); (and redress 69(c))

damages 76.1

dead reckoning 9.2

dead weight 22.1

decision: yacht's – to race FR B; *interested party*; not to be taken by interested party 71.2, 77.5; to accept protest 72.1; to refuse protest 72.2; when party fails to attend 73.4; re-opening after – 73.5; to be based on facts 74.1; whether finishing position prejudiced 74.2; on measurement protest 74.3; details to be communicated 74.7; appeal against – 77.1; appellant accepts original – 77.4; sustained or reversed 77.6; NA's – final 77.7

deck planking 64.2(b)

declaration 3.2(b)(xxii)

definitions (Parts I and VI – see each individually)

deposit: in lieu of certificate 19.3(b); late acceptance of – 68.8(b); on appeal 77.2; (see also **fee**)

designer's mark 26.1(b)

deviation in excess of tolerances 19.2

diagram: in protest 68.5(d); in appeal 78.1(d)

disabled 69(c)

disciplinary action 75

distribution of SIs 3.3

disqualification: (Fair Sailing FR C); when buoyancy signal late 4.1 "Y"; for non-compliance with Pt.III, Preamble to Pt.III; no – without prior warning 25.4; for infringing a rule of Pt.IV 31.1; before or after racing 31.2; right-of-way yacht in collision 32; after contact 33.2; right-of-way yacht not hailing 34.1; (when yacht renders assistance 46.2); (when anchor lost 53.3); (without a hearing by RC 70.1); measurer has no powers to – 70.4; infringement by yacht leads to – 74.4; (alternative penalties 74.5); retirement not to rank as – 74.6(a); – and placings 74.6(b); for gross infringement etc. 75; by NA on appeal 77.6

doors 22.1

dragging: yacht 46.1; foot in water App. 2.4

entry: rejected by RC 1.3; N of R 2(c)(h); in resailed race 12(a) new – in re-sailed race 12(b); – form 18; yacht to hold measurement certificate 19.1; ownership of – yacht 20.1; ranking as a starter 50; rescinded 70.4(a)

equipment: *starting*; *finishing clear-astern etc.*; – and advertising 26.1(b)(d), 26.2; contact 33.2; for increasing weight 61 (see also **hull**)

error: in timing signals 4.2(d); (in sound signals 4.7); abandon after – in starting procedure 5.4(a); general recall after – in starting procedure 8.2(a); leads to disqualification without hearing 70.1(a); causes re-opening of hearing 73.5

evidence: – of infringement permits action 70.1(e); given by interested party 71.2; on validity of protest 72.2; right to hear – 73.1; presented to and asked for by PC 73.2; from committee member 73.3; reopening for new – 73.5; when yacht materially prejudiced 74.2(b)

exoneration: for rule infringement 33.1; after contact 33.2(a); at obstruction or mark 43.3(b)(c); after touching mark 45.1, 52.2; after passing mark on wrong side 51.4; at marks 52.1, 52.2; at mark not surrounded by navigable water 52.2(c); protested yacht – 74.4; 720° turns App.3.1

expenses arising from measurement protest 76.2

extensions (of line): (4.1 "I"); through two posts 6(c); crossed by recalled yacht 8.1(a), 51.1(b)(c); crossed from course side at start 44.1

facts: known only after race 68.3(a); to be final 74.1; PC's to be accepted 77.3; appeal decision based on PC's – 77.6

fair sailing FR C (75)

fault: prejudiced yacht not at – 69; yacht at – to be penalised 74.4

fee: N of R 2(h); accompanies entry form 18; accompanies protest 68.7; accepted late 68.8(b); at measurement protest 76.2; (see also **deposit**)

fetching mark or obstruction 43.3(b)(c)

FINISHING: *racing; proper course;* 3.2(a)(vi)(vii); 4.1 "S"; within a time limit 10; after – rules of Pt.IV apply Preamble Pt.IV; as per definition 51.1(a); – and string test 51.2; marks lose required side when yacht – 51.3; clearing line after – 52.2(b)(ii); displaying protest flag until – 68.2(c)(i); single hander – with protest flag 68.2(c)(ii); without protest flag 68.3; protest time after, or after not, – 68.6(a)(b); no hearing when yacht fails to – 70.1

finishing line: *racing; finishing;* 3.2(a)(vi); for shortened course 4.1 "S"; committee boat at – 4.1 "Blue Flag"; types of – 6

finishing mark: *racing;* laying – 6; ceases to have required side 51.3; touching – after finishing 52.1(a)(iii); exoneration after touching – 52.2(b)(ii)

finishing position: to satisfy RC before awards 13; prejudiced 69, 74.2

finishing signal: for shortened course 4.1 "S", 4.1 "Blue Flag"

finishing time: adjusted by PC 74.2(c)

fixtures and fittings 22.1

flag: *mark;* visual signals 4.1; usage prescribed by NA 65; (see also **class, signal, protest**)

flag "A" 4.1 "AP"(d)

flag "B" 3.1, 68.2

flag "I": as national letter 25.1(c); when flown by yacht 70.1(b); App 3.2

flag "M" 9.1

flag "P" 4.2(a)

flag "X" 8.1(a)(ii)

flagpole *mark*

floorboards 22.1

flotation rule 74.3(a)

fog: hides mark 9.2; IRPCS – signals 66

forestays and jib tacks 27

foul: anchored yacht hails to prevent – 46.2; assisted yacht – 46.3; getting clear after – vessel 55; use of winch after – object 57; boarding by crew of vessel – 58; leaving to clear – vessel 59

foul weather 5.4(c)(i)

fundamental rules: – immutable, status of rules, 3.1

gear: inadequate 53.3; to be recovered 55; not aboard at start 60

general recall: *racing;* 4.1 "1st Sub"; after timing error 4.2(d); procedure 8.2

gross infringement 75

grounding 55, 59 (see also **aground**)

ground tackle, *mark*

guns: 4.4; mis-timed 4.5 (see also **sound signals**)

GYBING: *bearing away; on a tack;* new overlap after – 38.3; – yacht to keep clear 41.1; room required for – 41.2; onus of proof that – completed 41.3; simultaneous – 41.4; room for inside yacht to – 42.1(a) c-astern yacht keeping clear 42.2(a); as a means of propulsion 54.1(b)

hailing: 4.1 "L"(b); as recall 8.1(a)(iii); required 34.1; recommended 34.2; mast-abeam when luffing 38.4; before starting 40; before luffing to windward of mark 42.3(c); for room to tack at obstruction 43; not to – and tack simultaneously 43.1; obligations of hailing and hailed yachts 43.2; when obstruction is also a mark 43.3(b)(c); indicating yacht anchored or aground 46.3; when alternative penalty prescribed 68.4, App.3.1, App.3.2

hauling out to effect repairs etc: 53.2,59

headsail: changing – 64.1; sheeting – 64.2(a); boomed – 64.2(b); attached to spi boom 64.3; definition 64.4

hearing: bodies responsible for organising – 1.5; infringement acknowledged prior to 68.9; RC acts without a – 70.1; yacht demands – 70.1(a); RC or PC acts with a – 70.2; called after measurer's report 70.4; no penalisation without a – 71.1; by combined YC committees 71.3; called as soon as possible 72.1; protest refused without a – 72.2; time and place to be notified 72.3; right to be present at – 73.1; failure to attend 73.4; reopening a – 73.5; measurement – 74.3 essential for bad conduct 75; NA returns case for re-hearing 77.3

helmsman: to wear personal buoyancy 4.1 "Y"; abreast of mainmast when L luffing 38.2; hails mast abeam 38.4; abaft of mainmast, luffing before starting 40; obligations when handling a yacht PtV Title

hindering: 31.2; (8.2(b))

hull: advertising on – 26.1(e) 26.2(a)(i); wind and water on – 54.1; frictional resistance of – 63; bulwarks etc. not part of – 64.2

hull and equipment: *clear astern*

hull crew or equipment: *starting*; *finishing*; over line at start 8.1, 51.1(c); advertising on – 26.3; contact between – 33.2

ill 56,57

independent protest committee 1.5(c); *Protest committee* (b); 77.1(b)

infringement: before general recall 8.2(b); before re-sail 12(c); of rule 25 warning required 25.4; of Pt.IV while racing 31.1; of SI before and after racing 31.2; action needed after – 33; after realisation of – 33.1; after contact 33.2; of Pt.IV, right to protest 68.1; protest against – required flag 68.2(a); rule – to be in protest 68.5(b); acknowledged 68.9; not reported 70.1(b); committee aware of – 70.2; of measurement rule 74.3(a); penalties for – 74.4, 74.5; retirement after – not to rank as disqualification 74.6; gross – of rules 75; damages arising from – 76.1; – yacht disqualified by NA 77.6

injured 58,59

inside yacht: 42.1(d)(e), 42.3(a)(b)(c)

insignia – see **class insignia**

inspection 3.2(b)(xx)

intending to race preambles to Pts III and IV

INTERESTED PARTY: report to – not acceptable for initiating action 70.2(d); ineligible for discussion or decision, may give evidence 71.2(a); objection to – before evidence taken 71.2(b); not to take part in appeal 77.5; financial interest App.6.2.4; may retire from IJ App. 8.5.1

international class 25.1, 26.2

international jury: 1.5(d); 1.6; 1.7(a); *protest committee*; App. 8

international regatta 1.6 (a)(b)(c)

intervening yacht: *c-astern;* responding to luff 38.6

invalidating a measurement certificate 19.2

IRPCS: (3.2(b)(xxviii)), Preamble to Pt.IV; 66; App.9

IYRR: Status of Rules, 2(b), 3.2(a)(i)

IYRU: establishes rules Status of Rules; has jurisdiction over regattas 1.1, 1.6; approval required to refuse entry 1.3; rules accepted 18; recognises int. classes 25.1; informed of gross misconduct 75.2

jib tacks 27

judging: 1.1, 1.2, 1.5

jury 1.5, 1.6, 1.7, *protest committee*, App. 8

ladders 22.1

LEEWARD AND WINDWARD: L's rights when overlapped 37.1; L's obligations on establishing an overlap 37.3; L's right to luff 38.1; limitations on L sailing above a proper course 38.2; L's right to luff until hailed, L governed by hail 38.4; L restricted by obstruction 38.5; L on free leg 39; L's luffing restricted before starting 40; L luffs W to windward of mark 42.3(c); L's rights and obligations at starting mark (anti-barging) 42.4; L hails for water near obstruction 43.1; (see also **windward**)

leg of the course: yacht on free – 39; mark and –, starting mark and first – 51.3; touching a mark on a – 52.1(a)(ii)

letter of consent: 26.2(a)(c)

lifelines 62

lifejacket 4.1 "Y" (see also **buoyancy**)

LUFFING: *proper course*; exception to hailing rule 34.1; exceptions to limitations on altering course 35(a); exception to assuming proper course to start 35(b)(i); right to – 38.1; stopped by hailing 38.4; curtailed 38.5; – two or more yachts 38.6; – before starting 40; inside yacht without – rights at mark when gybing 42.1(e); limitations at mark 42.2(b); – opponent to windward at mark 42.3(c)

mainsail: *gybing; tacking; leeward and windward;* numbers and letters 25.1; (25.2); (54); only one to be set 64.1

making fast 53

man overboard (46)(59)

manual power 57

MARK: *racing; starting; finishing;* 3.2(a)(iii); 4.1 "M"; shorten course at – 4.1 "S" (c); to port or starboard 4.1 "red/green flag"; shifting starting – 5.2; changing course at – 5.4(b); shortening course at – 5.4(c); abandoning race because of missing – 5.4(c)(iii); finishing lines 6; starting area buoy not ranking as – 7.1; missing or shifted, RC's duties 9.1; unseen 9.2; hailing to claim room at – 34.2; assuming proper course after rounding – 35(b)(ii); rules applying at – Section C; rules at a starting – surrounded by navigable water 42(b) outside overlapped yacht gives room at – 42.1(a);

proper course to next – assumed by overlapping yacht 42.1(e); c-ahead and c-astern near – 42.2; limitations on overlap near – 42.3; taking other yacht to windward of – 42.3(c); at starting – (anti-barging) 42.4; when obstruction is also a – 43.3; touching and re-rounding 45; rounding – correctly 51.2; required sides of various – 51.3; passing on wrong side of – 51.4; touching a starting – 52.1(a)(i), a – of the course 52.1(a)(ii), a finishing – 52.1(a)(iii); causing – to shift 52.1(b); exoneration by rerounding 52.2(a), by rerounding a starting – 52.2(b)(i), by rerounding a finishing – 52.2(b)(ii), by 360° turn 52.2(c)

marks: sailmaker's 26.1(a)(i); builder's designer's on hull spars and equipment 26.1(b); clothing 26.1(d)

mast: main – luffing 38.2; '– abeam' hail 38.4; '– abeam' and luffing before starting 40; boom attached to – for sheeting headsails 64.2; sail tacked abaft formost –, spinnaker boom and foremost –, spinnaker boom attached to – 64.3; definition of headsail 64.4

match racing: *racing*, 2(i)

measurement (or rating); 2.1; 3.2(b)(xx); valid certificate to be held 19.1 certificate not to be invalidated 19.2; undertaking to produce certificate 19.3; procedure in – protest 74.3; expenses of – protest 76.2

measurer: *Protest* (e); authority 70.4; action before race 70.4(a); action after race 70.4(b)

member: of club for entry 20.1; of club in charge of yacht 21

minor and unavoidable 33.2, 68.9

misconduct: action by RC 75.1; by NA 75.2

moorings 53.1

name of yacht 26.2(a)(i)

national authority: prescribes to rules Status of Rules; organises races 1.1(b); approves CA 1.1(d); prescribes on rejection of entries 1.3; prescriptions of – to govern RC 1.4(a); appoints IJ 1.6(a); prescribes on denial of appeal 1.7; 2(b), 3.2(a)(i); permits experimental rule changes 3.1; observance of prescriptions to be checked 13; requires certificate 19.1, recognises club 20.1,21; allots sail numbers to Int. classes 25.1(c); allots insignia, letters, numbers to 'other' yachts 25.2; consents to advertising 26.2; 26.3; 26.4 prescribes on flag usage 65; *Rules*; informed of RC's action 75.1; disqualifies for gross infringement 75.2; prescribes on damages 76.1; receives appeals and references 77.1; prescribes time limit and deposit for appeal 77.2; withdrawl of appeal from – 77.4; upholds or reverses decisions 77.6 decisions final 77.7; receives particulars of appeal 78.1

national letters: in entry form 18; Int. classes to carry –, list of –, separated from number by hyphen 25.1; place on sail 25.1(d)(i), on spinnaker 25.1(d)(iii); when required 25.1(e); size 25.1(f); requirements for 'other' yachts 25.2

navigable water: starting mark surrounded by – 42, 42.4; touching mark surrounded by – 52.2(a); touching mark not surrounded by – 52.2(c)

navigation lights: (3.2(b)(xxviii)); (Preamble to Part IV); to conform to IRPCS 66

normal position: *finishing, clear astern* etc.

notice of race: to be published 1.1; to advise of IJ 1.6(c), 1.7(b)(c); contents of – 2; prescribes entry form 18; requires certificate 19.1; prescribes sail numbers 25.3; prescribes on period of ad. ban 26, announces dispensation 26.4; copy to accompany appeal 78.1(a)

notification (to yacht or party): of penalisation 70.1; of action and hearing 70.2; (of measurement protest 70.4); of hearing 72.3; of measurement protest result 74.3(b)

numeral pendants 4.1 "AP"(c)

number of entries 2(c)

object: *obstruction*; restricts responding to luff 38.5

object (verb): 71.2(b)

observers 73.1

OBSTRUCTION: hailing to claim room at – 34.2; causes luff to be curtailed 38.5; – on same side 42; yachts on a beat 42(a); room at – when overlapped 42.1(a); 2 overall lengths from – 42.1(b); onus at – 42.1(c); clear ahead at 42.2; limitations on establishing overlap at – 42.3; at a continuing – 42.3(b); hailing to tack at – 43.1; (responding 43.2); when – is a starting mark 43.3(a); when – is a mark 43.3(b); foul of an – 55

Official notice board 3.4, 4.1 "L", 26.2(c)

ON A TACK: *gybing*; *leeward and windward*; *clear astern etc.*: right of yacht – 41.1; room for yacht – to keep clear 41.2; c-ahead yacht stays on same tack or gybes 42.2(a).

onus: when changing tacks 41.3; when outside yacht claims overlap broken 42.1(c); when inside yacht claims overlap 42.1(d); when hailed yacht keeps clear 43.2(b)(iii) & see RYA Appendix D(b)

ooching 54.2(c), 54.3(b)

opportunity see *room*

opposite tack: *clear astern etc*: basic rule 36; exception to rule 42 for – yachts 42(a); when inside of two yachts on – must gybe 42.1(e)

oral instructions 3.5

organising authority: constitution of –, appoints RC, issues N of R 1.1; may direct RC 1.2; may reject entry 1.3; governed by rules 1.4(a); modifies class rules 1.4(b); appoints independent PC 1.5(c); appoints IJ 1.5(d), 1.6(c); denies appeal 1.7; N of R 2(a); requires deposit 19.3 permits advertising 26.3; of offshore event and clothing 61.4

outrigger 64.2(b)

outside yacht (and overlap): 42.1(a)(b)(c); 42.3(a)(c)

OVERLAP: hailing to establish or terminate 34.2; obligations and rights when – 37.1, when not – 37.2, in transitional phase 37.3; proper course limitations during – 38.2; limitations when new – begins 38.3; room at marks and obstructions when – 42.1; duty of outside yacht 42.1(a); outside yacht to give room when – broken 42.1(b); onus on outside yacht claiming – broken 42.1(c); onus on inside yacht to prove – 42.1(d); obligation on inside yacht to gybe 42.1(e); when not – 42.2; no obligation to give room before – 42.2(d); limitation on establishing – 42.3(a); a late – 42.3(a)(ii); at a continuing obstruction 42.3(b)

overall lengths: *obstruction*; 2 of longer yacht for overlap 38.3; within 3 of a leeward or clear astern yacht 39; 2 from mark or obstruction 42.1(b)(c) 42.2(a), 42.3(a); luffing before 2 – of mark 42.3(c)(ii)

overboard: 46, 55, 59

owner: responsible for qualifying yacht Pt.III title; – or representative signs entry form 18; maintains yacht as per certificate 19.2; signs form when certificate unavailable 19.3(a); lodges deposit 19.3(b); to be club or club member 20.1; has two yachts in same race 20.2; steers another yacht 20.3; – or representative aboard to be club member 21; signs protest form 68.5; corrects defect in protest 70.4

Part IV: immutable Status of Rules, 3.1; rules of – infringed 31.1; rules of still apply to infringing yacht 33.1; returning yacht regains rights of – 44.1(b); yacht failing to return keeps rights under – 44.2; rules of – apply to unexonerated yacht 45.2; protest under rules of – 68.1; alternative penalties for infringing – 74.5

PARTY TO A PROTEST: objects to committee member 71.2(b); notified that protest is invalid 72.2; brings evidence on invalid protest 72.2; right to copy of protest 72.3; right to be present at hearing 73.1; gives evidence 73.2; hears committee member's evidence 73.3; fails to attend hearing 73.4; hears decision, asks for decision in writing 74.7; right of appeal 77.1(a); may be penalised by NA 77.6; to receive appeal decision 77.7; comments on appeal 78

passing – see **rounding**

penalty: (see also **disqualification**) *starting*; *finishing*; 3.2(b)(xxi); for advertising 26.5; for Pt.IV infringement when racing 31; accepting a – 33.1; accepting – after contact 33.2; after receiving undeserved room 43.3(b); when hailed yacht fails to fetch 43.3(c); no – for fouling assisted yacht 46.2; after causing another to touch mark 52.1; after failing to recover gear 53.3; *party to a protest*; no – without a hearing 71.1; RC – yacht 74.4; alternative – 74.5; – to be in decision 74.7; – for gross infringement of rules 75; yacht – on appeal 77.6; alternative – (720° Turns, Percentage) App.3

Percentage penalty 70.1(b), App.3

person: in peril FR A; owning two yachts 20.2; onboard 24, 59; overboard 46

photographic evidence App.11

piece of string rule 51.2

places: after disqualification or retirement 74.6(b); after removal from series 74.6(c)

planing conditions 54.3

plank 62

points: divided in tie 11; PC may adjust 74.2(c); retirement – 74.6(a)(b); when yacht removed from series 74.6(c)

polymer 63

port tack: *on a tack*; 36

POSTPONEMENT: *racing*; and new start 3.2(b)(xvii); – signal 4.1 "AP"; – after timing error 4.2(d); sound signals for – 4.4; RC's powers to – 5.3; – for new course or other reason 5.3(b); – to a later day 5.3(c); time and place of re-sail 5.6; (when mark missing 9.1(b))

power pump (or winch) 57

premature starter: 4.1 "X"; (recalled yacht returning 8.1); general recall for unidentified – 8.2; (– continues racing 33.1); (limitations on an ex – 35(b)(i) – returning keeps clear 44.1(a); limitations on ex – 44.1(b); rights of – continuing to race 44.2; – to return and start 51.1(b); (– returning across extension of line 51.1(c))

preparation of defence 72.3

preparatory signal: *racing*; 4.1 "P"; shifting mark before – 5.2; timing and systems for – 4.2(a); (use of sound signal for – 4.4); new – after general recall 8.2; Pt.III applies before – Pt.III preamble; yacht nears start line after – 50; afloat and off moorings at – 53.1; crew not to leave after – 59; no outside assistance after – 60

prescriptions (see also NA and SI): permitted by IYRU – Status of Rules; to govern RC 1.4; 2(b); 3.2(a)(i); checked for observance 13; accepted in entry form 18; *rules*; on damages 76.1

prizes: 2(1); 3.2(b)(xxvi); when yachts tied 11; RC checks before awarding – 13

PROPER COURSE: altering course to assume – 35(a)(b); same tack, above a – after starting 38; luffing subject to – 38, 38.1, 38.2; – limitations 38.2; same tack, sailing below a – on free leg 39; gybing at mark to assume – 42.1(e); – completes re-rounding 45.1

propulsion: abnormal 54.1; prohibited actions 54.2; permitted actions 54.3; – when sounding 56

PROTEST: who may hear – 1.5; 3.2(b)(xxiii); when two yachts touch 33.2(b); remedy for improper "mast-abeam" hail 38.4; *party to a protest*; *protest committee*; who may – 68.1; intention to – signalled 68.2; grounds for – known after race 68.3; trying to inform protested yacht 68.4; particulars of – 68.5; time and manner for lodging – 68.6; fee 68.7; remedying defects 68.8; withdrawing a – 68.9; redress requested in accordance with – 69; statement contained in invalid protest 70.2(b) evidence at valid – grounds for committee's action 70.2(e); between yachts in different races 71.3; accepted 72.1; refused 72.2; to be available to parties 72.3; decided without full hearing 73.4; on measurement 74.3; not containing pertinent rule 74.4; expenses entailed by – 76.2; to accompany appeal 78.1(b)

PROTEST COMMITTEE: kinds of – 1.5; *interested party*; extends time limit for protest 68.6(a); sets time limit for non-finisher 68.6(b); permits correction of protest 68.8; decides protest when infringement unacknowledged 68.9; finds contact minor and unavoidable 68.9; redress requested from – 69; calls hearing when satisfied error made 70.1(a); acts with hearing against yacht, notifies yacht 70.2; initiates redress for prejudiced yacht 70.3; receives report from measurer 70.4(b); no interested party to serve on – 71.2(a); objection to member of – 71.2(b); (– of two clubs 71.3); decides protest is valid, calls hearing 72.1; refuses protest 72.2; (notifies time and place of hearing 72.3); when member of – is witness 73.1; may admit observes 73.1; takes evidence 73.2; member of – gives evidence 73.3; decides protest without full hearing 73.4; re-opens a hearing 73.5; finds facts 74.1; considers redress 74.2; takes evidence for redress 74.2(b); makes equitable arrangement 74.2(c); decides measurement protest or refers it to authority 74.3; penalises 74.4;

promptly communicates decision 74.7; endorses diagram 74.7(b) (ii); penalises gross infringement 75.1; allots measurement expenses 76.2; appealed against 77.1(a); RC appeal against independent – 77.1(b); refers decision to appeal authority 77.1(c); time limit for appeal after – decision 77.2; NA to accept –'s findings of fact 77.3; case returned to – rehearing 77.3; no member of – on appeal body 77.5; –'s decision upheld or reversed 77.6; observations of – on appeal, with diagram 78.1(c)(d)(f)

protest flag: "B" always acceptable 3.1; 4.1 "B"; displaying a – 68.2(a); in single hander 68.2(c)(ii); protest without a – 68.3; not required for redress 69; not required for sailboard App.2

protested yacht: *party to a protest*; right to be informed 68.4

protesting yacht: *party to a protest*; signifies intention to protest 68.2(a), 68.2(c)(ii); duty to inform 68.4; delivers protest 68.6; remedies defects in protest 68.8, 68.9

pumping 54.2(b), 54.3(a)

race committee (see also **protest committee**): *postponement*; *abandonment*; *cancellation*; authority and duties – Pt.II; appointed 1.1; conducts and judges races 1.2; rejects entries 1.3; governed by rules 1.4; hears protests 1.5(a); appoints PC 1.5(b); appoints jury 1.5(c); supervised by IJ 1.5(d); changes SI 3.4; calls attention to signals 4.4; signals the course 5.1; postpones or cancels race 5.3; changes, shortens course, abandons or cancels race 5.4; considers action under 74.2, 5.5; notifies postponement or abandonment 5.6; recalls premature starter 8.1; makes general recalls 8.2; repositions or substitutes marks 9.1(a); deals with missing mark 9.1(b); accepts new entries in re-sail 12(b); notifies yachts of re-sail 12(d); is satisfied rules observed 13; considers rectification of wear or damage 19.2; accepts undertaking to produce certificate 19.3; confiscates accompanying deposit 19.3(b); consents to owner with two yachts 20.2; consents to owner steering another yacht 20.3; is satisfied overlap broken or established in time 42.1(c)(d); penalises yacht that has lost anchor 53.3; *protest committee*; *party to a protest*; acknowledges protest flag 68.2(c)(i); notices protest flag 68.2(c)(ii); informed of protest by retiring yacht 68.2(d); receives protest 68.6; prejudices yacht by act or omission 69(a); acts without a hearing 70.1; acts with a hearing 70.2; initiates redress 70.3; receives report from measurer 70.4(a)(b); excludes for bad sportsmanship 75.1; appeals 77.1(b); refers case 77.1(c); notifies party about appeal 78.2

RACING: decision to – is yacht's FR B; RC to conduct and judge – 1.4; SI for each yacht entitled to – 3.3; life-jacket to be worn while – 4.1 "Y"; earlier start needs consent of all yachts – 4.2(c); rule of Pt.III before and while – Pt.III Preamble; rectifying certificate before – 19.2; shipping ballast/water before and while – 22.2; advertising rule infringed while not – 26.5(b) Pt.IV affecting yacht not – Pt.IV Preamble; disqualified while – 31.1; disqualified before or after – 31.2; persisting in – after infringement 33.1; yacht – anchored etc. to be avoided 46.1; Pt.V applies while – Pt.V Preamble; touching a finishing mark while – 52.1(a)(iii); anchored etc. when – 53.2; measurement rule infringed while – 74.3

rail 64.2

ranking as a starter 50

rating (see **measurement**)

recalls: 3.2(a)(v); individual – signal 4.1 "X"; with class warning signal at dip 8.1(a)(i); displaying flag "X" 8.1(a)(ii); by hailing 8.1(a)(iii) with other precedures 8.1(b); yacht's failure to see or hear – 51.1(d); (see also **general recall** and **premature starter**)

recovering gear: 53.3; 55

rectifying wear or damage 19.2

redress: 1.5; *protest*; finishing position prejudiced 69; action or omission of RC 69(a); rendering assistance 69(b); disabled by other vessel, definition of 'disabled' 69(c); prejudiced by yacht penalised under rule 75 69(d); initiated by RC or PC 70.3; eligibility for – decided 74.2(a); evidence at – hearing 74.2(b); PC makes equitable arrangement 74.2(c); – granted to be in PC's decision 74.7(a)(v)

reefing: 53.2, 59

reference – see **appeal**

refusing a protest 72.2

regatta: 1.1, 1.6, 2(b), 3.1, 26, (see also **race**)

regatta committee 1.1(c)(e)

rehearing protest 77.3

reject entry 1.3, 70.4

re-opening hearing 73.5

repairs 53.2, 59

request for hearing 70.1

request for redress – see *redress*

required side: *mark*; rounding or passing mark on same – 42; passing or rounding marks on – 51.2; beginning and end of – 51.3; leaving mark on – when re-rounding 52.2(a)

re-rounding: after touching a mark 45; exonerating yacht keeping clear until she has – 45.1; yacht clearly returning to – 45.2; one entire – in exoneration 52.2(a); 52.2(b)

re-sail: *abandonment*; 3.2(b)(xvii); 4.1 "N over X"; (5.3); 5.4(a); procedure 12

rescinding an entry 1.3, 70.4

responding by hailed yacht at obstruction 43.2

responsibility: – of yacht FR B; RC's – Pt.II Preamble; RC's – 1.2; of individual to to wear life-jacket 4.1 "Y"; of owner for qualifying his yacht Pt.III Preamble; of owner to keep yacht as per certificate 19.2

restrictions 3.2(b)(xxiv)

results: (13); 70.1

retiring: *racing*; Pt.IV rules continue after – Pt.IV Preamble; obligation to – after infringement 33.1; acknowledgement of infringement after contact by – 33.2(a); hailing yacht to – 43.3(b); hailed yacht to – 43.3(c); protest after – 68.2(d); protest without flag after – 68.3(a); after infringement not ranking as disqualification 74.6(a); places to be adjusted after 74.6(b)

returning to start: (8.1;) rights and obligations 44; premature starter to – and start 51.1(b)

right-of-way yacht: fails to try to avoid damage 32; not hailing before altering course 34.1; obligation not to alter course 35; luffs before starting 40; limitation on yacht tacking or gybing to become – 41.2; – after returning allows other room to keep clear 44.1; (45.1)

rocking 54.2(e)

room: hailing to claim 34.2; ample – and opportunity for windward yacht 37.3; – and opportunity for windward yacht before start 40; – at marks and obstructions when overlapped 42.1(b); – for inside yacht to round or pass, definition of – 42.1(a); clear-astern yacht has no right to – 42.2(d); at starting mark 42.4; close-hauled, hailing for – to tack at obstruction 43; limitation on right to – when obstruction is a mark 43.3; ample – and opportunity for correct starter 44.1(b)

ropes 23, 53.3, 55

rounding a mark: exception to altering course limitations 35(b)(ii); room to – when overlapped 42.1; – manoeuvre when not overlapped 42.2;

rounding or passing: *mark*; 4.1 "M"; RC's action if no mark to – 9.1(b); evidence for – 9.2; – marks or obstructions 42; overlapping yachts about to – mark 42.1; room to 42.1(a); clear-ahead and astern yachts about to – mark 42.2; keeping clear for – 42.2(a); exonerating yacht keeping clear of others 45.1; – each mark to sail the course 51.2; exoneration after – on wrong side 51.4

round-the-ends rule: – signal 4.1 "I"; rule infringed 4.1 "X"; – and recalls 8.1; (– when prescribed by SIs 51.1(c))

rubbing strake 64.2

rule numbers: **1**– status, 3.1; **1.4(b)**– 2; **1.5**– 1.6, *protest committee*, 77.1(b); **1.6**– 1.5(d), 1.7; **1.7**– 2, 3.2, 77.1; **2**– 1.1, 3.1; **3**– status, 3.1; **3.1**– status, 2, 3.2; **3.2**– 3.1, 11, Pt.IV Preamble; **4.1 "P"**– 4.2(b); **4.1 "1st Sub"**– 8.2(a); **4.2(a)**– 4.2(b); **4.4**– 8.2(a); **5.4**– 9.1; **8.1(a)(ii)**– 4.1 "X"; **19**– 70.4, 74.3; **26**– status, 3.1; **31.2**– 8.2(b); **33.2**– 68.3; **35**– Pt.IV, Sec. C, Preamble; **38.1**– 34.1, 35(a); **38.4, 38.5, 38.6**– 40; **40**– 35(b)(i); **41**– 42.2(c); **41.2**– 41.3; **42**– *clear astern*, 34.2; **42.1(a)**– 42.3(a); **44.1(b)**– 35(b)(i); **51.1(a)**– 3.1; **51.1(c)**– *starting*, 4.1 "I" "X", 8.1; **51.2**– 51.4, 52.2; **52**– 68.3; **52.2**– *finishing*, 45.1, 45.2, 52.1; **53**– 54.1(d); **54**– 56; **55**– 53.2, 54.1(d), 60; **57**– 55; **58**– 60; **61**– status, 3.1; **68**– 33.2, 52.1, *protest*, 72.1, 72.2; **68.2**– 3.1; **68.5**– 68.8, 69. 78.1; **68.6**– 69; **68.7**– 68.8, 69; **68.8**– 69; **69**– *protest*, 70.3, 74.2; **70.1**– *protest*, 70.2(a), 71.1, 74.4; **70.2**– *protest*, 26.5; **70.3**– *protest*, 74.2; **70.4**– *protest*; **73**– 75.1; **74.1**– 75.1; **74.2**– 5.5; 69; **74.4–74.6**, 70.1, 26.5; **74.7**– 74.3; **75.1**– FRC, 69, 77.1(d); **77**– 74.3; **77.3**– 78.1; **App.2**– 1.4; **App.3**– *protest*, 70.1; **App.4**– 1.4; **App.8**– 1.5(d); **App.10**– 61

safe pilotage 43

sails: maker's mark 26.1, 26.1(a); (27); natural action of wind on – 54.1(a); adjusted 54.1(b); rapid trimming 54.3; changed 64.1; sheeted to spars 64.2; spinnakers 64.3; tacked down 64.4

sail numbers: on entry form 18; allotted by NA, hyphen after letter "I" 25.1(c); positioned 25.1(d)(i)(iii); positioned on spinnakers 25.1(d)(iii); size 25.1(f); for 'other' yachts 25.2; when class rules may be contravened 25.3; (see also *class insignia* and *national letters*)

sailboard: 1.4, 26.1(f), Appendix 2

sailcloth 26.1(a)

sailing: above a proper course after starting 38; below a proper course after starting 39; above a compass bearing to first mark 42.4

sailing the course: premature starter – 44.2; touched mark and – 45.2; how to – 51; – when yacht exonerates herself 52.2(a)

sailing instructions: powers of – Status of Rules; *racing*; *mark*; *obstruction*; govern RC 1.4; to contain denial of appeal 1.6, 1.7; time and place for receiving in N of R 2(f); alter rules, to be in writing, to rank as rules 3.1; obligatory contents 3.2(a); obligatory contents when appropriate 3.2(b); distribution of – 3.3; changes in – 3.4; oral 3.5; prescribe other signals 4.1, 4.3; prescribe shortening course 4.1 "S"; except life jacket rule 4.1 "Y"; prescribe general recall signal 4.1 "1st sub"; prescribe starting signals 4.2(a); (alter starting intervals 4.2(b)); prescribe new starting procedure 4.2(d); explain other signals 4.3; shorten course 5.3(a); prescribe notice for change of course 5.4(b); identify ends of lines 6(a); prescribe limit marks 6(c); define starting area 7.1; prescribe recall procedure 8.1; prescribe general recall procedure 8.2; prescribe on time limit 10; establish method of breaking tie 11; observance of – to be checked before awards 13; form of entry 18; accepted in entry form 18; require measurement certificate 19.1; deposit 19.3; disqualification for infringing – before or after racing 31.2; accepting penalty when – infringed 33.1; prescribe alternative penalty instead of retirement 33.1, 33.2, 43.3(b)(c), 52.1, 68.4; prescribe 'other' systems for premature starters 51.1(b)(c); course sailed to be in accordance with – 52.2(a); prescribe on manual power 57; prescribe on boarding 58; prescribe on leaving 59; prescribe weight of clothing 61.1(b); prescribe on increasing stability 62; *rules*; powerless to disestablish flag "B" 68.2(a); prescribe method and time for delivering protest 68.6; prescribe protest fee 68.7; prescribe alternative penalties 74.4, 74.5; to accompany appeal 78.1

same tack: basic rules 37; when overlapped 37.1; when not overlapped 37.2; transitional 37.3; luffing and sailing above a proper course after starting 38; luffing rights 38.1; proper course limitations 38.2; overlap limitations 38.3; hailing to stop or prevent a luff 38.4; curtailing a luff 38.5; luffing two or more yachts 38.6; sailing below a proper course on a free leg 39; luffing before starting 40; when inside of two – yachts must gybe 42.1(e); hailing for room to tack when two yachts on – 43.1

scantling 74.3(a)

scoring: 2(e); 3.2(a)(viii); (ties 11); RC can adjust 74.2(c); 74.6(c); App.5

sculling 54.2(a)

serious damage see **damage**

sheeting – sails to spars 64.2

shifting ballast 22

shoal: *obstruction*; 42.3(b)

shortening course: 3.2(a)(vi); 3.2(b)(xiii); 4.1 "S"; RC's powers to – before start 5.3(a) after start 5.4(c)

signals: (see also *warning, preparatory, starting*): 3.2(a)(iv), (v); 3.2(b)(vi), (x), (xv), (xix); IC flags over class flags 4.1; other visual – 4.1; – for starting a race 4.2; 5-min intervals, system 1 flags, classes at 10 or 5 min intervals, system 2 shapes ditto 4.2(a); intervals not limited to 5 mins 4.2(b);

advancing time of warning – 4.2(c); errors in timing starts 4.2(d); other – 4.3; calling attention to – (guns) 4.4; visual starting – to govern 4.5; – the course 5.1; changing the course 5.1; postponement – 5.3; re-sail – 5.6; sound – on recall 8.1(a); general recall – 8.2(a); use of mark – 9.1(a)

simultaneous tacking or gybing 41.4

simultaneous hailing and tacking 43.1

single-handed yacht and protest flag 68.2(c)(ii)

skin friction 63

sound signals: one – for postponement 4.1 "AP"; one long – for start of round-the-ends rule 4.1 "I"; – for premature starters 4.1 "X"; one with lowering of 1st sub 4.1 "1st sub"; 1, 2, 3 or repetitive – specified 4.4; failure or mistiming of – 4.5; – for recall 8.1(a)

sounding 56

spars: maker's mark 26.1(b); natural action of wind on – 54.1; used in getting clear 55; sheeting sails to – 64.2

spinnaker: sail number and letters on – 25.1, 25.1(d)(iii); sail maker's mark on – 26.1(a); – staysails excluded 27; changing – 64.1; spinnaker and spinnaker boom 64.3; distinguished from headsail 64.4

sportsmanship 75

stability: (22); use of trapeze 62

stairways 22.1

standing on bottom: 53.3, 55, 59

starboard tack: *on a tack*; 36

STARTING: decision to – yacht's responsibility FR B; timing of yachts – 7.2; eligibility to – in re-sail 12(a); assuming a proper course to – 35(b); same tack, luffing and sailing above a proper course after – 38; luffing after – 38.1; new overlap when yacht – 38.3; same tack, sailing below a proper course after – 39; same tack, luffing before – 40; leeward yacht – 42.4; leeward yacht not entitled to room 43.3(a); returning to – 44; keeping clear whilst returning to – 44.1(a); reacquiring rights of way 44.1(b); until yacht returns to – 44.2; non-starter ranking as starter 50; complying with the definition 51.1(a); returning after – prematurely 51.1(b); conforming to the round-the-ends rule 51.1(c); failure to note recall and – correctly 51.1(d); string represents wake from – 51.2; required sides of mark at –, and approaching line to – 51.3; touching mark before – 52.1(a); re-rounding starting marks after – 52.2(b); no hearing after failure to – 70.1

start: 2(d); timing – 7.2; new – after general recall 8.2(b)

starting area 3.2(b)(ix), 7.1

starting line: *starting*; 3.2(a)(iv); shorten course signal at – 4.1 "S"; types of – 6; recall of yacht on course side of – 8.1; RC's procedure when yacht returns 8.1; in vicinity of – Pt.IV Preamble; luffing after clearing – 38.1; luffing before clearing – 40; approaching – to start 42(b), 43.4(a); leeward yacht approaching 42.4; course and pre-start sides of – when returning 44.1(a); in the vicinity of –, ranking as a starter 50; premature starters returning across 51.1(b)(c)

starting mark: in lines 6; rounding a mark other than a – 42; at a – surrounded by navigable water 42.4; when – is an obstruction 43.3(a); required sides of – 51.3; re-rounding a – 52.2(b)(i); (52.2(c))

starting procedure 4.2, 5.4(a), 8.2(a)

starting signal: *starting*; *proper course*; *abandonment*; one minute before
– 4.1 "I"; individual recall after – 4.1 "X"; for starting race 4.2; visual
signals to govern 4.5; postponing, cancelling or shortening races before
– 5.3, and after – 5.4; to time start of yacht 7.2; yacht on course side at –
8.1; leeward yacht before and after – 42.4; premature starter returning
after – 44.1(a); premature starter at 51.1(b); one minute before – 51.1(c)

status of rules – introduction; of SIs 3.1

steer 20.3

string 51.2

surfing 54.3

swimming 59

tack of sails: position of sailmaker's mark 26.1(a); spinnaker – 64.3, 64.4

TACKING: *on a tack*; new overlap begins on – 38.3; changing – 41; – yacht
keeping clear 41.1; room required for – 41.2; onus of proof that – completed 41.3; simultaneous – 41.4; – round mark when overlapped 42(a);
room for inside yacht to – 42.1(a); – round mark when clear ahead 42.2(b);
– inside circle 42.3(a)(ii); hailing for room to – at obstruction 43; when a
yacht may – after hailing 43.1; when the hailed yacht must – 43.2; yacht
not entitled to room to – 43.3(a); – when obstruction is a mark 43.3(b); roll
– 54.1(b) – affecting boomed headsail or outrigger 64.2

team racing: FR C; *racing*; rules of – govern RC 1.4; App.4

ties: 3.2(a)(viii); methods for breaking 11

time limit for finishing: 3.2(a)(vii), (b)(xvi); finishing within – 10; for advertising 26; for protests: PC extends – 68.6(a); set for non-finisher 68.6(b) (for
RC protests 70.2) for re-opening hearing: 73.5, 77.2

timing the start 7.2

tolerances in measurement 19.2

torso 62

touching a mark: re-rounding after – 45; obligation on yacht that – 52.1;
– surrounded by navigable water 52.2(a); starting or finishing 52.2(b); – not
surrounded by navigable water 52.2(c)

trapeze 62

unaffiliated body 1.1(e)

underwater surfaces 54.1(a)(b)

unwinding (51.4)

variable sail plan 25.1(f)

vessel: assisting a – FR A; *obstruction*; mark – 4.1 "M"; replacing mark 9.1;
– not racing Pt.IV Preamble; – forming continuous obstruction 42.3(b);
causing mark – to shift 52.1; yacht's action after fouling other – 55; yacht
boarded by crew of – fouled 58; yacht's crew leaving after fouling – 59; –
required to keep clear 69(c)

video see **photograph**

visual signals 4.1; – to govern starting 4.5

void see *abandonment* or *cancellation*

wake 51.2

warning before disqualification 25.4, 26.5

warning signal: changes in SI to each yacht before – 3.4; after postponement 4.1 "AP"; after abandonment and re-sail 4.1 "N over X"; desig-
nates class 4.1 "P"; life jacket signal displayed after – 4.1 "Y"; after
general recall 4.1 "1st sub"; in systems 1 and 2, 4.2(a); made earlier than
scheduled start 4.2(b); new – after error 4.2(c); course to be signalled
before or with – 5.1; course to be changed before or with 5.3(b); exception
to sound signals 4.4; class – left at dip 8.1(a)(i); new – after general recall
8.2

water 22.2, 54.1

water pockets 61(b)

water-tanks 22.1

wear and tear 19.2

weight 53.3, 61, 62

weight-jackets 61

wet suit 4.1 "Y"

wind: insufficient – 5.4(c)(ii); – on sails 54.1; head to –: *tacking*; *leeward and
windward* – aft *gybing* sailing by the –; *close-hauled, luffing*

windward: *leeward and windward*; *tacking*; *on a tack*; *close-hauled*; W's
obligations when overlapped 37.1; W's rights when keeping clear 37.3;
W's helmsman abeam L's mast 38.2; W hails 'mast abeam' 38.4; W
causes luff to be curtailed 38.5; W's rights if luffed before start, W's
helmsman abeam L's mast 40; inside yacht taken to – of mark 42.3(c);
W's rights and restrictions at starting mark 42.4

withdrawal of protest 68.9, 77.4

witness: Of incident 68.1; of infringement 70.2(d); (– an interested party
71.2); gives evidence or excluded 73.1; member of protest committee as
– 73.3, App.6, App.8

wrong side of mark 51.4

yacht appearing at start alone 3.2(b)(xxix)

yacht in distress 46.3

yacht involved: *party to a protest*; – in incident 68.1; infringes a rule 70.2(e)

yacht materially prejudiced: requests redress 69; RC considers redress for
– 70.3, 74.2

yacht's name 26.2(a)

yacht's type 26.1(e)